SOUTH TOWARD HOME

Tales from an Unlikely Journey

By Alice Joyner Irby

ALICE'S CHILDHOOD HOME, WELDON, NC

Outer Banks Publishing Group
Raleigh/Outer Banks

SOUTH TOWARD HOME. Copyright © 2020 by Alice Joyner Irby. All rights reserved. Published in the United States of America by Outer Banks Publishing Group—Outer Banks/Raleigh.

www.outerbankspublishing.com

No part of this book may be reproduced in any manner whatsoever without written permission except in the case of brief quotations embedded in critical articles and reviews.
For information contact Outer Banks Publishing Group at

info@outerbankspublishing.com

This book is a work of non-fiction. All the characters and events in this book are real; resemblance to actual events, organizations or actual persons living or dead, is intentional, and recounted as accurately as memory allows. Some names and identifying details of people described in this book have been altered to protect privacy.

Cover photo of the Roanoke River by Lee D. Copeland
Copeland Ltd Photography, Weldon, NC

FIRST EDITION - April 2020

Library of Congress Control Number: 2020935093

ISBN - 978-1-7341687-4-7
eISBN - 978-0-4635648-7-5

WHAT OTHERS ARE SAYING...

"From the parts of home that each of us takes with us no matter our travels through life, to the worries and wants parents have for their children, Alice captures a little bit about all of us in her masterful storytelling of her unique journey through life."
—Mark Elgart, President/CEO of Cognia, an educational services organization

"Alice Irby's memoir is a moving, inspirational, and entertaining chronicle of an educator, business executive, and mother who has made a difference—in education, in business, and especially in challenging social inequities. Her stories—profiling the genteel and the feisty in equal measure—are authentic and heartfelt recollections of a woman who lived, fought, and led through some of America's most tumultuous decades."
—Richard Swartz, former President, Riverside Publishing

"The stories in Alice Joyner Irby's new, and first, book are about a deep appreciation of belonging—to family, to place, and to community. The bond between mother and daughter is profoundly moving. Alice's bold journey north and then all over the world through her travels reveals her curiosity about people and place and the impact of both on her. I never had the pleasure of working directly for Alice, but as a woman CEO, and after reading these stories, I would have loved to have been mentored by her. I can only turn to the next generation of young women leaders and do what Alice did throughout her career—she led fearlessly and mentored those around her with her own caring and compassionate heart." —Karen Cowe, Chief Executive Officer, Ten Strands

TABLE OF CONTENTS

PROLOGUE — 1

STARTING OUT
The Church That Reached to the Heavens — 5
Partners in Crime — 30
The Funeral Foursome — 60
A Sound Like No Other — 75

MIXING IT UP
The Not-so-Friendly Skies — 91
The Great Game — 101
Just a Bowl of Peanuts — 119
My Love Affair with Learning — 135

ALONG A WINDING PATH
Off to War — 165
Welcome to Rutgers — 189
Second Time Around — 212

MY CELEBRITIES AND MY FRIENDS
Clearing Fences — 237
I Know Who You Are! — 254
Of Pies and Pine Straw — 266
Spunk—and Grit! — 279
Mary, Mary — 296
The Heart of an Angel — 314

MAGICAL HARMONIES AND CONNECTIONS

Music and Memory: For James	320
Awakened	329
A Big Part of Me	345
The Sound of Music	359
Amazing Grace	369

PAST AND PRESENT

My Christmas Angel	388
To Market, To Market	402
Of Fortitude and Courage	430
South Toward Home	453

EPILOGUE	487
ACKNOWLEDGMENTS	507
ABOUT THE AUTHOR	509
APPENDIX	511
ABOUT THE COVER	512

*For Andrea and James—
and our family past and present*

PROLOGUE

And in the sweetness of friendship let there be laughter, and sharing of pleasures.
For in the dew of little things the heart finds its morning and is refreshed.
—Kahlil Gibran, *The Prophet*

The depths of the Great Depression was not the best time to come into the world in Weldon, North Carolina, a small farm community a good bit east of Raleigh. But there I was, wild brown hair and eyes as dark as two holes burned in a blanket, screaming to awaken the neighbors early on the morning of August 29, 1932. My mother recalled it as the hottest week of the year, marked also by an eclipse of the sun, but it may have been that she just blacked out from an excess of baby daughter in a dearth of air-conditioning.

These stories span my lifetime of adventure, change, and even rupture in making my way from the protective cocoon of safety and love provided by my parents, teachers, and the citizens of my town, where I learned about discipline, loyalty, and friendship, into a worldly web of opportunities, risks, choices, and uncertainty. Tentatively at first, then with purpose, I metamorphosed into an intellectually curious college student and, in time, into an independent woman in a sometimes seemingly irrational world, a world in which men controlled the career ladders and leadership positions of influence. Several of these stories depict what it was like for a young Southern woman to work in a skewed world before the Women's Movement took off in the 1970s.

How would you have reacted if, in interviewing for your first job out of graduate school in 1955, you were told with a smile that you were qualified for a higher-level position but that it was not possible because you were a woman?

What would it be like to be a Director of Admissions at the Woman's College (WC) in Greensboro, N.C., shortly after the Supreme Court's *Brown v. Board of Education* desegregation decision? The University system, of which WC was a part, voluntarily desegregated its student bodies and admissions policies. Immediately, I faced both challenges and opportunities.

Soon there would be WC students joining N.C. A&T men in supporting the 1960 sit-ins at the Woolworth counter, prompting a crisis on campus. With my colleagues, I became involved in trying to lessen the tensions on campus.

How would it feel to be present at the creation of the Great Society in 1964 when Lyndon Johnson unleashed his enormous talents to extend civil rights to all our people, regardless of race, sex, or class? From dealing with college students in North Carolina, I went to fashioning programs in Washington, D.C., to help youth aged 16 to 22 who had dropped out of school and work but who were eligible for the new federal Job Corps.

Can you imagine how it felt, about that same time in 1964, to be denied a seat on an "executive" United Airlines flight, which my two male executive counterparts used routinely, because I was a woman? Or, later being denied a credit card at Rich's Department Store in Atlanta because I was divorced and could not use my former husband's credit—even though I was a young executive with Educational Testing Service in Princeton, N.J.?

Commuting from Princeton to New York for work one day, I was kicked out of a parlor car reserved for men. Just as well; it was filled with smoke. Neither the laws about equal rights nor smoking in public had reached the male upper-class elite riding in that car. But that was not as bad as the IRS auditing my tax returns for each of several years because they did not believe I supported a child and earned the income I reported.

New Brunswick, New Jersey, was a long way from my birthplace in Halifax County in rural Eastern North Carolina, but by 1972, I found myself at Rutgers University as the first female vice president of a major university in the United States. The times had indeed changed in the late '60s, but disruptions were still filling the air. I confronted familiar issues, this time in different shapes: a sit-in, the implementation of Title IX in an all-male college, the admission of minority students, and eligibility of athletes, to name a few.

Time after time, year after year, I found myself at the intersection of discrimination and liberation; of segregation and integration; of the pull of tradition but also the desire for change. Through it all, I tried to be true to my learning at the knees of my parents and mindful of the hopes and expectations of my teachers. And, time after time, I discovered that music sustained me and restored my soul. I came to realize that siblings and friends are the real treasures in life. And early in my adulthood, I came to appreciate the ramifications of the dreams Martin Luther King, Jr., spoke of in that speech he gave first in Rocky Mount, N.C., on November 27, 1962, and later to thousands in Washington, D.C.: "I have a dream that one day...."

These stories offer glimpses of the land in Eastern North Carolina where I grew up and into the ways of people there, then and now. Throughout my eight-plus decades, I have never relinquished the ties or the lessons I learned there from my family, my mentors, or my community. Yet I have also learned new ways of living and doing from people in the distant corners of this big blue Marble—and it has altered and enriched my life, feeding my soul and imagination.

Southerners go home, they say, even if it is in a coffin. People in that eastern corner of the state know what the dirt feels like under their feet. They know what the Roanoke River yields other than turbulence. They know the meaning of loyalty, the depths of sorrow, and the transcendent power of faith. And they know why there is an inscription on a local tombstone admonishing us all to "Leave them laughing when you say goodbye."

April 2018

STARTING OUT

THE WELDON METHODIST CHURCH

The Church That Reached to the Heavens

Hugging the banks of the Roanoke River, where rockfish swim upriver every April to spawn, Weldon in the 1930s was a small farming community in northeastern North Carolina with a population of 2,500.

I was born in Granny's boarding house at 401 Elm Street, the fourth street up from that river, in the depths of the Great Depression.

It was August 29, 1932, a sweltering day in the years before air-conditioning.

Giving birth on the second floor of a rambling, ten-room house, my mother suffered mightily from the heat, but two days later—the hottest day of that year—the temperature reached 101 degrees, capped by a total eclipse of the sun. The only coolant at 401 Elm Street was a fan blowing over a block of ice from the icehouse way down the dusty, unpaved street. Mother must have wondered, "What have I done to deserve this—having a baby during hard times and now the land is on fire? What does this portend for my baby and my family?"

Yet, even with shimmering waves of heat and labor pains clouding her vision, she saw through her bedroom window the spire of the Weldon Methodist Church reaching to the Heavens. All would be well.

The center spire of our church, built in 1908 and the tallest edifice in town, long cast its power and inspiration on those below. The pointed arches of the neo-Gothic structure dominated Washington Avenue, the main street, protecting homes and citizens all across town, and its richly toned stained-glass windows offered solace to all who walked or drove by. To worshippers inside, rays of light through the scarlet, golden, and French-blue windows spread across the pews and into the chancel, adding energy, mystery, and authority to sermons and scriptures as they were read. The twenty voices of the choir sailed out blocks away on summer Sundays through wide-open double doors, signifying that the Weldon Methodist Church could be counted on as a mainstay of life here.

Weldon had other churches—a small chapel-like Episcopal Church across the street; a spacious Baptist Church two blocks away; a red-brick Jewish synagogue with one large, golden stained-glass window; and several African American churches, one an A.M.E. Church a couple of blocks from our house on Elm Street. Members of all the churches, regardless of race or denomination, cooperated during the year, visiting each other's houses of worship on special occasions, especially funerals. Congregations were segregated by race—this was the 1930s—but mixing and visiting at times was quite natural.

That was life 75 years ago when I was a child. The members of the Weldon Methodist Church, built by visionary leaders of the congregation, had faith in its expanding role in the community. Two of the founders, in fact, were members of my family; dedications on giant stained-glass windows paid tribute to William T. Whitfield and Thomas F. Anderson. Six generations of my family attended services there.

My grandmother was a soloist and choir director. My mother taught Sunday school and led Women's Circles. My father, a devout worshipper, was a lay leader all his adult life. I was a lifetime member, too, until October 23, 2016. On that day, the church closed, leaving me feeling as if another anchor of my life had come unmoored.

For years, Weldon had been dwindling in size, from 2,500 to about 1,500 in the twenty-first century. It was as if a slow-motion, mini-tsunami overcame Weldon beginning in the 1970s. Farms were mechanized, resulting in lost jobs. The boll weevil decimated the cotton crops for years until a method was found to control it. Textile jobs moved to Mexico and then to Asia. The North-South trains bypassed Weldon, stopping north of Weldon in Petersburg and south in Rocky Mount. The result was not just loss of passengers, but the freight business suffered as well. Once young people graduated from high school, they went elsewhere for college or work. Finally, numerous downtown merchants could not keep their doors open as malls developed outside town.

As a result, the heart of the church, its large congregation and choir, had been shrinking in membership as well. The families of my youth, the girls and boys from my gang, the ministers and choristers no longer filled the sanctuary with stirring voices of celebration and communion, of faith and worship. Those folks are now scattered across the country, pursuing their dreams in far-off places; or at rest in the town cemetery.

But life in the church as I remember it still inserts itself subtly into the stories I tell myself today. My mother's voice calls down from the head of the stairs at home: "Alice, don't drink or eat anything now that you have on your church clothes. That's the only Sunday dress and coat you have—and it is Easter."

We dressed for church in our finest: soft faille or silk-like dresses, Mary Jane shoes with white-ribbed socks, white gloves, and straw hats in summer. In winter, we wore plaid-wool dresses, tweed coats with velvet collars, brown Oxford shoes, leather gloves, and hats down over the ears. Every other year, we got new church clothes, always a size too big so we would have room to grow into them the following year. Families had to stretch their pennies in those days.

ALICE, EASTER 1937

No female—lady or child—dared enter the doors of the Weldon Methodist Church without wearing her hat and gloves, her hair in place and controlled by nets or hairpins. Hairspray was unknown.

George, my brother, joined the family in 1934. When he was very young, he wore pants above the knees in summer with a sports jacket, usually double-breasted, and a man's hat like Daddy's. By school age, boys wore knickers with high-ribbed socks. Their knickers were down around their ankles more often than up under their knees, but the boys were handsome, even when they rumpled their Sunday clothes fidgeting in the pews. Dad watched from the back-row pew, pretending to act as a deterrent to their mischief.

Tiny tots met in the basement for Sunday school so as not to distract the adults. Once in grade school, we graduated to classes upstairs. Then we were permitted to attend 11:00 services in the big sanctuary, accompanied by our parents. Over time, demonstrating our good manners earned the confidence of our parents, and we could sit with our friends. Blanche and I liked to sit together behind Mrs. Nannie Spires and the other ladies.

"Alice," whispered Blanche, "listen to the ladies drag that song, 'Rock of Ages.' It's as if that rock is being dragged from here to Halifax and back." We snickered and mimicked them. Giggling was frowned on, but we couldn't help ourselves sometimes. If we made noise, Genie, my aunt who was in the choir facing the congregation, threw me an exaggerated frown of disapproval, meaning "Sit up straight and be quiet!"

Before the remodeling about twenty years later, pews were arranged in amphitheater style with the communion rail curtained around the chancel. Three vestibules with large double doors opened into the sanctuary. Ministers could see everybody from the pulpit at the center, in front of three high-backed decorative chairs positioned against a wall below the organ pipes high up over the chancel. The pulpit was so wide and tall that short preachers had to stand on a stool to see our entire congregation, numbering in the hundreds each Sunday.

Facing the congregation, preachers' eyes focused naturally on the two large stained-glass windows dominating the outside walls of the church. One scene depicted Christ praying, the other showed him blessing the multitudes. The elevated choir loft and organ console were to the left of the pews and pulpit.

Blanche and I tried several locations among the pews, trying to position ourselves behind a tall person or on the side beyond anyone's direct view, but not a single area was "safe" from the sight of an adult, no matter where we went. We ended up back in the fourth row, even though the ladies' singing was off-key and slow...slow...slow. Even so, their hat brims were big enough to give us some cover.

Anyone who misbehaved could not sit with friends the following Sunday, and any adult who napped was the subject of gossip after the service. Actually, the hard, freshly-varnished wooden pews wouldn't let worshippers nap too long. Snoring was discouraged by a hard elbow to the ribs.

Music was as important as prayer, scripture, and sermons. The congregation, as well as the choir, loved to sing. Over the years, our organists' sturdy hands and strong fingers found a use for every pipe in the organ, sometimes simultaneously, it seemed.

Mrs. Sawyer, Bill Pierce's maternal grandmother, was the liveliest organist in both body and sound. When she played, the volume from every pipe in the sanctuary was so loud we could hardly hear our own voices. But we youngsters loved it. We could almost dance to her movements as she glided her fingers among the three consoles and twisted her hips in stomping on the foot pedals.

Gwen Dickens, a well-trained professional organist, played the organ and simultaneously directed the choir. A woman of multiple musical talents, she played the piano in area restaurants and conducted community choral performances. Her tenure was the longest of the three music directors I remember well.

Gwen followed Josephine Pierce, a graduate of Westminster Choir College in Princeton, New Jersey, who married a Weldon man, moved to town, and became our choir director. She was not an organist, but she put to good use her own crystal-clear soprano voice with her flair for drama and choreographed elaborate Christmas pageants with ninety-voice choirs, composed of singers from the other churches in town in addition to our own.

Every chorister in the Christmas choir had to walk down one of the two main aisles in the sanctuary carrying a lighted candle while singing "O, Come All Ye Faithful."

"Be careful, Alice," Virginia Sledge admonished me one year. "You can easily burn yourself and your partner. You can even set the church on fire."

That made my hands shake even more. I remember walking down the aisle with the candle melting fast on my circular paper holder and fearing, "Suppose this tallow burns my hands and fire balls fall on my robe, my robe catches on fire, the fire spreads to the floor and then to the pews and then to the walls and then to the ceiling!"

I had visions of bright flames setting the church on fire and spoiling the program—in fact, spoiling all of Christmas for the entire town! Compared to walking down the incline of that aisle to my seat, singing alto with the adults was easy.

A short written history of our church, distributed at the last service in 2016, includes a description of the early building. The Sunday school area included a large assembly room with classrooms on three sides and a balcony above. A low-platform stage anchored the cavernous room. Big, sliding garage-like doors opened to the sanctuary as needed.

Dr. Guy Suiter, who brought me into the world, was also Sunday School Superintendent and presided over the general assembly every Sunday morning. The program began with everyone gathered in the big room, after which we divided into classes and listened, or tried to listen, to the lesson of the day. When the bell rang—just as in school—we bolted out of the door to meet our friends, though there wasn't much time to share the most recent gossip before the 11:00 worship service.

Hazel Neville also was a big part of my life at Sunday school. She was in charge of the programs for the 9:30 general assembly. On more than one occasion when I was in high school, she called me at the last minute on Saturday.

"Alice, can you help me out with the program tomorrow? I have a Bible passage and poem I would like you to read." She had the script; I didn't have to create it but I did have to stand alone on the stage when speaking. She knew I could memorize things quickly—those days are long gone—and that by starting time Sunday morning I would be able to recite whatever she brought by my house on Saturday night. No dates on those Saturday nights.

Hazel was also the Methodist Youth Fellowship (MYF) leader. Young people, often from three churches, met on Sunday evenings at the church, after which our gang went to someone's house for socializing and singing. Hazel never kept us very long so we could have the rest of the evening to ourselves. We walked over to a friend's house—with permission, of course. Blanche played the piano while we sang, often in parts. She played "by ear" as well as "by sight." Lots of times we sang hymns, other times popular songs of the day.

Dancing was not allowed on Sunday, but if we were lucky enough to be in Mrs. William A. Pierce's mansion, we could dance—quietly and secretively, of course—in her large entry hall. She pretended not to hear or see, so our parents never knew.

Her home was the most elegant in town, with steps as wide as the house itself rising to a covered portico supported by columns. The spacious, high-ceilinged foyer led to a staircase that could have been the model for Tara in *Gone With the Wind*. Blanche loved to play Mrs. Pierce's grand piano. We felt honored to be there, and we were always well behaved because we wanted Bill, Mrs. Pierce's grandson, to get her permission for us to return.

Hazel, a woman who had postponed marriage to stay home and care for her mother, became a dear friend, too, even though she was a good bit older than I. Hazel's industry and her devotion to the church and to our youth group were a marvel.

OUR GANG ON SUNDAY NIGHT, BLANCHE AT PIANO, ABOUT 1948

Every Christmas Eve, after we went caroling around town to serenade the shut-ins, we gathered at Hazel's for hot chocolate and cookies. By that time, it was almost midnight, time to go to the midnight service at the Episcopal Church. Christmas Day began for us in the calm of a cold night as we walked home to the accompaniment of caroling church bells.

Adults in the church seemed to us so wise and knowledgeable. The Board of Trustees, all male in those days, managed the finances and oversaw the upkeep of the physical plant, with help from the sexton, of course. Women took care of the education programs, the needs of the choir, and the many social receptions. They had their Circles, e.g., the Alice Anderson Circle No. 1, named for my grandmother. Because of their faith, good works, and dedication to the church, we looked up to those adults as the backbone of the community.

The men gathered in a space called the Baraca Room, a small chapel with its own altar, pews, piano, and stained-glass windows. It seated as many as forty at a time. We were afraid to go inside, fearful we would disturb something precious or get caught in forbidden territory. Indeed, the men frowned on us if we even pretended we were going to open the door. Occasionally, however, one of them would take us inside to look around. We didn't see anything special about the room, but some of the artifacts belonged to individual members who considered them priceless, even irreplaceable. I guess they thought we would damage or destroy the collection. "Baraca" comes from the Hebrew word "Berachah," meaning "blessing," and referring to Bible classes for young men. Our Baraca Room was for young and old alike, however—any adult male in the church.

Like most families, our family usually had Sunday dinner at home, both because our parents were frugal and because home cooking was better than what was served in the one respectable restaurant in town. By the time church services ended at noon, we were ravenous. Mother liked to socialize with her friends after the service and, admittedly, it did take her a few minutes to disrobe after singing in the choir. Home was only two short blocks away.

George and I would call into the church vestibule, "Mother, we are headed home." We were the first to start walking.

Then, Daddy tired of standing around and said, "Margaret, I am going to follow the children," hoping Mother would follow.

"I'll be there in a minute," she responded.

Soon, the minutes got longer and longer until Mother was the last one to leave the church, often leading the sexton to say, "Mrs. Joyner, can you continue your conversation on the sidewalk, so I can lock up the church?" She was never even aware he was waiting for her and her friends.

We couldn't put food on the table, much less eat, until Mother came home and organized everything, because she was in charge—always. But we might sneak a leftover roll or two. When she got home, George and I rushed to be helpful, more so before the meal than after. We dared not criticize, but as we got older, we did tease her now and then. A good sport, she laughed about her extended visiting, but over the years—even after Margaret Ray, our younger sister, came along—nothing changed. Our Sunday habits were fixed.

Neither did things vary regarding our Sunday afternoon activities. Daddy made sure of that. My siblings and I were forbidden to play cards, to go dancing, or to go to movies on Sundays. Weekend homework had to be completed before Sunday. We were allowed to visit friends and relatives, to take walks around town with groups of young people, or to hike along country streams and river paths. We could read the funny papers or library books and play the piano. At 5:00 p.m. we were expected to go to MYF, which we enjoyed. These were the rules for observing the Sabbath, not just in our family but in most Methodist families. For all that, the Methodists were not as strict as the Baptists. Sometimes we wished we were Episcopalian because they were the most lenient observers of all.

The walls of the Weldon Methodist Church framed the major events of life: from birth to baptism to marriage to death. A member of my family or I experienced all of them during the decades we worshipped there. When I was just a few months old, my birth was celebrated in the church by my parents and my grandmother, for whom I was named. Similarly, my brother and sister were baptized as infants. Baptism was such an important ritual that the Alice Anderson Hudson Circle, named for my grandmother, gave the baptismal font to the church in her memory. And that font remained in the chancel until the church closed.

"I wish there were some way we could preserve the baptismal font," I mused to my brother and sister in 2016.

"I'd like to take it to my church in Morehead City," George responded. "There is a spot in the sanctuary that would be just right for it."

With permission of the Church Board, he transported it to Morehead City and placed it in his Methodist church. The four-foot, white marble memorial font stands there now, within a few feet of the pulpit and ready for the minister's use in a ceremony.

A small farming community offers teens few choices of activities. We had one movie theater, a small community swimming pool, and a Boy Scout hut for meetings and dancing where we had to furnish our own Victrola and records—no D.J.s then. Activities centered on home, school, and church. We gathered in each other's homes for club meetings and bridge. We worked on the high-school annual and newspaper at school during the week, anxious to cram into our parents' cars on Friday nights for away-football games in nearby communities. The Junior-Senior Prom, in an elaborately decorated gym, was the climax of the year's activities. Mother was in charge of both the annual and the Prom.

MOTHER WORKING ON OUR ANNUAL, *THE LITTLE BREEZE*

Just as we were celebrating our high-school graduation in June 1950, the United States went to war again, this time in Korea. Little did we realize how it would disrupt and change our lives and plans. Within a year, the young men in our gang were drafted or dropping out of college to enlist in the Navy to avoid the Army's harsh basic training and deployment in the infantry.

A couple of girls dropped out of college as well, returning to Weldon to get married in their home church. Susan Shepherd married Roy Smith at the end of her freshman year at St. Mary's. He had just graduated from N.C. State but had a deferment to enter Harvard Business School, so they immediately headed to Boston.

Blanche married Thurman Bullock, a friend of Claud, my future husband, and a resident of neighboring Roanoke Rapids. They were married in the Weldon Methodist Church while he was in the Navy, after having left Chapel Hill right after his freshman year. She finished her Bachelor of Music degree at Greensboro College.

The War prompted many serious decisions that would otherwise have been delayed. We young adults, in turn, imposed burdens on our families.

On very short notice to my mother and father—three weeks, to be exact—I was married to Claudius Irby, also of Roanoke Rapids, in the Weldon Methodist Church on June 14, 1952, before he headed off to the Navy's Officers Candidate School in Newport, R. I. A recent graduate of UNC in Chapel Hill, Claud got a notice in May to report to the Navy on June 22. That changed our plans and rushed our decision to wed.

I returned to the Woman's College to finish my degree. It surprised everyone, including me, that I married while still in college, but I thought nothing of doing both: getting married and getting educated at the same time.

Panicked by my wish to marry in the church and have the reception at home rather than at the Country Club—so much easier—Mother set about trying to get the house ready and make all the other pre-nuptial arrangements: sending out invitations to most people in town; selecting gowns—hers, mine, and the bridesmaids'; and notifying the two local jewelry stores. Bridge parties and luncheons filled our days, sandwiched between necessary shopping and decorating the house.

"Alice, do you think I am Superwoman, trying to do everything in three weeks?" Mother said in exasperation. I guess I did think she was Superwoman; she always had been.

"I am sorry, Mother. I had no idea a wedding was so involved. I forgot we live in a small town where everyone knows everyone else, and they all get involved."

"And," she said, "that also means trying to find workmen to paint and sand floors on short notice. Having it at home adds a whole new dimension to a wedding."

Little did I realize what was involved until I saw Mother having all the floors refinished, walls freshened with new paint, unnecessary furniture stored, tables set up to display gifts and, later, to accommodate large platters of food for the reception.

Mother got her revenge—from the grave 58 years later—when Andrea gave me two, not even three, weeks to plan her wedding in the Village Chapel in Pinehurst, N.C., and to host her reception for 65 at my home.

Caterers were not a part of Weldon life, but no one needed them. Mother's friends helped with the food for the reception, and, of course, they prepared non-alcoholic fruit punch. Not only did the churches discourage serving liquor, no respectable Weldon family served liquor at a wedding reception. On occasion at a celebration, to no one's surprise, a few fellows sneaked into a backyard, pulling flasks out of their dinner-jacket pockets for a quick quaff.

Custom did not include sit-down dinners and dancing—that practice came years later. But, gracious style doesn't depend on money for extravagant affairs. The country was just recovering from the Second World War and money was not plentiful. Still, according to custom, the wedding was a formal affair, with long gowns for six bridesmaids, white ties and tails for ushers, and a lacy, full-skirted dress for my little sister, the flower girl.

June is truly summertime in the South. That Saturday night was a typical sultry summer evening, tree leaves drooping in the humid air, no air conditioning in the church, and only window units at home. I breathed a sigh of relief when the 54 candles in the six tall candelabra standing in the chancel of the church held firm without melting or at best bending over. My mind flashed back to the time years earlier, when as a child, I worried about the church catching fire from my Christmas candle.

The church was full of people decked out in long, sparkling gowns and tuxedos, the atmosphere full of energy, and the guests full of cheer—offering momentary relief from the anxiety of world affairs, though some of the young men in the wedding party and congregation were preparing to go off to war.

At home for the reception, we opened the windows and encouraged guests to enjoy the front porch—a spacious one extending across the front of the house. It never occurred to me that the population of Weldon could not cram easily into our house. It was, after all, a big house with big rooms.

"People don't mind being crowded if they are having a good time, and it is a good time," I assured Mother as she ushered people through the receiving line.

"But, Alice, it is so hot. The candles are melting and the cold food is getting warm."

"Don't worry, Mother, they can go outside to catch a slight breeze. Besides, they are used to the heat," I said, trying to calm her.

Claud and I were not anxious to leave the party or our friends but, when we saw our getaway car, hardly recognizable from the confetti, toilet paper, and who-knows-what inside, we had to escape before we got cornered. To think that we had trusted his dad with the keys!

"Addison Irby," admonished Ruby, his wife. "How could you let that happen to Claud—my only child!—and let them whitewash the car you care so much about?" Claud's dad smiled sheepishly. A quiet man, he had a sense of humor and liked a joke every now and then, even it if meant ignoring Ruby's attempts to control him.

We got away around 11:00 p.m. and drove to Richmond, only 85 miles away. Spending the first night of a honeymoon in Richmond at the John Marshall Hotel was *the thing to do* for newly-married couples in Weldon.

And Mother and Dad? Exhausted, but still standing, with proper smiles on their faces 'til the last guest said good night. Only then, after saying good-bye to their oldest child and grieving her loss amidst the joy, they were left to clean up the mess.

Forty-nine years later, in the spring of 1990, Mother, my siblings, and I buried my father with a funeral service in the

Weldon Methodist Church. Eighteen months later, my brother, sister, and I buried our mother. The ground beneath my feet nearly gave way entirely. Even now, I can't contemplate those times of grievous loss without tears swelling my eyes.

From the window in my upstairs room, the room where Mother labored during my birth, I saw the steeple reaching above the housetops, calming my grief and my anger by reminding me of the unconditional love of my parents over sixty years. Coming into sharper focus, the steeple of the church called me to honor their lives—lives devoted to others and to God. There, in my childhood room, images of our family, those present and those departed, whose lives were touched by that church, sustained me.

I can still see the drawn, sad faces of the townspeople entering the church for the two funerals in 1990 and 1991. And I recall the ministers' pained faces—Luis Reinoso, minister and family friend, presiding during my father's service. I remember that one of the songs used in my father's service was the hymn he loved most: "How Great Thou Art."

Caswell Shaw, Mother's former student and Methodist District Superintendent, presided during my mother's. I steeled myself to read from *The Prophet* at my mother's service because I knew she often quoted its sections on love.

Dad's death was not unexpected. He was 93 and had been in a nursing home for three years. We were as prepared as most families are for that time. Yet, one is never prepared to lose a much-loved parent.

Mother's death was a shock. Just before Christmas, on December 8, 1991, she died in a Rocky Mount, N.C., hospital three weeks after successful surgery for blocked carotid arteries. In preparing to go home, after being released by the surgeon, she collapsed to the floor.

I had gone home to prepare for her arrival and to cook Thanksgiving dinner when I got a call from the hospital. Pneumonia was the diagnosis. For the past week, she had complained about a hacking cough. I doubt x-rays were ever taken. I have never been back to that hospital and can't bear to drive by it.

She was 87, but just weeks earlier, she had given a stirring speech at a town gathering. Because her death was unexpected, we had not given any thought to a funeral service. Only a year later, when we were cleaning out the house, did we find a list of her wishes regarding her funeral; fortunately, we had guessed correctly on most choices of music and speakers.

So loved and admired were my parents in the community that the church was overflowing on both occasions. Dad was the oldest member of the church at the time of his death, and a devoted mentor for younger men in the community. Mother's former students came from all over the area to express their shock and disbelief, many saying over and over how she had been an inspiration and major force in their lives.

For days, George, Margaret Ray, and I received guests at home. Numerous floral arrangements decorating the house brought welcome reminders of the beauty of life, even in winter. Friends brought tons of food, a common practice in Southern towns. We had plenty of Ralph's barbecue and Brunswick stew, potato salad, coconut and chocolate cakes, and fruit pies. Letters came from friends and from Mother's former students across the country. It took me many weeks to write notes of thanks to all who shared our grief, but I enjoyed every moment of writing because their kindness and compassion helped temper my loss.

After that, the big house on Elm Street, just a couple of blocks from the church and filled over the years with celebrations of birth and life, was vacant. All the Thanksgivings and Christmases, with every member of the family home for the holidays, were holidays of the past, not lost in memory but occasions we'd never experience and share again.

To this day, without our being in that particular house, and without the people who made it home, something is missing at Thanksgiving and Christmastime, even though I continue to roast the turkey, make the dressing and gravy, prepare the chicken salad, and layer the ambrosia using recipes handed down by generations of family. Andrea cooks the collards just the way Mother used to do.

I am reconciled to the emptiness. Yet, in spite of that loss, every December wherever I am, I know that Mother's and Dad's spirits are with me, whispering over my shoulder, reminding me of how much they loved and valued me. I can feel their presence now as well.

Today I am holding in my hand the program and an "Order for the Leavetaking of Weldon United Methodist Church." Congregants used it that last day, October 23,

2016, when over one hundred members and former members of our church gathered in commemoration and celebration of its long life of 108 years. How greatly my parents would have lamented its closing!

How much I wish I had been there, but surgery on my left leg precluded it. Two weeks earlier, I had said goodbye to the few remaining members, to the minister, and to what for me was a sacred place. George was too saddened by the prospect of the church closing to join me. Jennifer, his daughter, and his granddaughter, Drew, met me there as we three joined the remaining ten or eleven members in worship.

Talking at length with the minister, Sue Owens, and Shirley Stowitts, a loyal, long-service member, we walked around the chancel and commented on the simple altar now at the center of the church, the powerful organ, and the red-carpeted choir loft. We marveled again at the commanding, familiar windows and told stories about our ancestors who contributed to this building.

"Ladies," I said, "you don't remember how the sanctuary looked in the old days. It did not have the typical architectural arrangement that you see here now."

"What was it like?" Jennifer asked, having been born after it was remodeled.

"Instead of the center aisle you see now, culminating in the chancel and free-standing altar with the cross, the old church was a semi-circle of pews descending in theater-style to the chancel, which served as a stage for Nativity scenes, Easter celebrations, and confirmation rituals for new members—also, for other plays and dramas. Back in the 1940s and 1950s, the choir was so large it could not fit in the space designed for it."

I described the young-people's choir having to sit in the pews. "The ushers sat on the back row right under the stained-glass windows—so they could nap, I think, without anyone but the minister seeing them.

JENNIFER, ALICE, AND DREW IN SANCTUARY, WELDON METHODIST CHURCH, FALL 2016

"We loved to run among the labyrinthine halls behind the sanctuary to chase each other or get to class," I continued. "Of course, the women tried to keep us out of the basement and kitchen, except when they had church suppers."

I paused, searching for words to impress upon Jennifer and Drew the spiritual significance of our church.

"It was the pumping heart of our community life, a vital place of worship and learning, a true sanctuary from pain and sorrow, and a hall for discovery and joy.

"It had everything we young folks needed and wanted. Our roots are grounded here. I thought it would go on forever."

We lingered for as long as we could.

Finally, when the minister had to close the doors, the three of us stood on the steps and took some pictures. With one final thing to do, the last mile of our journey routed us to the cemetery. Jennifer, Drew, and I walked among the graves in the Whitfield-Anderson plot, detailing aspects of our ancestors' lives and saying good-bye, but saying thanks as well.

I said a special prayer for my life, my family, my town, and all the people of Weldon who had enriched my life over three generations through their love for and devotion to this *Church that reached to the heavens.*

October 2016

Partners in Crime

My first crime—the first one I remember—and the surprising punishment that accompanied it, happened over something I loved, and still love: ice cream. I was a brash eighteen-month-old. The story goes, my father was churning the ice cream for Sunday dinner on the backdoor steps of our house. It was a hot summer day, and the ice packed around the ice-cream container also frosted the outside of the tin bucket holding the hand-crank ice-cream maker. The bucket was cool to my touch and so inviting that I thought it would be even cooler if I sat on top of the ice.

"Alice," Daddy reluctantly admonished me, "I can't turn the handle if you keep crawling on the top of the bucket," he said gently. Twice he had brushed me aside so he could continue turning the handle. The third time, I made no effort to climb down. Sighing, he stopped turning, picked me up, stood me on a lower step, and spanked me good.

My frilly lace panties turned hot instead of cold, and my legs turned red. I was stunned as I looked up at him, first in shock, then in tears. Daddy had never disciplined me in any way, much less spanked me. I screamed, which I think shocked him!

It worked: I never did it again. But I also recall that Daddy was uncomfortable playing the role of Enforcer. He never spanked me again. I like to think I never gave him reason, but more likely he just decided to turn the disciplinary duties over to Mother. Besides, Daddy had to work six days a week at Mr. Garlick's furniture store. He was grateful to have a job during the Depression years and certainly put his mind and attention to it. Even in hard times, his faith and confidence in the future carried him through those tough years, enabling him to one day have his own furniture store.

I wasn't a difficult child, just playful and inquisitive. Mother used to say I asked WHY so much she stopped answering because I would just continue with my WHYs.

She also got tired of changing my sun-suits twice a day because I snooped around, found the outdoor hose, and added water to my sandbox so I could make mud pies. I liked being outdoors by myself, playing and exploring our backyard. "Stop! Alice, stop!" Mother yelled when I started eating my mud pies. How did she know what I was doing? Later, I saw that Mother and Granny kept an eye on me through the kitchen window.

When I ventured into Granny's rose garden, her pride and joy, she came running down the back steps, "Quit, Alice, that's off limits. You will get stuck with a thorn."

"Yes," she may have thought, "but you will also damage my rose blossoms and my bushes." But I was fearless. And why not? Nothing bad ever happened to me, and I was surrounded with loving, if stern, family and helpers.

Well, actually, some bad things did happen occasionally. Or, I should say, I did some bad things. There was the time in the summer of 1935 when I investigated the paving of the street in front of our house. Big tractors and trucks making noise were going up and down the street and around the corner along the side of our house. They left black stuff on top of our pretty, rocky sand.

"Why mess up our street?" I wondered.

Left by myself for a minute, I ran down to the curb, stooped down to touch the black stuff and found it gooey and runny. I started stirring it with my hands.

"Stop, Alice!" Granny yelled from the porch. "And get back from the street before you get run over."

Quickly, I stood up, wiped my hands on my new Mickey Mouse dress and ran back to the front steps to meet Granny who was coming down the steps fast.

"Oh, Child!" Granny cried. "You have smeared your pretty red-smocked dress with black tar. Your mother will be distraught! She spent dear money to get that dress for you, and there are not many extra pennies around here these days.

"Come here right now," she ordered. "There is nothing to do but show you to her. What a mighty mess! We have to get that tar off your hands right away before you mess up something else."

Mother was crushed. "Alice, you have ruined your new dress! And your father and I don't have money to buy you a new one. How can you get into so much mischief? You are a menace to the family! What makes you so fearless? I will have to ground you again."

And, ground me she did. My boundaries, even with an adult around, were the sidewalk in front and along the side of our house, Nanny Kate's house next door, and the fence and woodshed in the back. Alone, I was limited to the front porch and steps—if someone was there to keep an eye on me through the screen door. There I sat, elbows on knees, head in hands, pouting, as I watched big children play in Mr. Garlick's vacant side yard across the street.

I cried but I was not shocked because by now, I knew Mother was the Enforcer. In truth, Mother gave me my deserved comeuppance. I wasn't really a menace. I didn't hurt anyone—except myself! If I had been older than my three years, maybe I could have explained that I was not a menace, just a little curious—and wasn't that good?

I didn't have playmates. I was an only child then and there were no young children in neighborhood families, but I had Granny and Mother and Sally Ann until my brother George was born two years after me.

Granny was usually occupied with her boarding-house business, but she took time to cuddle me and give me a treat, often a biscuit with some molasses on it.

GRANNY WITH ALICE, 1933

Mother was always busy helping Granny prepare three meals a day for about 30 people and make up beds in the five rented bedrooms. Geneva, our main cook, was a good-looking, full-bodied woman who could have been a model. She presided over pots boiling on two big wood stoves. Imagine working at that in the summertime with no air-conditioning!

Bessie helped with cleaning and eventually learned to be a great cook, too. She and Mother became good friends, and she stayed with us all her working years until she became ill. Henry was our handyman and wood chopper for the stoves. He always wore a hat and, when not working, a long-sleeved shirt and tie.

But Sally Ann, the woman Granny had hired to cook and help out around the house, was the real BOSS of the Realm. She gave me the treat I liked the most: coffee "saucered and cooled." She sneaked it to me so as to avoid Mother's eyes. It looked like cocoa but tasted even better.

"Sally Ann, don't you dare give that child coffee!" Mother exclaimed. "What sane person would give a baby coffee?"

"A li'l coffee 'n' cream not gonna hurt this baby," Sally Ann frowned, pursing her lips as Mother reprimanded her. Persisting, Sally Ann poured hot coffee from a cup into a saucer, blew on it, added a little sugar and milk to cool it, and spooned it into my mouth. It tasted like candy. Mother shook her head every time, disapproving vigorously but knowing Sally Ann did not have to obey anyone—except Granny. Sally Ann knew she was immune to punishment; so she stood her ground, claiming the coffee-milk would make me strong. She dipped her snuff, and I drank my coffee-milk.

Years later, when Sally Ann, always thin but becoming frail, was no longer able to come to our house, Mother took George and me to see her every month or six weeks. As we walked up the sidewalk toward her modest white bungalow atop a small hill, we saw her rocking in her chair on the porch, in total command of her surroundings, as she had been all her life no matter where she was.

"Well, look-a-here!" she called to Mother. "Margaret, come right up and set a spell. An' bring those children over here for me to see close up."

Mother told Sally Ann the latest news about our family: Daddy, our Uncle Bill and Aunt Doots, and Nanny Kate and Uncle George, our great-aunt and -uncle next door. Soon Sally Ann tired of all that and turned her attention to George and me. She was never too sick during those visits to give us a lecture about obeying our parents and following the Lord.

"Lawdy me," she said to George and me, "you just keep gettin' bigger and bigger. Now you obey your mother—you hear Sally Ann? Your momma and daddy are God-fearing folks and your grandmomma Alice was a saint. I *loved* her. She's singing with the angels in Heaven. I reckon she's sitting by Jesus right this minute. I'll be joining her 'fore too long, I reckon—and I'll be happy."

She went on, "Now, Alice and George, you promise? The Lawd watches over you, but He'll punish you if you disobey Him. He loves you, but you have to obey. And, you be good to your momma and daddy. They don't need no mischief from you. Read your Bible and learn the Ten Commandments. And be good to other folks.

"Margaret, you make sure these children go to church every Sunday, come rain or shine. And, Alice and George, promise me you say your prayers every night."

She stopped to clean one of her teeth with a small stick she had pulled from the peach tree and trimmed into a toothpick. She held the thin, handmade pick between her teeth most of the time now.

"You understand me? I pray for you and your folks *every* day. Come here, one on each side of me. Hold my hand! I'll pray for you right now, both of you." And she did for several minutes, praying for our futures and our souls, then praising the Lord.

Her sermons put fear in our hearts and had more lasting effect than any of the preacher's sermons at church on Sunday mornings.

But that was years later. Back to 1934.

Maybe Mother and Daddy thought having another child would bring calm to the household. "If Alice had a sister or brother to play with," they may have reasoned, "she wouldn't get into so much mischief." But, wasn't I enough? And anyway, I didn't lack anything or need anybody!

George came along about the time of my second birthday. I was thrilled but also curious. Now I had a playmate, but it was a boy! He was about the size of my biggest doll and much cuter. He also wriggled and laughed, making me laugh.

Word was then—and even now—George was a much better and prettier baby than I was. He weighed ten pounds at birth and developed into a big baby with chubby, dimpled cheeks and a strong, healthy body. His broad smile captivated everyone—and still does. All Mother's friends marveled at his sunny disposition—while they remained silent when observing me.

George liked noise. His favorite toys were pots and pans. In those days, there was no money for babysitters, but no teens to babysit anyway. So Mother put him in a cavernous cardboard box under the kitchen table with a few spoons and pots, and he conducted a symphony for hours for the kitchen staff. He didn't run around the yard like his sister, making mud pies and getting dirty or falling down on gravel and scratching both knees—at least not early in his life. I couldn't understand why they liked George's banging more than my staying out of their way, roaming the neighborhood. Now and then, I'd hear them brag, "George is such a good baby. He has such a sweet disposition. He never gives us trouble."

I didn't like it one bit.

Because I was two years older than George, I got a tricycle before he did—and before anyone else in the neighborhood, too. For a while, I knew no boundaries. In Weldon, everyone knew everyone else, so I decided to visit neighbors around the corner, riding my tricycle and ringing doorbells. That didn't last long.

One day, Mother suddenly appeared, "Cud'n Mamie, I 'pologize for Alice's botherin' you. She's not permitted to go down the street by herself. She should know better by now."

Grabbing me by the sash of my dress, Mother pulled me toward home, controlling the tricycle with her other hand. I was grounded: no more solo missions. After that I was allowed to ride only under watchful eyes.

Alice Joyner Irby

GEORGE, PLAYING WITH DIRT IN THE PLANTER
ON THE FRONT STOOP, 1936

Mother and Daddy made no effort to steer us into typical girls' or boys' activities. They just let us grow naturally, and our parents didn't think a lot about gender roles and age differences. They simply reared us according to what they thought was right and would work. They celebrated our differences, proud to have a son and a daughter, but in both praise and punishment, we were treated the same. Not one kind of discipline for the girl and another for the boy.

George and I were different, but we enjoyed many of the same things. We played together in the sand pile, sometimes throwing sand at each other if we were angry. Both of us played hide-and-seek and tag, scratching our knees and legs as we raced across unpaved streets, falling occasionally on the gravel. Both of us sailed our toy sailboats in the Roanoke River when, in 1940, it flooded our town, creating a river in the main street. Both of us had chores, the same chores. For example, we picked up sticks for kindling wood to feed eight fireplaces and the two kitchen stoves.

When we were toddlers, we both got dolls and teddy bears for Christmas, though neither of us spent much time with dolls. It wasn't long before George abandoned his for trucks and erector sets, and I favored skates and my speedy tricycle. As we grew larger, both of us climbed the pecan tree in the backyard to shake the nuts to the ground for harvesting. George went higher than I did because he was stronger, and I was afraid of heights. We raced to see who could fill up a bushel basket first. Daddy then cracked the nuts and Mother salted them for Christmas. Later in the year, she used them in pies and other desserts.

When we were six, each of us started piano lessons with Louise Farber, a well-known piano teacher and my mother's best friend. George gave it up at the beginning of his second year. I persisted for twelve years, giving an individual recital during my senior year in high school. Mother and Louise thought I should pursue a career in music. I probably should have, because looking back I realize how much joy it would have brought me—and perhaps others. But I lacked the discipline and self-sacrifice necessary to succeed in that career.

George enjoyed sports and a companion dog named Tippy, part chow and part collie, reddish brown and extremely protective of the family. Tippy, keeping guard as he lay on the wide walkway leading to the front steps, succeeded a troublesome white spitz given to George by a boarder the year before. No one dared try ringing our doorbell unless Tippy knew him.

George and I also guarded our neighborhood, and always in proper Wild West garb, making sure that anyone who approached our house could see the guns in our holsters. To avoid identification and to protect our parents' reputation, we covered our faces with bandanas so that the bad guys would not know who we were.

We both had lively dispositions, sometimes getting ourselves in trouble. Since George and I lived with my grandmother in her boarding house, we loved to hide behind the sofa as boarders gathered for their evening meal, snickering at the costumes some of them wore or mimicking their accents.

Sometimes, in good weather, when guests gathered on the front porch, we sneaked behind the tall, bushy shrubbery, planted on either side of the front steps, so we could overhear their conversations. Our mission was to get local gossip or information about far-away places we could pass on to our friends.

A major north-south highway, U.S. Route 301, came right through the middle of Weldon, a block east of our house. Often travelers stopped for the night in one of several "tourist homes" in town. When they did, they took their meals with us because there were no decent public

GEORGE AND ALICE PROTECTING THE HOMESTEAD

restaurants in town. Granny's boarding house had a reputation for being the best place in town to eat.

Present also were the "regulars," teachers who rented rooms in town, or local residents who needed to take their meals out. I remember well a couple of sisters, Mrs. Bertha Purnell, a widow, and Miss Emma Rodwell. They came every day attired in coats—even in summer, and with hats covering their black hair, and kid gloves on their hands. George and I snickered behind their backs because we were convinced they had to wear hats in order to keep their wigs in place.

In 1940, when Mother was pregnant with Margaret Ray, the sisters stopped coming. The joke around the house was that they were afraid of catching pregnancy. Truth was, more likely, they did not think it proper for a pregnant woman to be seen among the public, even in her own home. Back they came after my sister was born, pretending they had never been away, cooing over her heart-shaped face and the sparkling eyes of our newborn.

If we got caught eavesdropping on the boarders as they waited on the porch or in the living room for the next seating, we were sent to our rooms—sometimes without dinner—after having to promise solemnly not to tell tales or to gossip about them with our friends.

A favorite target of our clandestine eavesdropping was Evelyn Griffin, a third-grade teacher in Weldon, who lived with us. Mother gave her exclusive access to our living room on Wednesday nights for her dates with Mr. Horace Stevenson from across the river in Northampton County. We couldn't hide behind the sofa, but we could crouch at the top of the stairs, see their laps and feet, and listen to their conversation. We made up stories about their romance to tell her students at school.

For years, their weekly dates continued—even after George and I had outgrown spying—until Evelyn finally decided that since Mr. Stevenson had not proposed marriage, she was tired of his dithering and broke up with him. Shortly thereafter, they announced their engagement and were married.

One of the long-term roomers was a straight-backed, dark-haired, six-foot, well-built state patrolman whom we liked a lot. He was friendly with George and me, and he had a dog, a white spitz, that he let us pet. No one messed with Patrolman Hines and his dog, or with any of us when they were around. George and I were the envy of our peers, having a handsome patrolman living with us and a beautiful dog to pet. The spitz was a good watchdog, though nobody in Weldon in those days needed protection. Mr. Hines later gave the dog to George, and we loved playing with him, stroking his long white hair. He was a good playmate for us but he did not like strangers, so George had to give him away. We suffered a decline in popularity when the patrolman was assigned to another location in the state and moved away.

My mother was not the only matron in the household equipped with a sense of discipline—and humor. Mother's brother, Bill, and her sister-in-law, Doots, lived in Granny's house as well. Bill was a butcher in the local Acme grocery store, and Doots oversaw the dining room of the boarding house, as well as performed any chores that needed attention. She also kept a close eye on George, embracing him with all the love a mother would offer. In fact, when asked who his mother was, George often said he had two mothers, Doots and Margaret, our "real" mother. Doots was talented in thinking of ways to amuse him or for him to amuse himself while everyone was at work in the boarding house.

One couple living with us had an older boy, Billy, whom we considered ornery and mischievous. Guests were expected to use only the front door, but members of this family came in the back door now and then. For a while, no one said anything, but soon the boy developed a habit of coming in the back door to sample desserts Doots had put on the back-porch table to be out of the way of the people working in the kitchen.

Also, Billy often snitched sweets from the back-porch shelves before meals were served. Doots got tired of his ignoring her admonitions and decided to teach him a few manners. She couldn't spank him because he was not her child, but she could use other tactics to get his attention. One day, she took a package of marshmallows, inserted quinine in some of the pieces, placed those pieces at the front of the opened package and set them on the back-porch table. The marshmallows were waiting when Billy came barreling up the back steps, springing into the back porch, eyeing the treat, and reaching quickly for two pieces, stuffing both in his mouth at the same time.

Screaming, he let everyone in Weldon know something was terribly wrong! Spitting out the marshmallows as fast as he could, he ran to his mother, yelling and crying, calling Doots "a mean old witch." He knew she was the culprit and tried to get his folks to complain to Mother. They knew better than to do that, though, not wanting to jeopardize their food and shelter. Instead, Billy had to apologize to Doots and to Mother. After that, he was never seen again on the back porch or anywhere near Doots' homemade desserts, except at the dinner table.

Instead of getting mad, Doots often made her point with a practical joke. One roomer, a dignified though somewhat pompous gentleman, had a habit of never telling Doots, when she asked, how he liked his eggs prepared for breakfast. With good manners, deferring to her, he would say, "Any way is fine. You decide."

Each day, Doots repeated her question. "Mr. Zollicoffer, how would you like your eggs today?" She really wanted him to state his preference, but, each day, he left the choice to her.

One day, she had had enough. She said, "Fine, Sir, I will take care of it." She brought him a raw egg, cracked and floating in a saucer. What did he do? He was not about to appear flustered. Good naturedly, he gulped it down and said with a smile, "Thank you." Thereafter, every day, he specified exactly how he wanted his eggs prepared.

During the Depression and War years, George and I had few toys, certainly not bright plastic ones as children have today. Rubber and wood were in short supply, especially during the war. Though I don't remember many big toys, we did not lack for fun. We had an erector set, Tinker Toys, pick-up-sticks, playing cards, Monopoly, Chinese checkers, and Caroms, our favorite.

I had one doll I liked, "Scarlett O'Hara," a black-haired beauty for whom my Aunt Genie made a trunkful of clothes. My hair was almost black, and I pretended I looked like her. I liked her outfits and changed her clothes to go with the season, but I never played with her. I just liked looking at her all dressed up, imagining myself looking like that, too, in long dresses with tight bodices and skirts draped over crinoline petticoats.

Caroms is a great game, modeled on pool. A carom is a small donut-like wooden ring—or a disk—about 1¼ inches in diameter and 3/8 of an inch thick, similar to checkers disks but thicker and smoother. There are 18 carom men in a set, a striker for each of two players, and a queen. George and I played with our fingers on a hard-surfaced wooden board, about 30" square, bound by one-inch bumpers around the edges. The board had woven-net pockets at each corner. To position the lacquered board so the four pockets hung off the corners, we knelt on the floor with the board on the piano bench. Green and red caroms were divided between two players. The black carom was the "queen." The queen is analogous to the eight ball—or black ball—in pool.

The rules are similar to those of pool. The player positions his striker on or behind a line painted on the board, then shoots at his pieces, trying to get them into a pocket without his striker going in as well. The goal is to get all of one's caroms and the queen into the pockets before the other player can sink all his caroms and the queen.

It took all my finger strength to break up the pack and try to get some of my red or green rings in the pocket before George could score with all of his. George and I were pretty evenly matched; I had more dexterity whereas he had more power in his fingers. Each of us won some and lost some, but we liked the game so much we usually didn't argue or fight over the outcome.

We were not allowed to play "big" pool because the commercial poolroom in Weldon was the hangout for disreputable men, most of them drinkers and heavy smokers. Like other parents, Mother and Daddy did not want us to develop bad habits. Thus, we were not supposed to go near the pool hall, but it being off-limits made the place ever-more fascinating to us children.

About the only time we ever got a look inside was in the summer as we walked by the front door, generally opened wide to relieve the stifling heat inside. As we walked by, we hoped to get a peek at the players smoking their cigarettes and to eye the bottles of liquor lined up like choristers in ranks behind the bar. Just as with scenes in cowboy movies, lamps hung low over pool tables in an otherwise dark room. We walked by fast so our parents would not catch us near what they called a "den of iniquity" and what we saw as a place of intrigue.

Eventually, Daddy bought us a smaller-than-regulation pool set, one that we could stand to play with pool sticks so we would not have to crouch on the floor and use our fingers. It didn't catch on with us. Truth was, kneeling on the floor playing caroms was more fun, even though in playing the game, I developed a callus on the third finger of my right hand that I have today.

Five years ago, long after I retired, my daughter, Andrea, gave me a Carom set for Christmas. It's still fun to play with grandkids and family. I remained champion over them for a while, until my arthritic fingers shortened my reign. I was toppled by grandchildren.

About the time I was school age, Weldon opened a small community swimming pool. Mother took both George and me to splash in the water. I took to the water like an eager duckling, happy to stay there all day, but of course, that was not permitted. I did go often, learning how to swim soon after I started splashing around.

Not so George. He didn't like the pool because he sunburned easily. He liked animals, though. So, when he was several years older, Dad got him a blaze-faced bay pony named Tex. Tex's stable was in an extra garage on our property, converted for that purpose. Soon we had the Wild

West right in our backyard! George put on his cowboy outfit with holster and gun, mounted the pony in a Western saddle, called Tippy to join him, and headed across town for the cemetery.

He went there not to battle ghosts but because it offered the safest isolated dirt roads in town. It was also quiet: the dead didn't talk, and mourners didn't visit often. George could chase desperados all day, calling loudly for them to surrender, mowing them down with toy pistols as they tried to escape. Today, a child would not be safe riding his pony around the horseshoe loop in the cemetery. What a loss.

While we developed different interests, one thing remained the same for both George and me: *punishment*. Mother was the Chief Enforcer and the Judge. Living in a boarding house exposed us to lively language from time to time. My mother and father did not approve of bad language, much less profanity, including "Darn." Yet, somewhere George and I picked up words like "Darn" and "Hell." "Hell" we thought was okay because we had heard that in church.

On several occasions—probably more than a few—Mother caught us using those words in calling each other names. One time, she made us sit on the linoleum floor in the kitchen and put our hands behind our backs. She disappeared into the pantry, a big room off the kitchen, and came back with something red in her hand. Calmly, she ordered us to raise our heads and open our mouths and look up at her. Can't you just see our small mouths opening innocently, like little birds in a nest, trusting we'd get a delicious surprise? Surprise, yes, but of red pepper pods, not candy or cake!

After that, we laid off bad language for a long time. We also learned to count to ten before saying a cussword. Sometimes, though, we would get so mad with each other we just had to express our anger in colorful language. Out came the red pepper pods again. If not that, Octagon soap. It took another two or three times before we learned to have our fights out of Mother's ear and reach, or not to have them at all.

We had a habit of staying out too late in the wintertime playing baseball or hide-and-seek. Dark was our curfew, but we often stayed outside until it was dark night. Other times, we would go to a friend's house and not tell Mother where we were.

Arriving home, we pretended nothing was amiss, but when the screen door slammed as we walked up the stairs, the Enforcer ordered us to go back outside and choose our own switches. If we came back with branches that were too short or too thin, we were sent back to get bigger ones that would not break but would sting. Most times, I think Mother was half-hearted in her use of the switches because if George and I started crying quickly, she lightened up and soon cast the switches aside.

Looking back, I do feel guilty because I got George in a lot of trouble. He followed because I was the older one, and there were few children his age to play with in the neighborhood. But there was one time I did not lead him into iniquity—one time that he, a boy across the street, and I were equal co-conspirators—partners in crime.

"Alice, George! Come here right this minute," Mother called us in a stern, commanding voice.

"Where have you been?" she asked sharply.

"Nowhere," we answered in unison. "Just here in the backyard playing."

"I'm not talking about now. I mean yesterday afternoon. Where were you?"

We could not remember. To us, that seemed years ago. Then we remembered, "We were playing across the street with Forest Rowe, running around the telephone company building and the vacant house next door," George reported innocently.

"Yes, indeed, you were! And you broke into the vacant house, didn't you?" Mother alleged with cold anger in her voice. "Furthermore, you damaged the walls, didn't you? Do you understand what that means? Breaking and entering? Destroying someone else's property?"

The questions and charges were coming so fast, we couldn't comprehend what Mother meant. We were just having fun and, besides, nobody lived there. I had crawled through a window; George and Forest had found the back door cracked open. We did not realize there was fresh paint on the walls when we jumped up against them, hitting them and leaving shoe prints all over them. I also found a loose board and made a few scratches here and there. After all, the place was abandoned. Why would anyone care? Who could have seen us? Who would have told on us?

"Mercy me!" groaned Mother, with worry spread across her face. "What will I do? What will my friends think—that I am rearing juvenile delinquents? Criminals? Vandals?"

George and I could not understand the words and why she was so upset. We were only playing, not hurting anyone, and not even fighting among ourselves. Just running around an empty house with Forest.

"Mr. Musgrove called to tell me that he has it on good authority—an eye-witness—that you two and Forest Rowe vandalized that house. He was shocked that children from a good family would do such a thing. But he has agreed that if you pay for the repairs and fresh paint, there will be no charges brought. All will be forgiven. That means that you will have to stay home, do chores, run errands, and earn enough money to pay him back."

"Earn enough money to fix everything?" we asked. "We don't even work. How can we earn money?" George and I were getting scared. We knew we were headed for a Big Punishment.

"Each of you will have to raise $3.00. You can start by picking up a bushel of chips for the fireplaces. You can't go out to play until you earn the first dollar. Then, before you can go out to play each day, you will have to complete chores and add money to the pot. AND, you must promise never to do anything like that again."

We shook in fear...then, in relief.

"Whew!" I said later to George. "That was not as bad as I feared. At least, she didn't send us for the switches, or grab the red peppers, or ground us forever."

George demurred, "But that's a lot of chores at five cents apiece. We will be old by the time we finish."

We tried to stay out of the way when Daddy came home from work that day. He knew; he had a solemn frown on his face. He sat us down in front of him and gave us a long lecture about respecting others and their possessions, reminding us of the Biblical phrase to "Do unto others as you would have them do unto you." He was dead serious. He was not angry or shouting, but we knew we had to obey.

When we realized what we had done, we were embarrassed. We avoided our friends. We kept our heads down when we went to church. Adults were talking behind our backs; we could see them doing so, and we felt deep shame.

Lesson learned. Never, never did we do anything like that again.

In time, life became normal again, and we were back to playing in our own yard—staying away from other people's houses. We learned later that our $6.00 was just a pittance of what Mother and Daddy had to pay to fix the walls, but they never complained to us about it.

The punishment each of us hated most was "Kiss and make up" when we trashed each other's room. We never fought physically with punches and blows. We always thought of some other way to get revenge for what we thought was an offense. After Mother closed the boarding house around 1940-41, she gave us rooms on the second floor, next to each other. Bill and Doots had moved to Newport News so that Bill could work in the shipyard to support the war effort. George and I had the upstairs to ourselves, with the remaining rooms reserved for relatives or a couple of people who stayed with us during WWII when their husbands were overseas.

When we were at odds with each other, we messed up the other's room and then ran downstairs or out into the yard. Coming upstairs to put sheets and towels in the linen closet, Mother discovered the piles of clothes, sheets, and bedspreads scattered in our rooms. She found us, marched us upstairs and made us clean up each other's room. That was bad enough, but the last phase of the routine was that we had to hug and kiss each other and say we were sorry! Ugh!

Of course we weren't sorry! We did the fastest, most superficial hug and kiss possible, just to get Mother off our backs. Despite our dedicated plotting and rigorous fights, however, George and I did love each other, and still do—very much.

Later, when I was about 10 or 11 years old, the punishment I hated the most was inflicted when, in the wintertime, I stayed at a friend's house until after dark. I was usually home by suppertime, but not always. Mother didn't permit me to walk home alone after dark. She alternated two punishments: grounding me for two weeks, meaning that I had to go straight home after school and could not call or see my friends, *or* chopping wood. I preferred chopping wood any day. Today that punishment might rank as child abuse, but by chopping wood, I learned a valuable skill as well as a lesson about obedience. We had lots of fireplaces and stoves to keep stoked.

Logs were delivered to us having been cut into small logs that, lengthwise, were the width of the fireplace. My job was to split the small logs into strips of wood to fit those fireplaces.

George chopped too, though perhaps not as punishment; he wanted to grow strong. He could chop faster than I and handle logs too big for me. Once, there were about a dozen railroad ties piled up in the backyard. All by himself, George chopped all of those into logs for the fireplaces.

To chop wood, I propped a log on end against another bigger log lying on the ground. The axe had to hit the propped-up log just right to splinter it completely. It never occurred to me that I could have cut off my toe or my foot. In fact, I came to enjoy wielding that axe. I grew strong, too, and I felt I was as capable as any man doing the same job.

Only once in my many years did I meet another woman who knew how to chop wood. She, too, grew up in a farming area. We were not the only ones, surely, because I remember that Robert Morgan started his novel *Gap Creek* with a scene of a mountain woman chopping wood. He knows about us.

Not only did George and I suffer the same punishments for the same crimes, we also had some of the same pleasures. We both liked baseball, probably because our dad was a big fan who followed professional teams daily via radio. He and a group of friends gathered in his furniture store, turned on one of the radios, and listened to the game of the day, preferably one featuring the Yankees.

In fact, Dad made sure I learned to play baseball because he needed me to practice with George. George had real athletic talent that Dad recognized early.

Never mind that Dad was a Southerner pulling for a New York team. He was a lifelong fan of Lou Gehrig and the Yankees. They were the top team year after year, and Dad regarded Lou Gehrig as the most talented player in baseball, and a fine gentleman, too! Gehrig was a left-handed first baseman, and George was also left-handed. Dad wanted George to follow in Gehrig's footsteps, but George needed practice, and Dad needed a third person to assist him in training George. Playing with friends in pick-up sandlot games was not sufficient to develop his skills, and George was too young to play high-school ball.

Dad needed a pitcher, catcher, and hitter. If I joined in, we had a trio of Dad, George, and me. I jumped at the chance! Not only was I allowed to play, I turned out to be an adequate challenger for George. I learned to throw strikes and balls, to field his hits by chasing the balls down the block, and to hit the ball so that he could try to put me out at first base—the telephone pole a quarter way down the block.

Dad alternated between catching and hitting, depending upon who was at bat, because pitching meant he would have to run down the block chasing balls and he was not very fast.

Besides, George and I needed the pitching experience.

DAD AND GEORGE, AROUND 1939

Dad taught me the fine points of the game, which later enabled me to enjoy following major-league games on the radio in the summertime while sewing my clothes for the next school year.

Girls were not prohibited from playing baseball, but few wanted to do so. Only Gwen Richardson joined me in wanting to play. To do so meant playing with the boys. Little League baseball didn't exist then, so our games were pick-up games. I was not as strong as the guys and could not hit the ball as far, but I had a good eye and had been taught a good stance by Dad. I usually got on base, and if the fellows at bat next were any good, I could get home for a score.

George became a star in high school. By that time, we had students attending our school from Halifax, a town just seven miles down the road, which meant there were enough boys to field a competitive team for varsity play. The varsity teams played neighboring high-school teams.

In high school, girls were put on co-ed softball teams in intramural sports, and I pitched for a while. My crowning achievement was striking out Glick Price. He was the biggest player in the school, when I was in the 9th grade. Softball was not as much fun as baseball—quite a comedown. So I quit, which was okay. By that time, I was beginning to be interested in other activities, such as cheerleading, dancing, and dating.

By the time we were teenagers, George and I had been through a lot together: pushing the boundaries of permissible play in our early years, most times getting caught and punished—appropriately. We covered for each other when possible, but most times, we were partners in crime. Little escaped Mother's eye or her imagination when it came to fitting the punishment to the crime.

We were partners in our development as well, learning to climb trees, to play croquet, to compete in Caroms, to chop wood, to ride horses, and to play baseball. I enjoy the game of baseball even today. I remember with fondness taking my father to Yankee Stadium when I lived in Princeton, N.J., to see the Yankees play and to watch Catfish Hunter pitch. Catfish was from Ahoskie, a town not far from Weldon. Daddy had a casual acquaintance with Catfish's father. North Carolinians were proud of Catfish and his success in the big leagues. Every year, I still look forward to watching the World Series, especially to observe the pitchers.

Mother's balanced combination of unconditional love and fair discipline gave George and me a solid, well-grounded childhood. What strikes me about those years is that, in every way, we were treated equally before the bar...the bar of Justice, with Mother administering the sentencing and the punishment...the bar of Praise, with both Mother and Daddy rewarding us and considering us worthy...and the bar of Compassion, with each of us receiving sympathy and counsel when hurt.

GEORGE, MOTHER, AND ALICE, LATE 1939

As we matured, we developed different interests, displayed different talents, and chose different professions. But, before the Joyner Bar of Justice, because of our loyal, loving parents, each of us was accorded equal treatment.

Neither of us was disadvantaged relative to the other or treated unfairly.

Fairness is a worthy goal. As I think about it now, the example my parents repeatedly provided shaped my behavior during my professional life, whether in admitting students to college, or in mediating an employee grievance. They created a standard for our interactions with others through the way they lived: lives of Christian charity, of hope in hard times, of faith in the dignity of every human life, and of justice and discipline when required.

With our parents' steady guidance, a sense of fairness was burned into our souls. Even today, many years into my retirement, I am troubled and repulsed when I observe an individual being treated unfairly. I know George is, too.

March 2019

The Funeral Foursome

Regardless of denomination, nobody in my part of Eastern North Carolina would have thought of having a funeral without music. Even families of non-believers gathered for services in funeral homes while church music played in the background. Every small town had at least one church, and funerals were usually conducted in church sanctuaries to the slow rhythms of comforting organ or piano music.

Country churches, which may or may not have owned musical instruments, hosted formal burial services for their local families. Where there were no musical instruments, congregants found a way to sing hymns together. Yet many funerals out in the country were in homes, with family, friends, and minister gathered in the sitting room. A church may not have been nearby, or the deceased had left instructions not to have his or her last rites in the Lord's home, but in his or her own home.

Not until after the Second World War did North Carolina have a network of hard-surface roads. Thanks to Governor Kerr Scott, many of the state's roads were paved or "improved" in the late 1940s. Improved roads might be paved, gravel, or well-graded dirt roads, i.e., red clay if in Eastern North Carolina. Many, but not all, of the secondary "farm-to-market" roads were paved, as were the state highways connecting towns across the region. County and local roads were usually dirt, though graded—smooth until rain created puddles. Or, until dry, hot days blew up storms of dust capable of blurring a driver's vision. An extended national highway system did not exist until later, when the Eisenhower Administration launched a major continental road-building program from 1953 to 1961.

Even with the new roads, vehicles needed good shock absorbers and axles, especially vehicles used to transport relatives and guests to funerals out in the country. Some funerals were on small farms in "deep" country, back in thick woods along pastures and creeks. These homesteads were connected to improved roads by bumpy driveways winding down a long path filled with washboard ruts and large rocks. Branches and limbs fallen from trees often lay across the road leading to the farmhouse.

Even so, better to have bumpy, puddled driveways than to live too close to the road. The house and out-buildings needed to be near the chicken coop and the barn. Safeguarding animals, especially chickens and hens, from tramps, poachers, and foxes, was necessary to protect the family's livelihood. Living at a distance back from the road also kept the children out of harm's way. The back roads were not heavily traveled by automobiles, but the tractors, farm equipment, and pickup trucks bumping along could threaten small children. And, meeting horses pulling wagons and small equipment was common, too.

Most of the children back in the "woods" had to walk a half-mile or more each day to get the school bus—and that was after they'd milked the cows, collected eggs, and eaten breakfast, preceded by an ample family blessing, of course. Country folk valued education above all else but

God. Children did their homework at night by oil lamp if electricity had not yet reached the farm. To balance the need for learning with the need for harvesting crops, county schools closed for two or three weeks in the fall so that farm children could help pick cotton in the fields, a back-breaking job, or dig up rows of peanuts, hoisting them onto tall-pole frames for drying.

Three crops provided income for farmers in northeastern North Carolina: tobacco, cotton, and peanuts, known as the "money crops." Tobacco allotments carried high value, granting the owner the right to plant a specified number of acres. Tobacco was cut, "handed," and cured in tobacco barns during the summer. An acre of tobacco could bring thousands of dollars in revenue. But a single farmer was not granted enough tobacco acreage to rely solely on tobacco. Cotton and peanuts added diversification and major sources of income once they were harvested at the end of summer and in early fall.

Cotton had to be picked when the bolls were full and the weather dry. In those days, it was picked by hand, the cotton separated from its seeds by a cotton gin at a plant that could make cottonseed oil out of the seeds and then send the separated cotton to textile mills for converting into cloth. In a good year, before the picking began, the cotton fields were full of tall, drying plants with round, white puffs on their stems, looking like pastures of freshly fallen snow. Travelers from out of state, riding along U.S. Route 301, then stopping in local service stations, often inquired about the blanket of white fleece out in the fields.

Peanuts rotted in the ground—they are root legumes, not nuts—if not gathered when their hulls were full of meat, and before the fall rains. Northeastern North Carolina was known for growing the famous *Virginia* peanut, the kind that people eat at cocktail parties and baseball games. The vines with roots attached were plowed up, shoveled by hand, and hoisted onto tall stakes to dry. Timing was everything. Farmers feared any mistiming of their harvests and always worried about fall rains and hurricanes arriving too soon. All hands were ordered to work fast, including the children.

If farmers did not make their tobacco, cotton, and peanut crops, their income for the whole year was lost. Their individual losses rippled through the entire local economy. Merchants were not paid for that farm family's purchases acquired through year-long credit. School supplies and books were in short supply. Persistent family needs could not be met for lack of funding. The only hope was for better weather next year.

People stayed close to the land. Even their handling of the deceased occurred near their homesteads, either in a church down the road or at home. Most funerals out in the country were in the early afternoon, the morning being devoted to the arrival of guests and the preparation of volumes of food for later in the day.

In anticipation of the funeral, a family member contacted the minister to plan the service and arrange for scripture and music. Sometimes the call came to the Weldon Methodist Church, where my family worshipped.

One day in October, Mr. Thomas, our school superintendent, called out to his secretary, Katty Pierce: "Reverend Ruark at the Methodist Church just called and asked if Blanche Selden and Alice Joyner could be excused for the rest of the day to sing at a funeral out in the country."

"Mr. Thomas," replied Katty, "that's fine, but shouldn't their parents be notified because Blanche and Alice won't be here when the closing bell rings?" Permission was easily obtained for me; my mother, as the French and history teacher, was right down the hall.

Katty then called Mrs. Selden, who was usually home taking care of Little Joe, Blanche's brother. "Of course, Katty. I'm happy for Blanche to leave early today to sing at the funeral. I certainly want Blanche to be of service to the church," Mrs. Selden told Katty.

No one in town would deny a grieving family the solace of hearing Christian music at the service of a loved one.

Surprised by the call, Blanche and I realized we were not dressed properly and certainly could not appear in bobby socks and loafers. That would be insulting to the grieving family. We felt our dress was important to a grieving family, a symbol of our respect for them and an acknowledgment of their significant loss.

Each of us ran home—nothing in Weldon was more than a five-minute run from school—and changed into stockings and black pumps.

Ben Wyche and J. P. Ellis, two businessmen in town, were the bass and tenor voices of our quartet. Ben, a fair-complexioned bachelor with sandy-blond hair and a medium build, owned and operated Merchant's Distributing

Company, a wholesale distributor of canned foodstuffs, grocery supplies, and dry goods. He and his two salesmen traveled daily across two counties calling on the many mom-and-pop stores selling to farmers and other country folks.

Ben telephoned each of us to say, "I'll pick you up in my car after I pick up J. P., and we'll head out to a small farm beyond Pierce's Crossroads." None of us ever knew what to expect, but without thinking, we had voiced a ready "Yes" when the request came in from the minister.

The Weldon Methodist Church did not have circuit-rider ministers who preached among a circle of small country churches, but it did offer to provide services for individuals and families on special occasions. Sometimes the request was for a minister to conduct a wedding or a funeral, and one of the ministers from a church in town, depending upon who was available, would volunteer to help.

Sometimes the request included music at a funeral. That's when Rev. Henry Ruark got the idea of a quartet from the Methodist Church that could go, on short notice, to out-of-the-way places in the county. He organized the four-voice ensemble solely for the purpose of serving grieving families who lived in the country and who did not have access to suitable funeral music. Our quartet had just the four of us, no substitutes.

We soon became known among our friends as "the funeral foursome." When a call came to the church, Rev. Ruark called the school office. Each time, Mr. Thomas excused Blanche and me from school for the rest of the day.

After the initial request, our parents had given blanket approval for future assignments, trusting Mr. Thomas and Rev. Ruark to use their good judgment about the wisdom of excusing us from school each time our singing was requested.

Like the first time, in succeeding trips Ben and J. P. Ellis, manager of the Weldon Savings and Loan, picked us up. J. P., a slight, brown-haired man a few years younger than Ben, was the sole manager and staff of the local savings and loan. On these occasions, he simply locked up the building and hung out the "Closed" sign.

Because Ben traveled county roads over and over, visiting his customers in small country grocery stores, he knew the territory pretty well. That was a good thing because there was no GPS or even a handy commercial map. Maps that did exist of remote county locations were those archived in Raleigh by the N.C. Highway Commission, and they were sometimes topographical maps that made reading road routes and markers difficult.

Usually Ben had up-to-date information on washouts, detours, and crumbling shoulders. Cars in those days had been made either before or right after WWII, when materials and labor were scarce and quality-control questionable. Thus, not every automobile accessory worked every time.

At times, too, visibility was reduced to almost zero. A couple of times, when it was raining hard, Ben's windshield wipers stopped. Ben stopped the car. "J. P., can you get out and try to get the wipers going again?"

"You mean, get out of the car in this driving rain?" asked J. P., thinking Ben had lost his mind.

"I have an umbrella somewhere here in the car. Be careful not to get your dress clothes too wet." Ben spoke like a father. "I can't see how to drive if we don't have a working wiper."

Reluctantly and whispering a few uncommon words under his breath, J. P. crawled out of the front passenger seat into the driving rain, trying to fix the wiper with one hand; with the other, to prevent the umbrella from sailing away. Usually he was successful...for a while.

A few miles down the road, Ben had to stop again. J. P. ducked as if to disappear, knowing what would come next.

"O.K., Ben, you don't have to say anything this time. I know what I have to do. And, since I am already wet, since you are the driver, and since we would never ask Alice or Blanche to get wet, I am the Indispensable Man," J. P. announced ruefully before Ben could say a word.

"I hate to ask you to do that, J. P.," said Ben apologetically, "but we have to have enough visibility to stay out of the ditch."

Drying off as we rode along, J. P. pressed Ben, "Hurry, Ben, I've used up the towels and other gear you have back here. I don't want to have to get drenched a third time. I might get a sore throat and not be able to sing at all!"

Ben shrugged and smiled.

As we rode along, we selected the hymns to use—unless they had been chosen by the family ahead of time—and practiced our parts, singing at least two stanzas of each hymn to be sure we had the timing as well as the notes correct. The music we knew, because the hymns were well-known Methodist favorites, but we did not always know the lyrics. As a backup, Ben kept Methodist hymnals in his car. We often admitted our thanks to Charles Wesley, too, for writing so many melodious, uplifting, and easy-to-sing hymns.

We didn't have a metronome—just the pat of our feet on the floorboard of the car. Blanche and I alternated soprano and alto, depending upon the piece. Ben sang tenor; J. P. bass. Because all four of us were in the Methodist Church choir, we were familiar with the hymns and with each other's voices.

Ben and J. P. wore coats and ties, always a dark color coat and a muted tie. If Blanche and I knew a day in advance, we wore our Sunday clothes and stockings to school that day. Eventually, I got so I wore stockings almost every day in winter, pulling my socks on over them, just to be prepared. When pumps were not on hand, we wore dark-brown loafers, but we made sure never to wear saddle oxfords. If push came to shove and we were not dressed properly, Ben dropped us by our homes to pick up some shoes and jackets before we started out. Because we were the "choir" for the funeral, we did not have to wear hats and gloves as on Sunday at church—thank goodness.

Proper dress was important in those days, as were proper manners. We would never consider wearing pants ("trousers," we called them then) to school or anywhere else. Blue jeans, i.e., "dungarees," were for planting and harvesting, not for social occasions. I had one pair of jeans I could wear around the neighborhood, but it was not a common practice to go downtown in jeans. Miss Eunice Clark made sure of that! She was the town's self-anointed Manners Patrol, always in her pearls, hat, and white gloves when she walked downtown every afternoon.

One Saturday, she saw three of us girls a block from my house near the post office, and called out in a sharp, staccato tone, "Girls, what are you doing going downtown in dungarees? Don't you know that proper young ladies never wear work clothes to town? What would your mothers say? Turn around right now, go home, and change your clothes, or I am going to call each of your mothers."

"Yes, Ma'am, Miss Clark," we said in unison, doing an about-face and hustling as fast as possible back to my house.

"What audacity!" we agreed.

"Do you really think she would call our mothers?" asked Susan, a friend and classmate.

"You better believe it," Blanche replied. "She lives a couple of blocks from us and it is not uncommon to see her patrolling the neighborhood giving orders to children playing."

Men in the families we sang for did dress in dungarees and overalls for their work in the fields. But, for special family occasions, including funerals, both men and women dressed in their Sunday best. In warm weather, women wore paisley dresses with white lace collars, straw hats of an early 1920s style, and white gloves. Men wore loose, cotton twill suits, white shirts with starched collars tight around their crimson-red, sunbaked necks, knotted ties, and held crumpled hats in their laps. Their gaze was down, their faces tense and pinched with grief.

While singing was our major function, it was not the only one. Each of us had another role, too. Ben, the senior member of our quartet, introduced us to the minister and the bereaved family. Sometimes he knew the minister or someone in the family through his business.

J. P. rode shotgun for Ben, sighting landmarks, fixing windshield wipers to keep us out of the ditch, making sure we arrived on time. At the home of the deceased, J. P. located a place for us to stand, not too close to the minister or the casket, and arranged chairs for us to use during the service.

Blanche played the piano when there was one. We always used the piano, whether in tune or not. Upright pianos painted dark black or brown, their keyboards aged and their cushions uneven, were common in those homes. The pianos had been there for generations and were proud possessions. We could not ignore them, for doing so would have been impolite. Humidity and wide temperature differences made it impossible for the owners to keep the piano in tune for more than a few weeks, so it was difficult harmonizing when the piano notes were off-key. When there was no piano, Blanche, who had perfect pitch, gave us the pitch for each part.

I was the announcer, informing the congregation of the hymns, should there be no written program. I called their attention to any other significant facts as well, e.g., the hymn being a favorite of the deceased, or one frequently sung at family gatherings. Occasionally, we were handed a hymn we had never seen and had to do our best to sing the parts on key and in the appropriate tempo.

The minister helped us, too, outlining the service in advance. Most likely, he came from a church in Roanoke Rapids, Weldon, or Halifax. Occasionally, one of us had a connection with the mother or father, or the son or daughter might attend our school. Family members were always courteous to us, even when we did not sound very good. We sang at least two hymns and, occasionally, an anthem if the piano was in tune. The better the piano, the more music we provided. The music seemed to comfort the grieving family as much as any of the minister's words. That was true for me as well because singing always lifted my spirits.

Performing in a country church was much easier for us than in a home. For one thing, we were placed in a small choir section at any church, standing *behind* the open casket, not *beside* it. As a result, the grief of the family members was not as palpable from a distance. Neither did the smell of enticing food permeate the sanctuary as it did in the home.

In the home, the minister stood at the center, facing the family and guests, with the open casket on his left and us on his right. Avoiding direct eye contact with the audience was difficult. Seated in our chairs during the service, staring down at the floor, we became familiar with every color and figure in the living-room rug. We tried hard not to glance at the casket or to look in the dining room at platters piled high with ham, potato salad, beans, corn, deviled eggs, fried chicken, rolls, and pies of every kind. But the inviting smell of freshly fried chicken and bacon-flavored vegetables sorely tempted us. I could see Ben's eye on the chicken. J. P. ogled the country ham. My gaze always wandered to the deviled eggs and chicken salad. We were all in such close quarters!

Most people have heard about itinerant ministers who rode a circuit among several country churches, but few can recount tales of circuit-riding country choristers! We may have been the first—and perhaps the only—circuit-riding musical funeral foursome in all of Eastern North Carolina.

One day, during one of our performances, Blanche leaned over to me and said, "I can see we have started our own call service—of a much better kind—right here in northeastern North Carolina!" We were proud of what we did and the comfort we tried to provide. After Blanche and I graduated, I supposed others took our place, though I never heard.

I grew to have great respect for those country people and the simple but risky lives they led. They arose early, worked hard in the fields, ate heartily three times a day, lived quietly, and were devout in their faith. How they coped with their losses when hurricanes destroyed their peanut crops or the boll weevil gobbled up their fields of cotton, I can't fathom. Perhaps the Bible's stories about feast and famine gave them a sense of inevitability and reconciliation with the circumstances and vicissitudes of life, so that their faith carried them through the famine years. I saw that they walked humbly but steadily with their God. As the minister read one or more psalms, some of the congregation mouthed the words along with him.

They knew their Bible. When he raised his hands and said the benediction, "The Lord bless you and keep you, The Lord make his face to shine upon you...and give you peace," to a person, they accentuated his cadences with "A-men," some adding, "Hav' mercy 'pon us, Lawd."

I don't know whether we made any difference at all out in those farmlands. The host family was always complimentary of our singing and thanked us, though, inviting us to share a meal with the family and guests.

"We're much obliged to you for the singing. It was mighty pretty music. Won't y'all set a spell and break bread with us? We have more than enough food," the man of the house would offer.

The woman of the house generally added, "Yes, thank y'all very much. The songs give me comfort. Your voices were so pretty together. My mamma liked to sing 'I Come to the Garden Alone....' She's probably singing with the angels now, bless her soul."

She'd continue, "Please stay long enough to have a piece of fried chicken, some potato salad, and a biscuit. You got a long way back to town."

"How gracious of you. Thank you very much," said Ben, our leader. "We can stay for a little while and are so glad you like the music. We're honored to be with you here in your home. We want you to know we're very sorry for your loss."

We stayed around for a few minutes, greeting members of the family, nibbling a ham biscuit or eating a deviled egg and a piece of fried chicken. Then we excused ourselves, not wanting to intrude on their privacy or conversation.

Remembering now, I hope we gave solace and comfort to the bereaved, for they certainly gave meaning to my young life in a quiet but powerful way—and to a degree unlike any other experiences of my youth. I gained respect and admiration for the strength, courage, and faith of Eastern North Carolina country folks. Their lives were hard but leavened, too, with determination and promise of new life and hope in the circling seasons. For me, it was a time of personal discovery and sober awareness of death—inevitable change, tempered by the common bonds among people.

God Bless Them.

Amen.

July 2017

A Sound Like No Other

For its long, soulful cadence, its call to lands beyond, its promise of adventure, and its haunting line to the past, the train whistle is like no other sound: mournful, seductive, exciting.

As a young girl in Weldon, living near the High Track, I depended upon passing trains to lure me into dreams, to urge me to imagine hobos in boxcars escaping their painful pasts, and to fuel my curiosity when soldiers of WWII passed every eight minutes in 80-car trains curling round the bend like serpents. Handsome young men hung out the windows eager to see the world—and to go to war.

The trains were our lifeline, with the Atlantic Coast rolling on the High Track and the Seaboard on the Lower. All through the night they came, and the switching yards were busy all day. If you couldn't sleep with the sound of train whistles penetrating your ears, you needed not visit our house.

From its beginning as the longest railroad by track mileage in the world in 1861, to its packed boxcars of the Second World War from 1941-45, and then into peacetime and beyond, the train provided supplies for small-town merchants to sell, provisions for Lee's army, troops for both twentieth-century conflicts in Europe, and transportation for people going North and South.

So important was the High Track, linking Florida to New York and Boston—the latter two, major points of debarkation—that during WWII the roadbed was guarded 24 hours a day by military police. George and I heard stories of how German spies were attempting to sabotage the trains themselves and dynamite the rails. We imagined our police chief, a kindly but powerfully strong man, taking out the conspirators. We stood ready to defend our town and our country, eager to charge the invaders with drawn weapons, our BB guns.

"Stop imagining things," Mother would say, bringing us back to earth from our make-believe games.

But have you ever walked the rails? We children were *absolutely forbidden* to go close to the rails, though occasionally we sneaked over to the tracks and had contests among our neighborhood friends to see who could walk a rail the farthest without falling off. One of us served as stake-out in case one of our mothers saw us and called out. Once I walked nine sections, the farthest of any in my gang that day.

"Alice, George, where are you?" Mother called from our front yard. We didn't answer, but instead raced to our neighbor's yard pretending to play hide and seek. The ploy didn't work. Mother came dashing across the street, finding us with our collaborators and took us home.

"We were just playing in Forest's backyard," we protested.

"I know what you were doing! You may have been playing with Forest, but you were also down on the tracks behind his house. I know they are irresistible to you.

"But don't tell fibs. If you do, you'll get double punishment."

Immediately she grounded us for a couple of days. Mothers have a way of knowing; so, to avoid discovery and punishment, we stopped walking the tracks for a time.

Everybody in town, young and old, tried to help with the war effort. Even in school, time was allocated for knitting Red Cross squares to be made into blankets for the soldiers in Europe. After school, we roamed the neighborhoods and playgrounds collecting tinfoil to be recycled with other metal for use in making tanks and fighter planes.

Sirens screamed at night, just when we were ready for bed, notifying us of a blackout, a time when the entire town was to go dark and therefore be invisible from the air.

"Pull all shades down. Turn all lights out," came the order from Daddy, who was a neighborhood warden. The local War Administration Board specified that window shades in every home had to be opaque dark green or black so that light would not show through them.

Mother turned off the lights all over the house, except in her bedroom where she used a blanket to cover the transom above the interior door and made sure the shades blocked any light showing through the windows. George and I dived under the covers, while Daddy walked the neighborhood looking for planes in the skies and suspicious strangers on the street.

"It's okay, Children," Mother said, attempting to soothe our fears. "This is just a test, a trial run, so that we will be prepared in case of a real attack." My parents may have known that the blackouts were practice runs, but George and I were certain that danger lurked on the streets.

We were certain because sentries were stationed at the bridges over the river, and we had heard about the German submarines trolling off the North Carolina and Virginia coasts. Doots and Bill lived in Newport News, right there on the waters of the Chesapeake Bay, and Bill heard rumors and stories about the Germans when at work at the shipyard. Federal officials didn't admit to an enemy presence, but locals knew that enemy submarines were roaming up and down the East Coast. Enemy sailors had been taken prisoner off submarines and ships. However, President Roosevelt suppressed the news, presumably to prevent panic among the population and to protect his sources of intelligence.

Now that an enemy presence has been documented by historians, the courage and dedication of the people along the shore who patrolled the beaches nightly, saving hundreds of lives, deserves more notice and appreciation.

Today, riding the train again from Cary to Washington, I listen to its intermittent whistle announcing its arrival at a station, calling a greeting! Scenes of my childhood in Weldon return to my visual memory once more, such as this scene of the parade float in Weldon at Rockfish Festival time.

I search for familiar landmarks: Ruth Proctor's house by the tracks in Halifax, our house on Elm Street in Weldon within sight of the High Track, the freight and passenger stations down below serving shippers and riders from far-away places, the freight elevator we liked to ride to reach

ALICE, FRONT LEFT, ROCKFISH FESTIVAL PARADE

the street from the High Track—always more fun than running down the stairs. And, of course, the muddy, turbulent, fast-flowing Roanoke River cascading over boulders and large rocks, reminding me of swimming in the pool close to the shore and watching the fleet of fishing boats plying its waters daily.

The train whistle sounds the same, and the gravel and packed-earth roadbed ensures the constant swaying of the coaches, but the coaches now are more modern and comfortable. Also, there is a helpful and courteous attendant serving soft drinks and handing out newspapers. A café car provides snacks, sandwiches, and drinks. Many small signs tell me that I am on a different journey today than in the past.

Frank, my 98-year-old cousin, is in the last stage of life in George Washington Hospital, in D.C. But I remember him in his WWII uniform as he arrived on the train in Weldon to spend his leave with us.

FRANK IN UNIFORM, WWII, 1943

I remember him even earlier when, as a teenage orphan, he lived with us for short periods of time. I remember my dad helping him get a hand-up by hiring him as his bookkeeper. I remember when Frank married Pauline late in life, in his 40s, and brought his bride to visit us. I remember when he and Pauline invited us to Washington to celebrate Andrea's second birthday. Andrea says that visiting Frank and Pauline for her birthday party is her first memory.

I remember Frank moving into a fine new apartment building there in 1957 as one of the first tenants. He's lived there ever since. I remember driving with him to my home in Weldon for Christmas, when he spent the holidays with us after Pauline's death. I remember many other occasions with Frank.

Frank's life was full—and filled with daily habits he observed slavishly. He had a designated time for everything and kept multiple clocks in every room. Only once in his life was he late for work—by 15 minutes—and that was because the bus was late. In retirement, he had a specific time for breakfast, for lunch, and for dinner. On Saturdays he walked to the neighborhood 7-Eleven to get a beer and hotdog. Dinner was sandwiched in between his cocktail hour and his favorite TV programs, "Jeopardy" and "Wheel of Fortune." Every family member knew not to phone him between 5:45 p.m. and 8:00 p.m.

At 5:00 sharp, Frank started his cocktail hour of two gin-and-tonics. Only when I was coming to town did he wait until after 5:00 for me to get there and join him. In recent years, he moved the time back to 4:30 p.m. One day, I got stuck at the Pentagon City metro. "Frank," I called from my cell phone, "I am running a little late because of metro traffic, but I will be there no later than 5:00."

"That's okay, Alice," replied Frank. "I have already started." He waited for no one, not even me if I was already in town.

When discharged from the Army after serving in Europe during and after the Battle of the Bulge, Frank settled in Washington, using the G. I. Bill to get a degree in accounting. Frank never considered himself a farm boy, even though he had grown up on a farm. Once off the farm, he was determined never to go back.

Deciding to make his way in the city, he landed a job with John L. Lewis's United Mine Workers, which gave him both good job experience as well as health and retirement benefits. Eventually, he settled into work in the probate office of the District Court in Washington.

"Yes, Alice," he used to say to me, "I enjoyed that job not only because I learned probate law but because I was able to work on interesting cases and estates here in the District."

"What kind of estates?" I inquired.

"One I remember was Marjorie Merriweather Post's. It was fascinating because of its complexities, but also because she was such a well-known public figure here in Washington. Many lawyers and probate officers worked long hours on her estate."

Frank was not all business. Living in Washington turned Frank into an avid Redskins fan. He knew the identification of every football player on the roster and watched every game on TV, cheering praise or shouting complaints right there in his living room—even though no one could hear him. Not a single article in *The Washington Post* or a weekly show on TV, with Sonny Jurgensen, Frank Herzog, and Sam Huff, escaped his attention.

"They need a new quarterback," proclaimed Frank when the 'Skins lost several games in a row. "They are just no good, but I have faith in Coach Gibbs, the new coach. He'll turn us around."

Frank was right. Joe Gibbs produced a winning team that won three Super Bowls. The years of Joe Gibbs's tenure from 1981–92 were the golden years of Redskins football. Tickets were so scarce they were handed down from one generation to another. Scalping prices were out of sight! Occasionally, I would be able to buy tickets from a colleague; or my little sister, Monk, got a few through her business associates. Then we took Frank to the games. Rain or shine, Frank was always eager to go.

Pauline's death in the mid-1980s threw Frank into a deep depression that lasted for several years. He lost his appetite and grew thinner and thinner. Finally, the doctor prescribed a gin-and-tonic each day, hoping it would increase his appetite.

"Frank, you can't live on gin and tonic. Without food, strong drink will eat your stomach away," I said, trying to persuade him to eat.

While he nibbled on bread, chicken, and rice to stay alive, the only thing he seemed to enjoy other than gin and tonic was ice cream. Later, I teased him, "Frank, I have never known anyone who could survive for so long only on gin and vanilla ice cream."

He just smiled his tacit agreement.

An errand of mercy brought Frank out of his funk. In December 1988, I developed breast cancer and could not get from Princeton, where I had surgery, to Weldon for Christmas. George and Gwen came to Princeton to be with me at Christmastime. Andrea came home from graduate school in D.C. to help me out.

I called Frank and asked him if he would be willing to go to Weldon to stay with Mother and Dad because there would be no children or grandchildren with them for the holiday. Willing to do anything to help my parents, Frank drove to Weldon by himself, the first trip he had taken in years.

Knowing Dad was a teetotaler without a home inventory of spirits, much less gin, Frank was unsure about how to go about having his late-afternoon cocktail. Mother assured him that she would have a glass of tea at the same time and call the hour "tea-time" rather than "cocktail hour."

"Frank," said Mother, "that way William won't know or care."

On the first day, instead of tea, Mother sipped a mild gin-and-tonic that Frank made for her, her first ever. "This is better than Lipton's, Frank. I didn't know a little gin could taste so good!"

Tea-time became Frank's new habit and a new Joyner tradition, with Mother participating each day during his visit. He had many subsequent visits, not only at Christmas every year but when he came to see me in Pinehurst and Andrea in Apex. Today, any family member having a drink in late afternoon refers to the occasion as tea-time.

Once Frank recovered from his depression, his appetite returned, and he enjoyed going out to dinner. He took me to his favorite restaurant at the Watergate complex, and I took him to the Cosmos Club. He always had a gin-and-tonic before dinner and joined me in a glass of wine at the dinner table. He must have considered the entrée a necessary hurdle to reach dessert because, after eating about half his meal, he claimed he was full and could eat no more. Every time, though, Frank, a creature of his regular habits, ordered the chocolate dessert, chocolate being his favorite by far.

Once, when Andrea and Monk came to town, they joined Frank and me at the Cosmos Club for dinner. The main meal, accompanied by a recommended house wine, sated us to the point of our not wanting dessert. But I knew that Frank always liked dessert and was too much of a gentleman to order one without our joining him. The three of us complied.

"Why don't we each order a different dessert and then share?" suggested Monk.

Frank was silent.

The waitress brought four colorful, uniquely decorated plates to the table. Frank was served the chocolate mousse cake.

"Here, Andrea, try my strawberry tart," Monk said as she passed it to Andrea, who, in turn, passed her cheesecake to me.

"Mom, this cheesecake is as good as any in New York," Andrea said in offering me a bite.

I knew better than to pass anything to Frank. He had not said a word. He stared at his cake, took his fork in hand, and silently began to eat. He ate the entire slice while we three were fumbling around with the remaining desserts.

Not too long after that, the family celebrated Frank's 90th birthday. George Freeman Joyner, one of the nine first cousins of the Joyner family, came up the night before the party and took all the family to dinner at Frank's favorite seafood restaurant that served Crab Imperial. Our host, George, nicknamed "Little George" to distinguish him from "Big George," my brother, offered all of us dessert to conclude our meal.

Sitting to the right of Frank, Little George said, "I don't want any dessert. I will just have part of Frank's."

Again Frank was silent. I said, "George, if you want dessert, you need to order your own. Frank will consume all of his."

"No, he won't mind if I have just a couple of bites," insisted George.

"George, you won't get any of Frank's dessert. If you want some, place an order," I continued.

Little George decided not to place an order.

Dessert was served. Frank still had not said a word. When the chocolate cake was placed in front of him, Frank picked up his fork and proceeded to enjoy the entire piece of chocolate cake—every crumb—all by himself.

Frank's life fills my consciousness as I travel to Washington to help him face his limited future. He has left his apartment for a nursing home and is now in the hospital with a foot and leg infection. The circulation in his legs is insufficient to sustain the tissue, and his left leg has developed gangrene. He faces tough decisions about his health, a Hobson's choice about amputating his leg or accepting imminent death. He is a courageous man, having lived independently since Pauline's death. More than twenty years ago, Pauline faced a disease of the arteries, faced a similar choice, and decided not to have her leg amputated when gangrene developed. Frank cared for her at home during her last months.

Frank is ever decisive and resolved in his choices, but this one is not easy. He is unafraid of death, yet he loves life and makes a real effort to sustain himself.

FRANK'S 90TH BIRTHDAY PARTY

SEVEN OF THE NINE COUSINS, FROM L TO R: WHIT JOYNER, BECKY JOYNER SADLER, FRANK (SEATED), GEORGE JOYNER (BEHIND FRANK), ALICE JOYNER IRBY, NANCY PARKER GIERING, MARGARET JOYNER KINKER (MISSING: LITTLE GEORGE, MOLLY JOYNER REESE)

He has no children and has outlived most of his friends. We younger cousins—five of the nine—are rallying around, both for our own sakes but also to be sure he is not alone. Little George and Jean, his wife, took the train up from Raleigh. Becky Sadler and Andrea are arriving soon. His barber from the Watergate shop came to the hospital to shave him. Reverend Omholt comes frequently, as do people from Frank's former apartment building.

Frank is failing mentally as well as physically, but he is still perceptive enough to comprehend the seriousness of his general condition, and to know who is around him. Heavy medication dulls his pain.

He has been generous and attentive to us and our progeny. We love him and want to insure his comfort and his confidence in us. He knows we care. I hope that God will give me the strength to represent his interests to his doctors and to show my compassion for him, giving me the words to assure him that he will continue to be a meaningful part of our family.

A Year Later—Summer 2016

Frank lies in the National Cemetery in Lorton, Virginia, resting with Pauline, the love of his life. Both were veterans of WWII. He died of gangrene in the Methodist Home, comfortable and bathed in kindness. Andrea was the last family member to see him, on the afternoon before he died. He died with the TV playing church music—a genre he loved, especially organ music—and his nurses kept it going day and night. The Lutheran Church he attended was right across the street. Rev. Omholt, the minister, had Frank's healthcare power of attorney and cared for him when I could not be there.

Frank never complained about the circumstances surrounding his dying. He commented on the pain in his leg, quite naturally, but not with the expectation that anything could be done about it.

Now, a year later, George and I have been to my Washington apartment—four floors directly below Frank's—to ready it for HVAC reconstruction. Everything has been pushed against the walls. How empty it seems! Somehow, today I imagined I'd see Frank about "tea-time," his usual cocktail hour. He often brought his gin-and-tonic down to my apartment, sat in the red chair so his highly polished shoes would not stain the skirt of my white sofa, lamented the condition of politics in Washington, and related the latest gossip at Potomac Plaza, his residence. I had real tea, not by choice but because of lingering side-effects of shingles in my trigeminal nerve.

Frank's apartment has been emptied of his furniture, clothes, American Legion mementoes, and pictures. It has been sold and is now occupied by a stranger.

We don't see Frank's friends, Harry and Rita Aid and Wendy Pallet. They are out of town or sick. We do see the staff of Potomac Plaza: LaVon Banks and Sherika Hagan, who attended Frank's funeral and were always kind and helpful to him. One friend of mine, Vivian Kilner, who was helpful throughout my time of transition and grief, helped me finish cleaning out Frank's belongings. She brought food to George and me while we were working in the apartment and has kept in touch. I will see her in D.C. again.

But it is not the same. Andrea and I stayed in my apartment on our way to and from Greece. We restored the apartment more or less to its pre-HVAC installation condition. Then, we left, and it will be a long time before I go again. Nothing pulls me in that direction anymore.

I did not expect to lose interest in Washington because I lost Frank. But that's the reality. What's there now except government buildings, monuments, memorials, and some lovely grounds and gardens? Yes, the Cosmos Club is still there, and I used to enjoy it, but now even its stimulating programs and good food don't hold any attraction. How is it we know but don't know until a sudden awareness hits us in the face that dear family and close friends make a place not only inhabitable but also desirable?

Frank's spirit lives with me. I find myself saying some of the same things he used to say. When someone tells me how well I look, given my age, I say "Looks can be deceiving." That was Frank's stock answer when people throughout the building told him how good he looked and what a dandy he was. He thrilled at the flattery, but I know also that he hurt most days from arthritis and other ailments, just as I do.

I have concluded, however, that what kept him going in his later years were his walks in the hall every day at 10, 2, and 4 o'clock, *á la* the old Dr Pepper ad, and his double gin with a little tonic and lime every afternoon at tea-time. To this day, when I pull out my teapot at 4:30 in the afternoon, I offer up a toast: "Here's to the good life, Frank, and to loving cousins!"

I probably have one more train trip to Washington in my future, if for no other reason than to pass through Weldon. Of course, I want to see the home in which I grew up. But even more, I long to hear that mournful sound, a sound like no other, of the train whistle and the clickety-clack of the wheels on the High Track.

November 2016

MIXING IT UP

The Not-so-Friendly Skies

In the early 1960s B.C.—before cocaine, cohabitation, and the crises of riots and protests—it was business as usual for the airlines. At United Airlines (UA), that included *Executive flights*, code name for "men only."

Two colleagues, Dick Watkins and Dick Burns—both heavy-set, tall men—and I were working together on a college grade-prediction study for Educational Testing Service (ETS), where I was then employed. The study included all four-year colleges in Indiana, 19 of them. Its purpose was to study the relationship among students' high-school grades, SAT scores, and first-year grades in college.

Our fieldwork included visiting each college, explaining the project to participating administrators, and collecting data on freshman classes for analysis back in Princeton at ETS. Over a period of three years, the three of us regularly flew together to Chicago and then to various cities in Indiana.

At least it started out that way. Then, one day, the two Dicks were booked on a flight different than the one on which I was ticketed. Pleased that she was able to offer an upgrade, the travel agent arranged for them to go on something called an Executive flight. I did not qualify and instead had to go on an earlier flight and wait for my colleagues in O'Hare Airport so that the three of us could take a puddle-jumper down to an Indiana city.

"This won't do," I thought—even though the Women's Lib movement was only a gleam in Betty Friedan's eye and did not get into full swing until the early 1970s. And, it wasn't until the Civil Rights Act of 1964, Title VII, that federal legislation called for equal treatment in employment regardless of sex, race, color, religion, or national origin. Other legislation followed concerning housing, creditors and credit availability, and the well-known Title IX (1972). I was not an activist, but I expected to be treated fairly, and in this case, that meant being treated on a par with my peers.

For a while, I did nothing other than complain to myself and a few friends that every time I started out for Indiana, I got a little hot under the collar.

"Let's see what we can do," said Greg, a friend. At the time of our next scheduled trip, Greg and I decided to go to Newark airport to seek booking for me on the Executive flight scheduled to leave later that day. I already had a ticket on the earlier flight, knowing I would probably have to use it—but hoping an enlightened agent would rally to my cause.

"I am booked on Flight UA 323 to Chicago but want to change that to Flight UA 829 to be on the same plane as my colleagues." I explained at the ticket counter. "My colleagues are Mr. Richard Watkins and Mr. Richard Burns," I elaborated.

The United Airlines agent explained that the flight was not open to me.

"I know there are seats available, because I checked before I came," I countered.

"It's an Executive flight," she stated.

"What does the term 'executive' mean? Is it a title?" Greg asked. "Or a level of education? Or size of desk or office? Or having supervisory authority? If so, Mrs. Irby has the same credentials as her two male colleagues."

The ticket agent paused, somewhat taken aback, then was clearly unable to give us a definition of "Executive." She fumbled her words, saying something like, "The men on these flights have to work while in the air, and it is very distracting for women with small children to be on the same flight. They need quiet. You have a seat on the plane that is waiting to take off now...," the agent attempted to explain.

"You mean Flight 829 is for men only? Is that right?" I asked with an edge in my voice.

When we didn't leave and continued to press the issue, the agent excused herself and disappeared behind the partition at the back of the counter. A second agent came out, another woman, who reiterated the first agent's words: "The flight is for executive men who need a quiet atmosphere when working, and United Airlines wants to make the flight as conducive to work as possible." She could not tell us how she determined which men were executives who needed to work while in flight.

"Is every male passenger an executive? It seems that any male qualifies as an executive and no female does. Is that correct?" I asked.

Greg asked to see the written policy. Then, she, too, disappeared behind the partition.

We were left standing at the counter while other customers were being helped by an agent several feet away from us. A few minutes passed and a third agent, this time a man, came out and told me the written policy was at United headquarters in Chicago and I would have to inquire there for a copy.

"And, Madam, if you don't go ahead and board the plane for which you are ticketed, the flight will leave without you. We have already held the plane 45 minutes for you," the agent spoke in a sharp voice. Not taking that flight meant that I would not be able to meet my colleagues in Chicago later in the day.

"Well, I have to get to Chicago, but I do intend to inquire about the policy when I get there. After all, I will have two hours to wait until my colleagues meet me," I spoke just as sharply.

Dutifully, I walked to the gate with Greg by my side. The tactic of protesting "victimhood" was not yet in vogue until the twenty-first century. This was a new situation for me; I was not combative nor given to protesting, and I didn't know quite how to proceed. Greg and I discussed what I would say to the attendants, if anything, as I walked up the steps of the plane to board. We decided I would stay mum except to greet them cordially.

In the 1960s, passengers boarded planes by departing the waiting room at the gate, going outside, walking to the parked plane, and then mounting steps attached to the side door of the plane. I gave Greg a hug, leaving him in the waiting room, turned around, and walked to the plane. At the bottom of the stairs, I put on my best smile.

I was the only person with a smile. At the top of the stairs, the pilot, the co-pilot, and the stewardess stood in the doorway, staring at me with scowls. No one said, "Welcome aboard." Instead, the attendant said, "Mrs. Irby, your seat is 8B and you need to seat yourself promptly because we are running quite late." Her harsh tone was not lost on me.

No one helped me to my seat. Passengers stared at me as if I were an angry or an uppity, trouble-making woman. Apparently, word had spread that I was holding up the plane. I did get my free Coke—but mine came with a splash and a snippy word from the stewardess. I was grateful that my seat partner did not scorn me—outwardly, anyway. He was quiet.

United Airlines headquarters was on the second level of the Chicago O'Hare Airport. After I disembarked, I found my way to the United office. Again I faced another counter with a partition behind it, a place to hide! A male clerk was standing there, idle and seemingly approachable.

"I understand that United Airlines has an Executive flight, and I am interested in knowing the provisions of that policy," I said pleasantly.

Clerks there had been notified. They were ready. "I'm sorry, Ma'am," answered the agent on duty. "It is filed away in another building. We will be glad to send it to you."

Even though they had my name and could look up my address, I wrote down my name and address and handed it to the clerk. Most likely, that little piece of paper found its way directly into the trash can. I was not naïve enough to expect to receive the policy, which, of course, never showed up in my mailbox.

"What was so special about the Executive flight?" I inquired of my colleagues when we met in the O'Hare terminal.

"Oh," Dick Watkins said, "its purpose is just to pamper men. Passengers are given socks to use if they take their shoes off, and pillows, free drinks, and snacks to go along with their cigarettes."

"Nothing special," Dick Burns chimed in. "United thinks that paying attention to men gives them a competitive advantage. And, as you know, most business travelers are men."

Dick W and Dick B were not impressed with the perks and agreed with me that Executive flights did not make sense, especially since they were clearly discriminatory. Both of my colleagues were tall, large men and would have preferred more seat and leg room rather than the pampering.

What went unsaid was that the flight attendants, by United policy, were single women, very attractive and practiced in providing good service. I'm sure they were not flirts. Neither were the men, but doesn't anyone like to be pampered? Discrimination thrived inside the airline companies as well as in policies affecting their passengers: no men or married women were hired by the major airlines in that decade to serve as flight attendants. If a woman married, she had to resign her position.

I put the matter out of my mind and continued my work on the project with the two Dicks. Later that year, as I prepared to go to Washington to join the Johnson Administration for a year, the situation popped back into my awareness. I felt a twinge of resentment. Executive flights were not only discriminatory on their face but affected business arrangements and relationships as well. I deserved to be treated fairly, on a par with my colleagues. How could airlines get away with such policies? I was convinced they shouldn't.

Maybe I was just sensitive to the winds of change as I prepared to go to Washington, on leave from ETS, to assist in establishing the Job Corps as part of President Johnson's War on Poverty. Once there, I began working with a young lawyer, Stan Zimmerman, who was also on the Job Corps Director's staff.

One afternoon, as we were idly chatting, I told him about my experience with United's Executive flight.

"Let's have some fun," he said, upon hearing my story. We determined that the Executive flights were still in use. Using his law firm's letterhead, Stan wrote to United Airlines, representing me as his client and raising the question of the legality of their practice. He insisted the airline cease such discriminatory flights, pointing to the proposed civil-rights legislation that President Johnson initiated and was beginning to move through Congress. Quite likely, United's practice was not yet illegal, but that did not stop Stan and me from rattling our sabers.

United Airlines acknowledged receipt of the letter but that was all: no admission of anything. That's what we expected. Life went on and, in fact, became all-encompassing at Job Corps headquarters as we worked feverishly to develop the infrastructure of the program.

To our surprise and pleasure, a couple of months later we determined that, quietly, the UA "Executive flight" had taken a nose dive into the dust: no widely distributed press announcement, not even a newspaper article. Nary a murmur from a traveling businessman that elimination of the Executive flight reduced his productivity—remember, they were supposed to be segregated from women so they could work! The flight merely disappeared from the list of arrivals and departures at airports and was no longer listed in the airline guide used by travel agents.

After work that day, Stan and I raised our glasses with a toast: "A Hand Up for Women's Rights, and a new nail in the coffin of Inequality!"

About the same time, another woman from Weldon High School stuck her neck out. Jean Satterthwaite moved to

New York City after graduation from the Woman's College, married a school counselor/writer and, when looking for work, realized that *The New York Times'* classified employment ads were divided according to MEN and WOMEN. In other words, not only was employment policy discriminatory in many places, job descriptions and classifications were as well.

Occasionally, the policy disadvantaged men, as in the case of UA's policy on flight attendants needing to be women, but, by far, its sword fell most punitively on opportunities and prospects for women. Jean and a few other women organized a protest of *The Times'* classification system by gender, which had been copied, quite naturally, by every other major paper in the country. They wrote letters, made telephone calls, and brought the policy to the attention of civic clubs and business associations, urging them to write and call as well.

The women were successful. After some foot-dragging and flimsy excuses, *The Times* backed down, realizing it lacked a defensible business reason to continue the practice. Things changed—want ads were listed by job classification, not gender. Eventually, other major newspapers followed its lead. Jean went on to be the first president of the NYC chapter of the National Organization for Women (NOW).

Greg, who came to know both Jean and me, vowed there was something in the water we drank in Weldon or the food we ate in the dining halls of the Woman's College. Where had the seeds of that independent, assertive, spunky spirit been planted?

Who knows?

Maybe the seeds were borne by the fast-flowing, powerful waters of the Roanoke River. Or by the toil of strong-willed, independent farmers and merchants, laboring without a government safety net to help them in hard times.

Maybe they were passed along in the discipline that Mr. Thomas, our school superintendent, enforced with his reliable sense of fair play.

Or maybe by the demeanor and actions of our role models, the women faculty at the Woman's College, or the history and philosophy professors there who awakened dormant portions of our minds to show us new horizons. Or maybe the seeds germinated first in the rich black dirt of Eastern North Carolina that stuck to our feet and made us independent, adventurous Tar Heels.

September 2017

The Great Game

The Great Game, to me, is not the nineteenth-century one among European nations when unnatural allies carved up national boundaries. The really serious game—the one that pits friend against friend weekly for life; the international game that spawns entrepreneurs to teach and sponsor tournaments; and the social game used as cover for neighborhood gossiping is *Bridge*, the seducer of young and old alike.

I confess that I was seduced at an early age. But then, every young woman in the South, especially in Eastern North Carolina, learns how to play bridge. In Weldon, we could not have gotten married without knowing how to play bridge, because no one would have given us a bridal shower or luncheon. Bridge parties for brides were how we collected the gifts to set up housekeeping.

The two local jewelry stores delighted in our parties; the more the better. They kept records of what had been purchased for each bride so they could advise purchasers. In the days before bridal registries came along in the 1960s, brides would never be so presumptuous as to enumerate their desires. Without the detailed records of the jewelers, a bride could end up with two sets, twelve each, of crystal glasses while not getting enough silver place settings to entertain two couples.

BRIDGE BRIDAL SHOWER FOR ALICE, BOTTOM LEFT, 1952.

And milk glass was popular and in abundant supply. Extra boxes of occasional pieces in milk glass stayed packed in attics until it was long out of style. Visit antique malls today to see enough milk glass to sate your curiosity.

I knew well how to play bridge when I went to college, but I was so busy meeting new friends and trying to keep up with my assignments—I signed up for extra courses—that I dared not engage in such an addictive pastime until my junior year. Neither did I knit argyle socks for my boyfriend, the other favorite pastime of freshmen. I was a nerd, trying to master the academic work assigned to me, though I did find my way to Chapel Hill now and then for a weekend. My home at the Woman's College (WC) was the Jackson Library, not the dormitory-parlor bridge tables.

My roommate, Ann, asked me one day, "Alice, do you still live here? Do you even know where your dormitory is located?"

I was away from 7:00 a.m. until 11:00 p.m. when the library closed. So were my new friends. "It's easier to pack up for the day and spend my extra time in the library than it is to come back to the dorm in between classes. Besides, the library has comfortable chairs for napping when necessary," I said, reassuring her that I was not unhappy in our room. Actually, I loved Cotten dormitory; it was where my mother had lived when she was a student in the 1920s.

"And, I meet Mary Lib and Nancy in the alcove of the library to go over our history lessons. For me, Western Civ is the hardest freshman course at WC. It's used, I'm told, to weed out students unlikely to make it through four years—and I don't want to be one of them," I explained.

"Macie Collins and I compare notes after Dr. Hook's French class. The library is the best place to meet since the soda shop is so noisy. We were put in his advanced class, and, while he is a terrific teacher, his accent is tough for us to understand sometimes."

That was more than Ann wanted to hear. She had her own challenges to manage.

My load lightened in my junior year when I took only one extra course, not two.

One of my classes got out at noon each day, Monday through Friday, whereas others started at 2:00 p.m. or not at all on those same days. A dash through the Soda Shop to get a grilled-cheese sandwich and Coke on my way to the town students' lounge next door got me to the lounge by 12:15 p.m.

That's when the game started.

I could have gone to the library during the break between classes, but the library had a "no food or drink" rule. I would have had to go without lunch or get there with only an hour at most to study. Thus, getting out my books and settling into a carrel was hardly worth the effort before I would have had to pack up and leave for my 2:00 p.m. class. Anyway, that was the rationale I used to give myself an excuse to spend time in the town students' lounge playing bridge.

Of the 2,500 students at the Woman's College—at that time the largest college for women in the U. S.—about 100 were students living at home. Most students studied in their dorms' small parlors or study rooms. Others were in labs and class most of the day. In Elliott Hall, the student union, student government offices occupied the third floor. On the second floor, a luxurious ballroom and two lounges were large, comfortable spaces but closed to students except on special occasions—probably because there were often major works of art hanging there. The one large daily gathering place was the town students' lounge on the first floor.

Often, I met Lou Bradley there after class to chat and compare notes about our unusual physical education class, modern dance *á la* Martha Graham. Physical Education was a degree offering at WC, and two years of physical education were required of all students. Some students coming to the lounge just hung out, reading magazines or sleeping. A few claimed to be cramming for their next class.

Card games occupied foursomes at several tables set up for that purpose. It was during a bridge game at one of the tables that I met Barbara Beasley. Barbara, a biology major, liked to play bridge. I could tell because she concentrated and didn't chit-chat during the game. I liked bridge, too, and I didn't talk during the game except to bid and keep score.

"You come here often?" I asked her when she finished her hand.

"Almost every day, in between my morning classes and afternoon labs," she answered. "There is no point in trying to study during my break. Besides, I need a diversion before I head back to the Petty Science Building for an all-afternoon lab."

"You play a lot of bridge here? Every day?" I asked.

"Not every day but often. I just pick up a game with anyone who happens to be interested," she said. "I would play more if I had a serious partner. Playing with somebody different all the time is frustrating. And, I am not a talker."

"I'm not sure how often I can play, but I do enjoy the game and the competition. I played a lot in my hometown during summers but haven't had time since I've been at WC until this year," I explained. "I'm pretty rusty but would like to try my hand at it again."

"How about meeting here again tomorrow at 12:15 and we'll try to get a game started," she offered.

That was the beginning of The Great Game.

Her schedule was about the same as mine most days, and we liked playing together. Before long, we decided to play as exclusive partners, taking on any comers on any day, Monday through Friday, just for the prize of winning. That September day was the beginning of a collaboration—

some say conspiracy—that lasted for two years, until Barbara and I graduated.

We started winning. And we kept on winning! Word got out—almost the way word of a floating craps game spreads around. Students from all around, not merely town students, came to the lounge to take us on. Seldom did they win, even if they had chosen their partners. No one else knew Goren's rules as well as we did, and by that time we had created a few subroutines of our own.

As our reputation grew, the spectator gallery grew, and more and more students came in to watch the games. That put enormous pressure on us to excel. But, excel we did. During our senior year, I think we lost one rubber. There were no prizes—just the satisfaction of knowing we knew The Game and each other's bidding as if we were clones.

"Alice, Barbara, congratulations on your graduation," several students approached us. "You deserve all the glory you receive, graduating with honors and being the bridge champions at the same time."

"Thank you," we said. "You will pick up the mantle without a minute's pause. Have fun next year—and best wishes for phenomenal success."

Juniors, especially, congratulated us on getting our degrees, but we knew their good wishes were half-hearted because they wanted us out of The Game. Some of them were standing in the wings, salivating, waiting to occupy the Champions' seats.

I don't know where Barbara went, other than home, for we had not been friends socially. Instead, we came together to be serious about bridge. I don't know where she is now either, but I remember those days with refreshing clarity. Those lunchtime hours were my relaxation, a time when I could close out everything else completely. Bridge was my main pleasure and my time-out from worry.

By the time I graduated, Claud had come home from the Navy. Until he was discharged, I lived in the dormitory, which required a special exemption at the discretion of Katherine Taylor, Dean of Students. By policy, dormitories were for single women only. For the two years I was in school after I married, the bridge game forestalled my anxiety about Claud's going to war and my isolation as one of a handful of students who were married, Doris Kearns being another. She and I consoled each other when we met on campus.

Claud and I bought a modest starter home in the northwest section of Greensboro, and he accepted a position in the underwriting department of Jefferson Standard Life Insurance Company. Knowing I would otherwise stay at home reading or working in the yard, he urged me to make friends with the neighbors during the summer months between college and graduate school. I didn't like shopping, nor did I crochet, knit, or quilt. I waited to go to movies until he could join me. I did know how to play bridge, though, and when I was invited to join the neighborhood club that met on a rotating basis in each member's home, I jumped at the chance. There were eight members plus a couple of substitutes; the group met twice a month.

The young women in the club were engaging and intelligent, fashionably attired and socially adept. And, they served refreshing desserts. Several were good players, but that was hard to discern because the casual conversations—often gossip—dominated the game. I was not used to that. Accustomed to concentrating on the game in silence, my eyes wandered around the room, analyzing paintings on the wall. My left thigh started bouncing; I had what Mother called the "jeebies." I couldn't concentrate on the game in the whirl of all those voices. In that particular social context, I was lost.

What to do? What to tell Claud? He was disappointed and wondered whether I was giving my new life a chance to succeed. We came up with a plan. Between June and graduate school starting at Duke in the fall, I would spend time with my folks in Weldon and then go with him to the beach for a week or so. That left only four weeks at home with only two more bridge games to play. I could do that, even host the group. I liked the women; I just did not like all that talking while I was trying to concentrate. That kind of social bridge was not for me. The bridal-bridge parties in my hometown had been much more fun, maybe because I had grown up with those women. There we played bridge first and then talked during dessert time. We talked about our men friends and our future life, not about people in the neighborhood who did not play bridge.

In spite of this blunder, I still liked the game.

That fall, I started classes at Duke, majoring in economics. I spent all day either in class or at the library, getting home around 11:00 p.m. via public transportation to my rented single room in Mrs. Bishop's house, having to prepare for an early rise around 6:00 a.m. One day, about a month after classes started at Duke, Claud called from home in Greensboro to suggest I take the weekend off and try to relax. He invited a couple from Weldon living in Greensboro, Joan and Johnny King, to come to Durham to join us for a game of bridge.

What a great idea. Freedom and relaxation, if only for a weekend. And, pleasure with friends.

Johnny worked for Blue Bell, an international manufacturer of blue jeans and overalls. Joan was busy night and day with active children at home. They were ready for a break, too. They were good players—they had to be if they were from Weldon—and liked the game. Neither did they spend all the time talking. I looked forward to a diversion and change of routine. They came over Friday evening, expecting to depart Saturday afternoon so that I could get back to my studies. Claud left work at Jefferson Standard early so he could arrive in time to greet them.

By dinnertime Friday, we were well into the game. We were nip and tuck, Joan and Claud on one side, Johnny and I on the other.

Johnny stopped and spoke up, "Instead of going out for dinner, why don't we order carryout pizza so we can continue playing now that things are just getting lively?"

The adrenalin was flowing in all of us.

"Great idea," agreed Claud. Joan and I nodded.

By 9:30 p.m., we were still at it—in heated, friendly competition. Not realizing the time, we were surprised when we saw that it was 11:30 p.m. and we had not stopped. Claud and I went back to my room across town. Joan and Johnny stayed at the motel.

Saturday morning could not come too soon. We were eager to resume The Game. While visions of winning hands did not spin around in my head all night, I did wonder what the next day would bring. By 9:30 a.m., we had finished breakfast and met to continue the game.

I don't remember the exact setting of the game—somewhere not too far from campus. Johnny and Joan had a small motel suite, outfitted with modest, dark furnishings, including a card table with light sufficient to see the markings on the cards but not much more. It was simple but okay. It was probably one of those Duke-subsidized motels used by families of hospital patients. We didn't choose it for partying or even for enjoying the few amenities that might be there. In those days, most motels offered plain and plainer.

About 1:00 p.m. on Saturday, Johnny raised his eyes from the scorecard, "Anyone plan to eat lunch?" Who had thought of food? But he was hungry.

"The student union is not far away; we can get carryout lunches there," I responded. We rushed over and back.

By 4:00 p.m. there were no clear winners. The lead bounced back and forth.

"We can't quit now," said Joan. "Let's just play 'til after supper."

Since lunch had been late, supper was later—as it turned out, too late for the Kings to drive back to Greensboro. We hadn't been mindful of the elapsed time all afternoon.

Interstate 85 was still on the drawing boards then— maybe not even that, given that it was not until 1956 that President Eisenhower initiated the new interstate highway system. The major highway between Durham and Greensboro was U.S. Route 70, winding through every town—Efland, Mebane, Haw River, Burlington, and Sedalia on the way to Greensboro.

"What are the choices for carryout around here, Alice?" Claud asked as we stopped to consider supper.

"Nothing that I know of except McDonald's and pizza. And, there is a Toddle House a couple of miles away: good hamburgers and great chocolate pie," I replied.

We chose hamburgers and pie; Claud and Johnny went to pick up the orders. They wasted no time and we were back at the card table in 45 minutes. By bedtime, Johnny and I began to edge out ahead, but not by much.

"Alice, if we can just play a few hands in the morning," Johnny whispered in my ear, "we should be able to seal their fate." Mrs. Bishop, a devout Methodist with a son in the ministry, would've thought I was a heathen, playing cards on Sunday morning. But, I figured the Lord would forgive us just this Sunday because, as Mother used to say, "When the ox is in the ditch, you have to pull him out, even on Sunday."

Clearly my ox was going to be in the ditch if Johnny's and my luck did not change. Our fortunes declined in the morning and we fell behind. We determined we would not quit until we could see a clear win. By then, it was obvious to our foursome that Johnny and I were the more aggressive partners.

On into the afternoon we played. Exhausted, we finally stopped to think about work and school the next day. Johnny and I were able to claim victory, though by the most narrow of margins. It was more like a draw—a whole weekend for a draw! On top of that, we were not even playing for money, just for pride and bragging rights.

Midafternoon, Johnny and Joan headed back to Greensboro. Claud stayed long enough to have a light supper, then headed back home as well. I tried to study. No such luck; I fell asleep, having been filled with adrenalin for two nights, thus deprived of sleep.

On a normal school day, homework consumed at least three hours every night, and there was more work waiting for the weekend. I had not opened a book since Thursday, despite the fact that I needed to prepare for two of my classes scheduled for Monday morning. I had to get the bus at 7:30 a.m., catching a bite to eat at the nearby Toddle House. I was not prepared for class, and it showed—to the professor, to my fellow students, as well as to me.

Not only was I embarrassed, for the first time in my life, I faced real academic failure. Prospects of dropping out, disappointing my parents, letting down the sponsors of my scholarship and fellowship, and fear of the future shook my confidence and filled me with alarm. I was physically dizzy. I had to step away from my seat in the conference room of the economics building for some fresh air.

Since childhood, I have occasionally been haunted by the prospect of failure, not failure in the public sense but failure to meet the expectations of my mentors. That failure, I realized, might result from my playing bridge, and who knows where that would lead.

"Olga, I can't join you today in the conference room for lunch," I announced to a student friend.

"I am not feeling well and need to be outside in the fresh air for a while."

"Okay," she replied. "Let me know if you need help." I needed help but not the kind she could give. I know she wondered what was wrong, for we usually ate together and went over our class notes, but I was mum. I didn't even have any notes to share that day.

The Duke Gardens were right behind and below the economics building. From the conference room windows, I could see flowering shrubs, perennials in the borders, and graceful weeping willow trees. I took my sandwich and Coke down the steps to a bench in the middle of the garden. Fall colors of rust, orange, and yellow had painted leaves on the trees and ground with an Impressionist's imaginary brush. Beautiful and serene, with total privacy for me.

The sunshine and warmth wrapped around me the way a blanket hugs a baby. I wanted to stay there; I wanted to make time stand still. What was I going to do? I felt like Ray Milland's character in *The Lost Weekend*, the 1945 Academy Award-winning film about an alcoholic on a weekend binge. I had binged on bridge and was painfully depressed by my hangover.

"Mother, Granny, Help," I called on their spirits for guidance. They did help—in the sense of my gaining inspiration from recalling their lives of courage and determination. How could I forget the courage with which my grandmother bore her illnesses during the last years of her life? And, what about my mother, losing her mother at age 32 with two children of her own to rear, all the while facing large debts for Granny's medical care? Courage is a fundamental quality because without it, there can be no action. I needed to act, and I needed to act with courage.

"Act how? What are my choices?" I wondered.

I realized that I was too easily distracted from my goal of getting my degree. Yet, being isolated in a dark carrel in the stacks of the Duke library, away from Claud, my friends in Greensboro, and a nascent social life was unsettling. Was I missing out? Bridge had evidently been my escape at first but now was a real addiction.

"I face a binary choice," I concluded. "Go back to Greensboro, rear a family, lead a full social life with our artist and faculty friends there, become a competitive bridge junkie, or commit myself full-time and wholeheartedly to succeeding at Duke and getting my degree."

What would my mentors have done: my mother, my grandmother, Louise Farber, Mrs. Wallace, Mr. Thomas, Warren Ashby, Miss Craig—especially the women? Intellectually, the answer was easy, but my will seemed unable to commit to it.

Sitting there that day for a long time, I made a pledge to myself, but also to the people who had shown faith in me. I chose the latter path: get my degree and see where fate leads me. I determined to go cold turkey; no more bridge.

It was clear that I had an addiction because I could not stop playing once I got the cards in my hands. That day, sitting on that bench in the Duke Gardens, I decided to create my own *Bridge AA*, the *Bridge Abstinence Association*,

U.S.A. No more bridge for the rest of my life. I was too easily seduced by The Game.

Have I been tempted since then? You bet I have. For years, I was too busy working, fulfilling my career commitments, and rearing a daughter. There wasn't time for bridge or any other game, and I didn't circulate among people who played bridge. There were a few faculty and many students at Rutgers who kept bridge games going, but my colleagues and I in administration did not have time for a lot of socializing. There was an occasional poker game at our officer retreats. I limited myself to five-card stud, which I know could never become a habit. It wasn't even much fun. Nor was I good enough at any other game to be a danger to anyone or to myself.

Life abounds with temptations. The Great Game is one of mine. When winning, it is sweet. When competing, it is spellbinding. But, when losing, it is depressing: from a titillating high to a bottomless low, like alcohol. But in my case, an external stimulus wasn't necessary; the urge to compete was all coming from inside.

In many retirement communities, such as Pinehurst where I lived for 17 years, bridge games are pervasive. When I admitted to local residents that I did not play bridge—or any of the other all-consuming games of the area, i.e., golf, or tennis—I got a puzzled look or a snappy remark, "Then why did you bother to locate here?" I thought to myself, "Was that the price of admission—and my notice of exclusion?"

I did learn to play golf at the novice level, and I could have picked up bridge again. There were always groups looking for members or substitutes. One thriving business in town employed professional teachers to coach newcomers to play duplicate bridge. There were weekly competitions and regional tournaments. Had I chosen to join friends to play The Game, I might have fit right in from the beginning. It was a good way for a newcomer to make friends.

"Alice," said Sara, "you don't have to play duplicate bridge to enjoy the game. My group is quite casual. We play rubber bridge, and our members play any convention they know; we play for fun. It's relaxing."

"How well I know it can be fun, too much fun," I responded. "But, there is a risk. I can become addicted again. I might become so serious about it, you would end up wanting me to drop out. It might even destroy our friendship. I can't risk it."

I knew that, given my competitive spirit, I might alienate players that wanted a social outing with lots of conversation. Shades of 1954 all over again. By this time in my life, I knew all too well that the word Moderation is not in my bridge glossary.

My life was full without an activity that threatened my equanimity. After a busy career, I was enjoying a calmer life: two book clubs with intelligent, well-read women, and soon a third with men and women who studied foreign affairs. And, I participated as a volunteer in a community organization, reestablished a relationship with my *alma mater*, UNCG (formerly WC), and used my professional experience to serve on the board of a company in New Hampshire. I traveled there four times a year. I also began making international trips for my own pleasure.

It wasn't just that my time was fully occupied. Down deep, I knew that addictions never really die, whether from alcohol, gambling, or bridge. When growing up, I had witnessed alcohol addiction among troubled men in my hometown—some close to my family. I remembered Pete Rose's ejection from the Baseball Hall of Fame for gambling. My life had been full without bridge, or any other card game. Oh, I had played an occasional game of poker or solitaire, but I had not even felt the need to do crossword puzzles. I had seen people addicted to those as well. Why chance it all again?

Entering my eighties, I did not want to have to acknowledge—even to myself—an emptiness from an addiction. Many of my friends play either bridge or mah-jongg and are able to do other things as well. They are not driven to win, as I am.

Sometimes I ask myself, "Should I chance it? Is the joy of making new friends at the bridge table sufficient to renege on my promise of years ago?" I wrestle with myself. After all, that promise was many years ago and life has taught me a thing or two since then—self-discipline being one. Surely I can control my appetite for winning. I know how to lose, having experienced that on more than one occasion. The Great Game can't be such a temptation now, decades later, can it?

Mom and Granny might let me off the hook; they were forgiving. But I would know. I would know that I had failed, failed to keep a promise—to them and to myself.

All my life I had aspired to being useful in some way to others. How useful would I feel if I spent several days a week playing bridge? Being *Useful*, after all, was a tenet of my Methodist heritage and of Protestant Christianity in general.

No, I would not play again. I kept my membership in the *Bridge Abstinence Association*. Now, 63 years later, I have not held a bridge hand since that Sunday in Durham in 1954. I decided to stick to my books, as I had done years before at Duke when, at age 22, I sat in the gardens and chose my life's path.

August 2017

Just a Bowl of Peanuts

"Where you from, Young Lady?" asked the customer who had just entered the Merrill Lynch office in Greensboro. He took his customary chair in a semi-circle in front of the big blackboard used to record stock prices.

"From Halifax County, Sir," I said, feeling his question as more of a demand.

"Then you are from peanut country—up in Eastern North Carolina where the land is flat, the summers hot, and the soil forms the delta of the Roanoke River."

"Right," I said proudly. "Best land in the State of North Carolina."

That short conversation was the beginning of a friendship that grew as I got my bearings in the brokerage business. He was one of the "Regulars" who watched the stock market every day. They sat around the office, gossiping about events in town, checking their favorite stocks on the tickertape, and occasionally making a trade. Most of the time, they just sat and talked.

I was an assistant to the account executives who dealt with customers and managed their accounts. Because I worked with all five of the account reps in the office, I got to know them, their habits, and their customers. When the reps and the Regulars found out about my "roots" in peanut country, I got a lot of teasing. Of course, those guys were not so sophisticated and worldly themselves. It was not as if they were from the Big Easy or Gotham! They had lived and worked all their lives in Greensboro, a mid-size North Carolina city bordered by farmland.

Had I been a man, I would have been offered a job as account executive, not an "assistant to." Mr. Shelley, the manager, had told me so.

"Mrs. Irby, I am happy to offer you the position of Administrative Assistant. In fact, your credentials are on a par with my male account executives, especially having studied economics in graduate school at Duke. But our employment practices don't consider women for account executive positions. Besides, a national examination is required for certification."

It was the first time I had been denied an opportunity because I was a woman, and I was surely taken aback. All during my school days, my years at the Woman's College, and my experience in graduate school at Duke, I felt I was treated equally and fairly among my peers, both men and women. I had also competed successfully among my male colleagues.

Mr. Shelley was, however, following corporate practices of the time, not being intentionally misogynistic. He did not express his personal opinion. Classifying career positions within companies according to sex was often a matter of employment policy. It was the 1950s, after all, and laws prohibiting discrimination by gender were not yet on the books at either the state or national level.

When facing Mr. Shelley across the desk, I thought to myself, "I'll show you!" But I did not challenge him and told him I would take the assistant's job. I needed a job and decided it would be a good way to learn the brokerage business. My major in college had been economics, not business. In this job, I could learn about everyday business: corporate America; the New York Stock Exchange; and other securities markets. There was a lot to learn, too, about trading municipal bonds from the bond specialist employed in our office. And it would be fun to learn to read the tickertape, the way trades were reported nationally at the time.

In front of a semi-circle of wooden captain's chairs facing a long wall the length of the office was a ceiling-to-floor black chalkboard that one of the clerks, Mary Alice, used to record successive prices of the Dow Jones stocks and also of local favorites, like Burlington Industries, Cone Mills, and R. J. Reynolds. Every fifteen minutes, she climbed several steps to reach the platform to post current prices on the board as they were shown simultaneously on the moving tickertape above the board. Successive prices posted on the blackboard enabled a customer to observe a stock's performance in sequence throughout the day until the market closed, not just the most recent sale shown on the tickertape.

Facing the board, but behind the customers' chairs, were cubicles partitioned by glass screens where account executives monitoring the market phoned their customers with buy/sell advice or answered incoming calls from them.

To the right of the cubicles, near the street-front of the office, was "the cage," a large, secure open area behind five-foot wood-paneled partitions topped with glass panes —the operational heart of the business. One glass divider contained a window for account execs to use in submitting orders to Nita, the office manager, who sent them on to New York via teletype. All the confidential client-orders and daily transactions, whether on paper or by wire, took place in the cage.

Nita also managed the clerks in that area and took personal responsibility for the teletype machine. The cage was off limits to customers, to account reps, to everyone except Mr. Shelley, Nita, and the others working inside. Mr. Shelley often admonished the account reps not to enter that inner sanctum; he didn't want them hovering over Nita or confusing things by trying to send orders themselves. Heaven Forbid!

Initially, I worked with all the account reps except, of course, Mr. Shelley, who was sufficient unto himself—a very organized, efficient man. Occasionally, I typed a letter for him, but otherwise was engaged by the reps. My role was somewhat unusual in that I was the only female who worked outside the cage. As I learned the ropes, I began to communicate with the Regulars about happenings in the market. Often, they would ask me at the beginning of the day, before the index averages were posted, how the market was opening. I got so I could read the tape pretty well. I had to, because I surely didn't want to look stupid to my bosses or to the others, my new friends.

Once I proved my mettle, the major producer in the office asked Mr. Shelley if I could work more or less exclusively with him. That was quite a compliment, for he was the most productive Merrill Lynch account executive in North Carolina. My in-depth education began then, because

I listened to him as he talked with his customers analyzing particular companies, their earnings, the stock movements, and the market's trends and predictions for the future.

Company "guidance," as it is commonly known now, was not a common practice then. Personal computers and laptops were years in the future. We had to try to keep prices and price/earnings (P/E) ratios of stocks in our heads. I learned to plot charts of individual stocks using bi-log paper, and I learned to read charts of market movements. This was practical stuff I had not learned in college or graduate school. I was having fun!

The more I learned, the more the guys coming in daily talked with me, sometimes requesting information but often joking or teasing me about being from peanut country. They wanted to know about my youth in Halifax County. Most, but not all of them, knew how peanuts were harvested and dried. Driving through Eastern North Carolina, they had seen mounds of plants, both leaves and roots—the legumes themselves, piled high on giant-sized stakes in large, empty fields. A few of them had eaten raw or roasted peanuts in the shell. A very few had tasted peanuts boiled in their skins, whereupon they usually turned up their noses, or spit them out.

That tipped me off that they were novices. They liked only what most people liked: salted, roasted peanuts that had been through a processing mill. What they didn't know was that while the variety grown in Eastern North Carolina was called the Virginia peanut, more peanuts were grown in North Carolina than in the state due north of it! The processing plants, such as Planters, were located in Southside Virginia, but the peanuts for those plants were harvested in North Carolina.

Not only did we grow them, we knew how to turn them into specialty snacks, or at least Mrs. Eure did. Mrs. Eure of Halifax County, fifteen miles below the Virginia border, sold homemade salted nuts in pint and quart jars, the best ever. A smart entrepreneur, she also packaged them in small paper bags and sold them over the counter for five cents a bag in filling stations, drug stores, and truck stops.

Every student at Weldon High School, indeed everybody in town, knew about Mrs. Eure's peanuts and where to find them. With our weekly allowances, we could afford the five-cent bags. Several times a week, when the school bell rang to let classes out for the day, we raced across highway 301 to People's Filling Station for an afternoon snack. Some of our crowd bought an RC Cola and a MoonPie. Why waste money on that, I thought, when *peanuts* were available? MoonPies were the same the world over; Mrs. Eure's peanuts were unique to Halifax County.

Most of us bought a Coke and a bag of Mrs. Eure's nuts, leaving Planters cans to grow stale on the shelves. The boys poured the nuts into their Cokes and then drank and ate at the same time. I didn't want to spoil the crispness and saltiness of the nuts by mixing them with the sweet acidity of the Coke, though. We bragged that Mrs. Eure was probably making a fortune because she won every salted-peanut competition around.

On a lark, I decided to bring the Merrill Lynch Regulars some of Mrs. Eure's peanuts, picking up a few pints when I went home to see my parents one weekend. Then I had second thoughts because, having tasted the best, they might want more every time I went home. Eating good peanuts is an easily-acquired addictive habit. I couldn't afford to keep them supplied all the time. I took what I thought would be enough for several days. Between the Regulars and the Merrill Lynch account reps, they gobbled up my supply in one day. To a person, they admitted they were the best peanuts they had ever eaten. And, to a person, from that day on, they called me "Peanuts."

Every morning, as I set foot in the Merrill Lynch office, someone greeted me by my nickname. One day, after my husband and I had had lunch together in a nearby restaurant, he headed back to his office on Elm Street in the Jefferson Standard Building and I headed down Market Street to the Merrill Lynch office. As I rounded the corner onto Green Street, I heard a loud yell: P E A N U T S!

Everybody on the street stopped and looked around. What was going on?

Who was that clown? I turned around, too. Lo and behold, it was the dignified Mr. Boyce, one of the Regulars, calling "Hey, Peanuts, hold up! I'll walk back with you." I waited and walked back to the office with Mr. Boyce, chatting about the market and my weekend trips to Halifax County while the onlookers stared at us, an unlikely pair. 'Til then, I never dreamed I would acknowledge such a nickname when called. After that, for the two years I worked at Merrill Lynch, I accepted the name "Peanuts," used by everyone in the office, even by some acquaintances once they heard the story.

I read somewhere that nicknames are put-downs. I disagree. Maybe so if they are intended as signs of opprobrium, but certainly not if prompted by affection. My sister Margaret is nicknamed "Monk" because she scampered around like a little monkey when she was a toddler. My daughter Andrea is "Andi," so named by my best friend on the day of her birth. My nephew is "Pooh" because his sister could not say Robert. And I'm "Peanuts." I consider all of them terms of affection.

However, I was not "Peanuts" to my husband's boss at Jefferson Standard Life Insurance Company. Claud, my husband, was a junior executive in the Underwriting Department, and we had been invited to the annual dinner celebrating the successes of the sales agents. Nametags for each of us were on a table at the door, and mine read "Alice, Claud's wife." Instinctively, I felt offended, as if I were suddenly someone's chattel. My name was not "Alice, Claud's wife," and I tucked the tag away in my handbag.

In the receiving line, the president of the company, Mr. Holderness asked me, "What happened to your name tag—did they forget to give you one?"

"No, Sir, is in my pocketbook," I said, "I took it off because it did not carry my correct name."

He apologized and then, he asked what my name was. I said, "I'm Alice Irby. Not 'Alice, Claud's wife.'" His face turned red; he seemed perplexed; he stammered, and then he graciously recovered and offered me a greeting of welcome. Embarrassed, Claud turned away from me and rushed into the ballroom alone.

No real damage had been done. We were not blacklisted from future celebrations, and Claud went on to become a vice president of the company. At the time, I felt I had struck a blow for women and wives! To the President's credit, my name tags for subsequent events had my correct name on them: "Alice Irby." Had that not been the case, I may not have attended any more company events, but I concluded that the practice was just a thoughtless act, a moment of blindness to others' identities.

Some of my friends, including a few women, thought my protest was overdoing it—an unladylike gesture. Still, down deep in my consciousness was a core principle that my mother and my Aunt Genie taught me during my formative years. Whenever I felt wounded because of undeserved criticism or gossip, they would say to me, "You can't let others define you, Alice. You must define yourself." I took that advice for my own life and chose not to look back.

The Regulars kept enjoying the peanuts from Halifax County. In time, Mrs. Eure grew older and tired of getting up early each morning, standing over buckets of boiling water, vats of deep grease, and pans of salt. Cooking and frying peanuts and packaging them was a labor-intensive enterprise. To be fresh, the peanuts had to be processed every day. That was required of anyone dealing in specialty peanuts, including my cousin in Hampton Roads, Virginia, who had a similar business. Like Mrs. Eure, Mary Lou Jones turned her kitchen into a processing plant every morning at five o'clock.

Waiting later meant working in heat around 100 degrees in summer with no air-conditioning, and reaching the retail customers too late in the day. The nuts had to be ready for sale by mid-morning. I remember as a child visiting my cousin, seeing her perspiring, her clothes damp from head to toe, moving the pots of boiling water around on the stove. She was strong and hearty, though. Imagine the strain on Mrs. Eure as she aged.

Ruth Gregory Proctor, a former student and friend of my mother who grew up in Halifax—a few miles from Weldon—knew Mrs. Eure. Ruth lived in Charlotte then, though she planned to retire to her family home in the historic town of Halifax. Mrs. Eure offered to give Ruth her recipe for the salted nuts so that Ruth could keep the business going. To get it, Ruth had to pledge total secrecy. Mrs. Eure would not reveal her secret to anyone because she didn't want competitors to encroach on her dominant market share. Ruth agreed to the terms and set up a small business in Charlotte until her retirement back home in Eastern North Carolina.

Upon moving back to Halifax, Ruth continued the tradition of making Mrs. Eure's peanuts for friends and for her children but discontinued the salted-peanuts business. She prepared jars and cans of the specialty as gifts at Christmastime. Every year, I looked forward to dropping by her house on my way to Weldon for Christmas with my parents. She always had a box full of goodies for me: pickled okra, hot pepper jelly, relishes, and, of course, peanuts.

RUTH ON THE RIGHT, WITH HER SISTER, JESSE

In time, Ruth, like Mrs. Eure, also grew old and, after suffering a series of small strokes, decided she should not attempt to deal with the boiling water and grease again. By that time, there was not a young person interested in the sweaty business of salting peanuts by hand. What to do with Mrs. Eure's recipe? She had promised not to disclose the peanut recipe, but she didn't want it to disappear. She wanted future generations to enjoy the unique taste. She described the process to me one day, revealing the extra step that she employed before the peanuts were dipped in hot fat. Without writing it down, I could never get all the steps just right. I think she knew I was not the one to carry on the tradition.

She decided to teach her son and grandson how to process them. They came to the family home in Halifax, spent a weekend with her, and went home practiced in the art of making Mrs. Eure's and Ruth Proctor's peanuts. With luck, the secret of preparing and the pleasure of eating the best salted nuts in the United States will be preserved for future generations, but possibly, never be for sale again.

For all the time I was at Merrill Lynch, the Regulars got a taste of Mrs. Eure's peanuts every time I went back home for the weekend. At the office in Greensboro, with Peanuts as my moniker and with experience under my belt, I did become an accepted member of the group of account reps at Merrill Lynch: Stewart, Brother Bill, Freddie, Neal, and Ridey. Never insulted, put-down, or harassed in any way, I was included in conversations about business, politics, and the topics of the day.

All of us liked sports, too, especially ACC basketball and national-league baseball. In those days, every North Carolina kid played baseball—well, not all the girls. When it came to baseball, I could keep up with the most knowledgeable and enthusiastic of them all, having been trained by my Dad from an early age.

One memory stands out. In October of 1956, we all hovered around Neal's radio to listen to the World Series. There were no TV sets in offices then. Games were often in the afternoon during working hours. Neal brought a radio in just for the occasion. Mr. Shelley turned his back and acquiesced in our break from work. During Game 5, suddenly the office grew quiet; customers and staff drew around the radio as their jaws dropped open. Don Larsen of the New York Yankees was headed toward pitching a perfect game of the World Series in Yankee Stadium—the Yankees vs. the Dodgers.

When he did it, cheers went up all over the office. That achievement still holds the record as the only perfect game pitched in the World Series and one of fewer than two dozen in Major-League-Baseball history. That day, no one paid attention to the stock market, not Mr. Shelley and certainly not many folks in the Wall Street office of Merrill Lynch, either.

Regardless of team preferences, we cheered for Larsen, as we would for anyone who could pitch a perfect game. We couldn't believe it! Dad and I were Yankees' fans, which made it especially sweet. Although Southerners through and through, Dad and all his buddies in Weldon pulled for the Yankees. They appreciated excellence—and winning. I called home immediately after Larsen's win. Dad and his merchant friends had also taken the afternoon off and were listening as they sat in his store huddled around the cabinet-style Zenith radio.

One Monday morning as I walked into the Greensboro office to begin work, Mr. Shelley, who occupied the first cubicle when he was not in his private office, called me over. What had I done? Normally, Mr. Shelley was taciturn, speaking only when giving directions or handling a trading matter. No small talk.

"I see that you wrote a letter to the editor of the paper," he said. "It's in today's edition." I had written to the editor of the *Greensboro Daily News* about something having to do with government tax and spending policy. Right now I can't remember why I wrote it.

"Yes, Sir," I replied. "If they want full employment, they are going about it the wrong way."

"Well," Mr. Shelley commented, "while I don't agree with your position, you certainly made your case well."

I was surprised and touched by his compliment; he didn't have to say anything about it.

On another occasion, he asked me if I would like to attend and record a business-strategy planning session he had scheduled for the account executives, a mini-retreat at a local hotel.

"Yes, Sir, I would be delighted," I responded before he could change his mind. I interpreted that as a vote of confidence in my understanding of the business and my ability to write the record of a technical business meeting. Though he would never say it, I think that was his way of including me as a member of his team, granting me a kind of equivalent status regardless of Merrill Lynch's benighted employment policies. Or, maybe he just wanted a good scribe. Who knows, but silently I cheered.

With P/E ratios dancing in my head, I climbed deeper and deeper into the world of investments and stock trading. I liked it, but was that to be my future? What about all those developments in the political and social world that had concerned me when I was in college and in graduate school? The previous year, I had done a study for the Planning Department of the City of Greensboro that examined the economic base of the city and prospects for growth. I liked that kind of research.

I considered applying for a government job but there was none in Greensboro that fit my interest and talent—and I did not want to risk hiring-discrimination again. One possibility, which would have meant a major change for Claud as well, was to apply to the Research Division of Merrill Lynch in New York. Instead of trading stocks, I could research companies and markets. Women were eligible to apply for those jobs.

Then, out of the blue, I got a call from Mr. Charlie Phillips about joining the staff at the Woman's College. He had a half-time position, assisting him in traveling around the state to inform students and parents about the college. The other half was teaching economics. It seemed like a dream job for me, a chance to start out on an academic career. It combined action with study. It involved limited travel within the state with few nights away from home. It offered opportunities to get to know students and faculty. Hastily, I accepted.

The downside was saying good-bye to my friends at Merrill Lynch. I had spent two full years there, learning a lot, enjoying my colleagues, and kibitzing with my pals. It was a great first job. I proved to myself I could make the grade. I think I proved it to my bosses as well. Maybe, in a small way, I paved the way for the next generation of women to be hired as account reps on an equal footing with men. I look on the industry today with pride and satisfaction: women are front and center. They are account execs and on boards at Merrill, right along with the "Boys." They have their own TV shows discussing economic issues and policies that affect viewers and the country at large—and now thousands of financial advisors and managers across North America tune into their shows on business channels.

I was happy and sad at the same time. I hated to leave my friends at Merrill; I held them close to my heart. They were the real thing—no guile. The Woman's College offered a very different world and one that was more formal than the environment at Merrill Lynch. I was not sure I would develop friends as easily. While the Woman's College was just across town, it was a world away, but a world that drew me to it. Not only did I leave my friends at Merrill Lynch, I left "Peanuts" behind as well. But not the memories; they went with me and are alive today.

Every time the supply gets low, I dump a bag of salted peanuts, in their shells, into a green handmade-ceramic bowl purchased from a North Carolina potter for that purpose. Visitors see them on my table and join in shelling and eating, while I tell them stories of Merrill Lynch and my roots in the peanut country of Halifax County where the land is flat, the summers hot, and the black delta of the Roanoke River feels cool to our bare feet—and where the boys are good dancers and the girls are light-hearted beauties, all of them nourished and delighted by fresh-roasted peanuts.

January 2018

My Love Affair with Learning

April 13, 2015

Author's Note:
This story is derived from a speech to the Phi Beta Kappa (PBK) initiates at the University of North Carolina in Greensboro on April 13, 2015. Phi Beta Kappa is a society honoring excellence in the liberal arts. I was asked to share with the young students how the liberal arts led me to a lifetime of learning. I had never spoken about myself before that night but agreed to do so with the hope that my life experiences would encourage young scholars to pursue their dreams.

Below is my story; at the end is my call to the PBK initiates.

I want my future grandchildren and those of George and Margaret to know about our mother and father and the kind of home we had; about my schooling, which I think was exemplary; and about the guiding role my college played in my maturity. To do that, I have added information about my early schooling.

Even though located in a small Southern town, my high school was much like a private school in that it focused on the classical basics with just enough athletics to make life lively. Yet academic life dominated.

College mentors, especially the warm and dedicated Professor Warren Ashby and Dean Mereb Mossman, the latter of whom I did not describe in depth for lack of space, encouraged and nurtured my growth into adulthood.

For all these reasons, I want this chapter to work both as a story and as a message to young scholars.

My learning began first with my family in the 1930s and 1940s. We lived in Weldon, North Carolina, tucked up under the Virginia border directly below Richmond. My mother was my first dedicated teacher and role model. That I spoke to UNCG's PBK initiates on April 13, 2015, carried special meaning for me. That date was the 110th anniversary of my mother's birth. The location, the campus of the University of North Carolina in Greensboro, was also significant. My mother, Margaret Hudson Joyner, was a 1926 graduate of what would become the Woman's College of the University of North Carolina.

Like her, I'm lucky to have lived during the Great American Century—in fact, for two-thirds of the twentieth century. During much of that time, the Woman's College and my family made it possible for me to benefit from this country's generosity and its historic abundance.

In my early years in Weldon, learning was painless and a natural part of life. It was an *unspoken expectation*, not a requirement. No one admonished me to do my homework or search the encyclopedias on our bookshelves. Growing up two years apart, my brother, George, and I were naturally curious. Our questions were encouraged. In fact,

Mother sometimes looked exasperated when we fired questions one after another. But she was also amused, so learning became *a habit* of mine quite early.

By the time I was sixteen, I had lived through the Great Depression, during which able-bodied men knocked on our back door offering to sharpen knives in exchange for a meal—and WWII, when young men from my hometown did not return from the skies over Europe or D-Day and its aftermath.

In those years, our resources were limited, especially compared to today...but they were plentiful enough to excite and nurture us. TV may have been on the drawing boards somewhere but there were no sets for sale in stores. Cell phones, the Internet, and social media were merely dreams in inventors' minds. We had rotary-dial phones and radio, which we gathered around every night for news and for weekly mysteries like "The Shadow" or "The Thin Man" with Nick Charles. To this day, I prefer radio to TV.

Sundays were reserved for church, friends, and conversation. Saturday was the only day we could go to movies, where we watched cartoons, newsreels depicting war battles in the Pacific and Europe, FDR's speeches, and black-and-white Western shoot-'em-up cowboy movies. We had Big/Little Books, the forerunner of comic books. When comic books did appear, Wonder Woman was my heroine. Whatever she could do, I thought I could, too—when I grew up!

A defining characteristic of our home was its egalitarian environment. I was never made to feel inferior to my brother or any boy simply because I was a girl. My father, who left school in the eighth grade to work on the family farm and care for younger children, insisted that each of his children go to college and have opportunities he was denied.

MOTHER   DAD

My parents' attitude, largely unspoken—that each of us should dream and strive to fulfill those dreams—was vital to my early development and later to my becoming an independent woman which, incidentally, happened well before the Women's Lib movement made waves in the 1970s.

My mother insisted that I make myself dependable and self-reliant. I can hear her now:

"Alice, get a good education and be prepared to make your own way. People can take many things from you, but they cannot take your mind and your education."

Mother made sure, too, that George and I learned about our past. During WWII, gasoline was scarce, but she saved her ration coupons to get enough gas to take us to Richmond to concerts or to visit historical sites—and to do a little shopping at Miller & Rhoads. We became familiar with St. John's Church, where the House of Burgesses met before the Revolution, and where Patrick Henry gave his famous speech on the theme of "Give me liberty or give me death."

I spent weeks in the summer at Colonial Williamsburg—only 65 miles from Weldon—where I came face to face with leaders of the Revolution. Weldon and Halifax, the town next door, were not without their own significant history. The Weldon-Wilmington Railroad, completed in 1840, was at the time the longest railroad in the world, 161.5 miles long, and a critical line for supplying the Southeastern seaboard and General Lee's army, 1860-65. And, Halifax was, ninety years earlier, a center of revolutionary zeal when citizens passed the Halifax Resolves in April 1776, months before July 1776, in Philadelphia.

For the longest time, I couldn't understand why everyone didn't know what happened in Richmond and Williamsburg at the time of the Revolution. It was such a part of my early life that I assumed everyone knew about it.

There was school, too.

Weldon School, with a student population of about 300 students in Grades 1-12, could not afford frills and extras in its curriculum. Teachers had additional duties, such as coach, principal, and guidance counselor. There was one paid administrator, the superintendent, in our high school and three paid principals in other schools in the system.

Our curriculum included the basics: 4 years of English, 4 years of math, 3 years of history, 2 years of science, and 2 years of French. Facilities were simple: classrooms, an auditorium, and a separate gym for physical education and dances; a football field, a basketball court, and a baseball diamond. That was enough.

Mr. Thomas, the superintendent, taught math; Mrs. Wallace taught English. Every Friday we had quizzes in math and a writing assignment in English.

Did they ever seem stern! There were times when we did not please them. Most of the time, they were simply very dignified, inspiring respect and commanding attention. You can be sure there were no discipline problems in their classes.

Mr. Thomas was formal and serious but had a twinkle in his eye. He made each of us go to the front of the class, take chalk in hand, and prove a theorem or solve an algebra problem, teaching us to think on our feet and to solve problems without help. He was also the enforcer when students misbehaved. Just walking into his office made the toughest boys' knees shake.

A couple of boys, Glick Price and Bill Rightmeyer, tested the patience of Mrs. Wallace, who taught us English all four years of high school.

"Glick," admonished Mrs. Wallace. "If you and Bill don't stop talking, I will have to give you a demerit. And if I see you floating paper airplanes again, I will have to send you to Mr. Thomas's office. You know what *that* means!"

"Aw, yes, Ma'am," answered Glick, "I don't mean no harm, but Bill here, he's botherin' me with his needlin'."

"Well, stop anyway," insisted Mrs. Wallace, "and go to page 87 to Hamlet's oration and start reading aloud."

The whole class snickered when Glick, a chubby farm boy who cared more about sows than Shakespeare, had to read sections from *Hamlet* aloud to the class. Glick chuckled, too.

I learned later from my mother, who was friends with Mrs. Wallace, that she could hardly keep from laughing when she reprimanded the two boys. We girls always thought she was partial to boys in that she seemed to pay more attention to them. Instead of admonishing them, she would turn her head every now and then to hide a smile when one of them played the fool. Nevertheless, she was fair to all in her grading.

Mrs. Wallace was a stickler for good grammar and manners as well as a taskmaster in drilling us on the components of good composition. Her shorthand version of Strunk and White's *Elements of Style* was "clear, concise, and coherent." If a composition did not have those characteristics, we had to do it over or get an F.

These two teachers, along with my teacher-mother and my piano teacher, Louise Farber, cultivated my intellectual growth, sparked my curiosity, and endured my inquisitiveness. And, each of them laid down the *rules*...of behavior, of study, of courtesy, and of community responsibility.

This is how learning shaped my early life. Even so, I had not yet learned to *love learning*. That happened at the Woman's College.

Attending WC was my own choice and I have never for a moment regretted it. Duke was runner-up. I was fortunate to have a choice between a good single-sex school and a good co-ed institution. Women could not attend Chapel Hill as freshmen until 1963.

When I arrived on campus, I had not anticipated the cornucopia of offerings and possibilities at WC. It was like putting Alice *in* Wonderland! However, I soon learned that my course offerings were somewhat limited because all freshmen and sophomores, except music majors, had to take a liberal-arts core curriculum: English, history, including world history, math, science, foreign language and, of course, physical education and health. It struck me that it was like the high school curriculum all over again except at a higher and more demanding level.

WC became my protective cocoon, enabling me, in safety, to craft a springboard from which future learning could lead me down any one of several paths. I developed an intellectual framework I trusted, one in which I could confidently welcome new adventures, evaluate future professional challenges, and discover new sources of knowledge.

"The Woman's College is *your legacy* as well as mine," I reminded the Phi Beta Kappa initiates. "Here's why and how."

Even though the University, now the University of North Carolina at Greensboro (UNCG), has changed in size, has become co-ed, and has added significant graduate and professional programs, its foundation *is still that core of liberal education* that permeated and defined it from its beginning in 1890. In my time, the College had three key attributes: a liberal arts core at its center, an honor code, and a commitment to pedagogy.

"Classroom learning was only one component of the 'liberating arts.' I hope that is true for you today," I emphasized. "Aycock Auditorium was a college-and-city center: for the performing arts of drama, music, and dance, for mind-expanding lectures, and, of course, for required assembly on Tuesdays...for all 2,500 of us.

"Elliott Hall, constructed in the early 1950s during my time here, housed art exhibits as well as offices for student activities," I explained. "Witherspoon Gallery was not even on the drawing board, but the visual arts were on display everywhere. Parlors in Elliott Hall housed traveling exhibits of famous artists, frequently the Cone Collection of Impressionist artists. In fact, there was an original de Kooning hanging on the wall of the freshman art lab, unprotected! That would raise hairs on the heads of every art professor here today," I explained.

The center of the campus, for me at least, was Jackson Library, a hard-to-reach building during freshman year because of the mud. In 1950, the new building's grounds had not yet been landscaped with walkways. Rain turned dirt trails into a sea of soft mud, requiring boots or galoshes every winter day.

Every afternoon, I read and studied there, taking naps frequently in the overstuffed, comfortable leather chairs. It was a place for meeting friends who gathered to study each day and to argue about issues and world developments. Reference librarians were my helpful guides in using the card catalog and discovering the stacks.

Today, Jackson Library is like hallowed ground to me. When I walk into the front door, I scan the rooms with an architect's eye to visualize the way it looked seventy years ago...and I look around to see who is sleeping in comfortable chairs. And I wonder who is spending time sitting on the cold cement floor in the stacks, browsing among the books on a given topic—so much more fun than searching the Internet!

The convenient physical facilities were important, but they served only in support of the intangible learning atmosphere of the College. A sense of studied inquiry; of faculty commitment to students as fellow scholars; of the welcoming friendliness of seniors and administrators; of respect among all students for one another, regardless of background or predilections—all this created a warm yet powerful living and learning residential community.

There was tolerance, not permissiveness but understanding; an appreciation of differences, not separations based on identity; an effortless commitment to impartiality, not simply advocacy of pre-set notions. The freedom to inquire, to speak freely, to challenge, to argue—all existed within the context of an ethical code based on honor and respect. The honor code was very real for us, a living code of behavior.

This was not accidental; it was nurtured by wise faculty and administrators over many years. Some of those individuals changed my life by living according to these precepts: Professor Warren Ashby, my philosophy professor; and Dean Mereb Mossman, my boss and friend; mathematician Anne Lewis; scientist Laura Anderton; historian Gene Pfaff; economist Eleanor Craig; poet Randall Jarrell; and Romance languages professor Malcolm Hook, to name a few.

Having placed in an advanced French class because my mother, who taught French in high school, had prepared me well, studying under Dr. Hook was an honor and a challenge. Writing home was expected of students, and when I wrote, Mother answered me in French. I responded in French. She marked each grammatical mistake, and I stretched to learn her vocabulary. My grounding in French was such that, when I went to graduate school at Duke, my professor exempted me from taking the foreign language exam when, on the spot, I translated for him a passage from an advanced economics text. Years later, following in Mother's footsteps, my daughter, Andrea, majored in French at the University of Virginia.

Several remarkable women became models for me, especially Mereb Mossman, Dean of Instruction, who, a few years later, chose me as Director of Admissions. She was second-in-command to the Chancellor, serving in positions now known as provost or vice chancellor. She became my most significant role model for years to come.

Eleanor Craig was another female mentor vital to my development. As an Economics major, I had limited choices of upper-level courses because the department was small. There were upper-level business courses available, but not many economics courses, and no advanced theory classes.

For my senior year, Dr. Albert Keister, the department head, suggested I undertake an Independent Studies program, involving research and writing a thesis first semester and studying economic theory the second.

Dr. Craig, a young assistant professor, offered to tutor me in economic theory, aware that such knowledge was vital to my success in graduate school.

Coaching me meant adding to her regular duties without extra pay.

"Can you imagine having your own personal tutor in college, and a professional woman at that?" I exclaimed to Claud.

What encouragement for a college senior: having a very able young woman in my field show enough interest in me to give me a foundation for graduate study! Observing her competence, her willingness to give a young student a hand up, and her skill in choosing study topics important for my development fueled my own ambition to advance and succeed.

Through a philosophy course, I came to know Dr. Warren Ashby and his wife, Helen. They were hospitable to students, inviting them to come to their home for conversation. Their home became Grand Central for a number of us, my home away from home. With their guidance, we discussed unfolding events, expressed our anxieties, and prepared for the unexpected. We learned facts, we voiced opinions, we speculated about outcomes.

Faculty and students at WC and at Bennett College, a college in Greensboro for African American women, met together from time to time to discuss the school-segregation case pending before the U. S. Supreme Court. In the spring of 1954, the Court handed down its first decision outlawing school segregation, and a second one in 1955, insisting on implementation. We cheered.

Implementation followed methodically in a few places; it came slowly in others; in still others, there was defiance and schools closed. Greensboro was well positioned to accommodate change. Several of its municipal boards had been integrated. Community organizations such as the then-segregated YWCAs were discussing merger. Faculty from surrounding colleges met in formal and informal gatherings, working collaboratively to smooth the transition.

About the same time, a political crisis was unfolding before my eyes: the McCarthy hearings on anti-American activities, calling out specifically those suspected of membership in the Communist Party.

"Alice, we have a TV and you are welcome to come over to the house to watch the McCarthy hearings that are underway," Dr. Ashby said. "I know there are no TVs on campus, and these hearings are important."

"Thank you," I replied. "I'll take you up on the invitation because I am concerned about the threats Senator McCarthy is making and what might happen to our guarantee of freedom of speech. I have read about some of McCarthy's tactics." I watched the hearings while sitting on the floor of their living room.

Little did I know then that the nationally publicized trial of Junius Scales, alleged Communist Party agitator fingered by McCarthy, would be held in Greensboro in the summer of 1954, right after my graduation, and that I would be able to attend the sessions. I sat in the federal courtroom in Greensboro every day of the trial, mesmerized.

The legal issue was not Scales' membership in the Communist Party, which was not illegal—contrary to what most people believed. The issue was his violating the Smith Act, his actively advocating the violent overthrow of the Government. Everything I had learned or valued about free speech and right of assembly was debated in that trial. McNeil Smith, a well-known Greensboro lawyer, and Telford Taylor, a famous civil rights defense lawyer from New York, were counsel for the defense. In spite of their elegant arguments for free speech, and distinguishing speech from action, the jury ruled the weight of evidence was against Scales, who was convicted and served time in prison. What a learning laboratory for me!

Dr. Warren Ashby

Big things were unfolding in the 1950s. Contrary to the label the press gave us as The Silent Generation, we were actively engaged in many aspects of public life. My friends, my brother, and my future husband were drafted to serve in the Korean War. Having lived through WWII, I knew what war could do to families and communities. On campus, we prepared ourselves to be active in the affairs of our communities, writing letters to our Congressional representatives and debating important issues of the day in club and civic organizations.

During my senior year, Dr. Ashby and I met occasionally in the Soda Shop to chat about my future and about his dream of a residential college—a college within the larger college to cushion the increasing size of the student body and to create a different model of learning.

"Alice, you have the ability and opportunity, given the changing times, to create a pathway for other young women to follow and to flourish. Don't give up," I recall him saying.

"That's a tall order," I said. "I'm not sure I'm capable of doing that." Trying to live up to his expectations has been an honor as well as a heartfelt duty, though I have not always measured up.

Weldon and the Woman's College got me on my way. In graduate school, Duke opened the doors of opportunity and discovery even wider.

I met students there from other countries, including a young German-Jewish woman who escaped Nazi Germany when she was 12 years old. She was enrolled in a Ph.D. program.

In addition to my courses in economic theory, I took classes in Asian history and economic history. Dr. Calvin Hoover, head of the Economics Department, excited my curiosity about comparative economic systems at a time when Nazi fascism and Stalinist communism dominated headlines daily, and when the Cold War was threatening global conflict. My faculty advisor, Dr. Smith, suggested I explore Duke's recently acquired manuscript collection of the Socialist Party U.S.A. as a primary source for my thesis on the relationship of the Socialist Party U.S.A. and the U.S. labor movement, once headed by Samuel Gompers.

Reading the original documents was like eating candy. Letters and position papers from Eugene Debs and other socialists as well as non-socialists, revealed vividly why the Socialist Party, even at its heyday around the turn of the twentieth century, could not penetrate the labor movement successfully. Samuel Gompers' banner of "More Now" forestalled the Socialists' "Boring from Within" ideological campaign.

At the end of my year at Duke, Dr. Hoover offered me an opportunity to work with him in his field of comparative economic systems. I was honored and excited, eager to start. Continuing in the academic world of teaching and research offered the prospect of a very satisfying life. I liked the lives my professors lived.

Circumstance put the brakes on. I was married, with all the ramifications that entailed. I needed to consider my husband and the fact that I had a home back in Greensboro. Also, given my active days at WC, I had envisioned a different life—one in public service, business, or community affairs.

"Do I take the more contemplative path of academic study?" I wondered. "Or do I chance it and take a less solid and predictable but probably more active path in the public arena?"

As Zorba said in the movie *Zorba the Greek*, "Go for the 'full catastrophe'"—a life in flux, taking chances, reaching for the unknown while fully aware of potential failure as well as potential triumph. One life offered stability; the other uncertainty and high risk—an oversimplification, I now understand, but I knew the choice would determine my life's path.

I chose the latter. But next time around, I intend to become a scholar!

In a couple of years, after a stint in the business world, my career path steered me back to the Woman's College. I began to study again, this time to prepare for teaching part time. The other part of my workday, I spent assisting Mr. Charlie Phillips in representing WC at college days throughout the state and attending gatherings of alumnae. The world was turning my way: being among students and faculty again, meeting new colleagues from other colleges, and developing new relationships with Claud's friends at work made the sun shine every day.

One day, Dean Mossman called me into her office. Knees shaking slightly, I wondered if she had received negative reports from alumnae or students.

"Alice," she started, "I have heard good things about your work with Mr. Charlie, and I want to invite you to apply for the position of Director of Admissions."

"I didn't know the position is vacant," I answered, puzzled. "Just yesterday I was talking with Miss Newton about our new freshmen students."

DEAN MEREB MOSSMAN

"Miss Newton is retiring early, and we would like to have the new director by September when school begins," the Dean explained.

"Of course, I would like to apply. I am flattered that you would consider me."

When she made the appointment, she said, "Alice, you can be a role model for other young women as you undertake your own career. Be aware of that and aspire to become a mentor to others."

"Well, maybe," I thought to myself. "My own mentors made a difference in my development. Why not try?"

I was young and inexperienced when I took over, not fully aware of the complex situation I confronted. But I jumped in with gusto, ready to follow Dean Mossman's guidance.

At that time, in the late 1950s, the Consolidated University (UNC–Chapel Hill, N.C. State, and the Woman's College) faced greater demand for enrollment than it could accommodate and had begun to use test scores as well as high-school grades to select entering students. Again, I returned to the classroom. I took courses in statistics and educational measurement while, in my new role as Director of Admissions, I developed new procedures for processing students' applications. I wanted to be sure that I used test scores fairly, according to professional standards of the American Psychological Association.

Simultaneously, the Consolidated University was integrating its student bodies, and WC had admitted two young black women.

I traveled all over North Carolina visiting high schools and attending college days to spread the word about WC. I went to many African American high schools—most schools were still segregated in North Carolina—recruiting able minority students. Not only did we want to admit more than a handful of minority students, we wanted to identify students who could succeed in college and thereafter.

The winds of change were blowing in Greensboro in 1960 when civil rights protests in the form of "sit-ins" occurred at the Woolworth lunch counter downtown. Some WC students were involved, not sitting at the counter, but meeting and appearing in public with protesters from N.C. Agricultural and Technical College, a predominantly black institution across town. Our students were easily spotted because they wore their WC jackets with the college emblem on the breast pocket. Soon they were reported to the Dean of Students. Their offense was violating the honor code by falsifying their destination when they signed out of their dormitories. Knowing the whereabouts of students at all times was the responsibility of the university administration operating in those days, like universities across the country, under the prevailing doctrine of *"in loco parentis."*

Violation of the honor code was a very serious offense, and, as a result, the young women were scheduled to be expelled. Several of them approached three of us: Professor Warren Ashby, Professor of Philosophy; Robert Greenfield, a faculty member in Sociology; and me, Director of Admissions. Multiple times, we met with the students, and with the university administration. Clearly, two values were in conflict: the importance of adhering to the honor code on the one hand, and citizen participation in the very important developing civil-rights movement on the other. We, along with others, urged the Chancellor to permit the women to remain in school—one was scheduled to graduate that spring—even if it meant punishment of some kind.

Chancellor Gordon Blackwell was worried about potential repercussions from parents and possible unrest in the community. Haltingly, Chancellor Blackwell, a steady and thoughtful man, came down on the side of the students. He supported their reasons for participating in the sit-ins: to recognize the equal rights of all citizens. At the same time, he had a responsibility to uphold the rules of the college. He grounded the students and required them to inform their parents, but they completed the academic year in good standing.

Students and faculty from the other four colleges in town, as well as community and religious leaders, worked to ease tensions in the city and contributed to the peaceful nature of the protests and calm in the city.

My years back at the Woman's College were the most intense, exhilarating, and liberating of my professional life. I grew up fast.

In 1962, Educational Testing Service (ETS) in Princeton, N.J., offered me another learning opportunity. Having used SAT scores in admitting students to the Woman's College, I decided I might as well learn the inner workings of high-stakes testing. By that time, I was a single mom and free to locate where opportunity led.

"I will stay a couple of years before returning to North Carolina where my roots are," I told Mother.

"Princeton is a long way from Weldon, and you have a small child to rear. I'm worried," she replied.

"Mom, it will be good for me—broadening, as they say—to live outside North Carolina for a while and to make my own way. Don't worry. I know people there."

Two years grew into thirty-seven, living either in Princeton or Washington, D.C. Like Zorba, I followed my nose. And, like Zorba, sometimes the outcome was, indeed, close to a catastrophe—or at least a big problem I had not anticipated.

ETS, at the time, was exploding with growth, adding staff almost daily. Tests were a viable means of identifying talent for colleges that were faced with more applicants than they could accommodate. Henry Chauncey, founder and president of ETS, set high standards of performance.

He was an egalitarian. All employees were treated fairly, in compensation as well as in opportunity. My colleagues, experts in their fields, were generous in helping me learn the ropes and settle in. I soon felt very much at home, appreciating being a part of such an organization.

Early on, though, I discovered that the situation was different in the surrounding area. Not everyone was all that mindful of equal treatment. Princeton University was still all male. It admitted women in 1969. I found that surprising since the University of North Carolina system had admitted women to all branches in 1963.

Occasionally, a few people I met in town made fun of my Southern accent and assumed, because I came from the South, I was prejudiced against minorities, whereupon they felt free to express their own biases. Quickly, I learned about discrimination above the Mason-Dixon Line!

I learned when I visited Andrea's elementary school that I was classified as a "secretary" on its records. The secretary in the principal's office told me that since I was a working mom and not a nurse or a teacher, it was assumed I was a secretary.

And then there was the train to New York City....

Early one morning, headed to New York on business, I drove to Princeton Junction to catch the train to Penn Station, waiting on the Junction platform with hundreds of other commuters for the next train. Every day, people rushed, shoved, and scrambled to board the train and get a seat. Mornings found commuters standing in the aisles when the train was full.

When the train stopped, I hopped up the steps and turned to my right into the nearest car. "Wow, what a nice car—unlike any I have seen before," I thought to myself. "And, there is a seat near the door to ease my exit at Penn Station."

I settled into one of the swivel armchairs. There was plenty of leg room. People were reading the paper and drinking coffee, placing their cups on small tables beside their chairs. They were smoking, too, which was then normal.

"I didn't expect this luxury. I'm going to find out how to get this spot next time, too," I decided.

Soon a conductor faced me with a smile. "I am sorry, young lady, this car is for men only. You will need to go to another car to find a seat."

"Why?" I asked. "I'm not disrupting anything and there is likely no seat in another car by now." Awkwardly, he restated he policy that women were not permitted in the car, "That's just the policy, Ma'am. I don't make the policy," he said, waiting.

Looking around I noticed that the male passengers were either hiding behind their newspapers, staring off in another direction as if embarrassed or miffed, or looking at me and smiling. It was obvious my protest was going nowhere.

I picked up my briefcase, smiled at the conductor and said, "The smoke in here is terrible anyway. I hope the fellows enjoy it while their lungs hold out." I never could find out what happened to that exclusive service but, years later, no one knew anything about it.

My years at ETS were filled with opportunities for growth and advancement.

After a leave of absence to work in the Johnson Administration during the mid-1960s, I returned to ETS to direct projects that required travel for business meetings or to visit our offices. Occasionally, my travels took me to Atlanta.

One spring day, with peach trees in bloom along the streets of Atlanta and fresh-green leaves glistening in the sunlight, I decided to take a walk in the downtown area to shop at Rich's Department Store. I needed a couple of tailored shirts. Typically, women executives in the mid-to-late 1960s, following the passage of equal-rights legislation, wore tailored suits and collared shirts with either a small tie or pin at the neck. Brooks Brothers was my go-to store for suits, but Rich's also had a brand of shirt I liked. The salesclerk suggested I get a Rich's credit card so that I could get a discount.

The clerk in Customer Service greeted me pleasantly and asked for my identification. When I presented my driver's license and the American Express card ETS provided executives, she asked for evidence of my husband's credit.

"What?" I exclaimed. "I am divorced and a single mom who supports herself and her child. My former husband and I are not in communication with each other."

"I am sorry, Madam, we cannot offer credit to a woman without the credit security of her husband, even if divorced, unless we have independent evidence of your credit worthiness. The American Express card, or other credit card, is not sufficient," she explained.

I asked to see her supervisor or the vice president. How does a young woman starting out ever get her first credit card? Sitting across from the vice president, I suggested he call my bank in Princeton. He squirmed, trying to decide what to do.

He thought about it and finally decided, "I'll accede to your request, but only because of your association with ETS." I got my credit card and, in time, so did many other women. The law caught up with Rich's and soon with all the others.

A decade after I left the Woman's College, I returned to the academic world. I was named Vice President for Student Services of Rutgers University, the first female vice president of a major American university. If my time in Greensboro had been filled with enormous change, my six years at Rutgers brought another kind of upheaval: Student protests on my first day on the job put me on the firing line. Reorganization of the colleges and university administration made me a target for protesting deans. Controversy over big-time athletics threatened the standards of our admissions policies. Passage of Title IX led to integrating Rutgers College, the original all-male Queens College chartered in 1766.

Intricate and complex problems consumed me, day and night, testing my energy, my imagination, and my creativity. I tried to keep my focus on students.

We implemented Title IX, admitting women to Rutgers College right away, even though under the law, we could have delayed for several years. We upgraded athletic facilities to accommodate women's sports and introduced women's teams to begin to balance those for men. We designed programs for veterans returning from the Vietnam War. We implemented academic programs to give minority or economically stressed students an early start in summer before freshman year. We held to academic standards in admitting athletes.

I knew that our choices affected lives in significant ways, and those choices had to be right. I pushed myself to my limit. But it was all to the good. I sharpened my skills and developed an executive-management style that served me well for the rest of my career. I survived—and, I think, made a difference in students' lives.

Each position I held over the years involved learning new things and developing new skills and ways of strengthening relationships. There were down times—way-down sometimes. But the dark days were many fewer than the bright ones.

If liberal arts learning had provided me only with personal pleasure and intellectual pursuits, that would have been enough. But, more than that, it gave me the foundation for adventuring into an uncertain but rewarding path of professional and community life. It taught me to appreciate the unknown, to discipline my mind in searching for the truth, and to cope with the unexpected once I ventured into that unknown.

In no other country could I have lived as free, with as many doors opening as I matured, and with as many opportunities to uphold my values in service to others and to my community as in America during the twentieth century. Every day bears witness to my gratitude for being steeped in the liberal arts from my early high school years through my time at the Woman's College. Because of that, I am still learning. And I love it.

Now, a few words about you and the future.

My life has spanned decades of great change: threats of war and violence to our nation; the expansion of civil and human rights; unprecedented stresses in the body politic; and the explosion of economic growth improving life for billions of people, to name a few.

In the 1930s and 1940s, we survived the Great Depression and WWII, stood in shock at the development of the atomic bomb, feared conflict with Russia when it developed its own atomic bomb in 1949, and felt anxiety daily during the early years of the Cold War.

In the 1950s, we watched with dismay Senator Joseph McCarthy investigate accused communists and Communist Party activity in the U.S.; began implementation of the *Brown v. Board of Education* Supreme Court decision outlawing school segregation; and sent our young men and women to fight in Korea, 1950-53.

In the early 1960s, we engaged in the sit-ins at the Woolworth counter in Greensboro and the protest marches in Washington for civil rights; passed new civil rights legislation and enforced executive orders; again, went to war, this time in Vietnam; and we watched with horror the assassination of a president in 1963, a leading civil-rights leader in 1968, and a presidential candidate two months later.

In the 1970s, student sit-ins still took place on college campuses, climaxing in the killings of four students at Kent State University; President Nixon left office in early August 1974 under the cloud of the Watergate break-in cover-up; and President Carter presided over stagflation and the hostage-taking of Americans at our embassy in Tehran.

In the 1980s and 1990s, the Berlin Wall came down, ending the Cold War, while another kind of war started: foreign terrorists attacked the United States for the first time at U.S. Marine barracks in Lebanon in 1983, next at the World Trade Center in 1993, then at the American embassies in Kenya and Tanzania in 1998 and the USS Cole destroyer in 2000, culminating, as you know well, in a full-scale attack on the World Trade Center and two other locations by the al-Qaeda network in 2001. At the same time, economic growth lifted millions out of poverty around the world.

Now, we come to the twenty-first century—your century.

It's time to ask: Can the twenty-first century be another Great American Century? It depends, I believe, on what its own generations make of it. It depends on you and others like you.

America is well positioned, with varied resources and enormous affluence, rapidly advancing technology and universities rich in pedagogy and research—all in a country that has provided greater-than-ever liberty, freedom, civil rights, economic plenty, and advancement of living standards to many around the world.

But progress is never inevitable. We are experiencing unprecedented changes and they are daunting. The question is whether positive forces will coalesce into a common purpose and a harmony that offers psychological and spiritual security; a balanced order insuring freedom of inquiry and liberty; and a common appreciation of justice and equality of opportunity. Or whether we slip further and further into disillusionment, disruptive behavior, and global conflict.

Based on what you have read and studied, what do you see? Where is the sense of community, upon which individual lives depend? Have wise voices been drowned out by the celebrity culture that entertains us? As an older American, I worry that the social media that offer us the ease of staying in touch with thousands of friends can easily preoccupy our minds with the present and the trivial. And, does that easy focus preclude learning the lessons of history and contemplating the future needs of our society informed by those lessons?

Securing freedom, ensuring liberty, expanding opportunity, and building community take strong leadership and vision as well as a focus on the ethical underpinnings vital to every successful civilization. Preserving the foundation of our republic falls to you and your progeny, the newest generations of this young country. *You* are the ones to bring order out of the chaos we sense and the rootlessness we feel. I know you will be able to do so as long as you remain curious, open-minded, and true to your moral code. Your liberal-arts foundation, with its emphasis on discovery, objective inquiry, and continuous learning, will serve you well.

I leave you with a thought of Greek biographer Plutarch. He writes of learning, "The mind is not a vessel to be filled, but a fire to be kindled."

I know that UNCG has kindled your fire. Keep it burning by continuing to learn, using that learning to enhance your lives and to contribute to your professions and your communities. I wish I could be around to watch you light up your world. Congratulations to you on being recognized for your achievements and for your initiation into the Epsilon chapter of Phi Beta Kappa on this April day, 2015.

April 13, 2015

ALONG A WINDING PATH
Off to War

Washington in 1964-65 was the deceptively clear-blue eye of a storm gathering up swirling winds of change from every point of the compass. Still reeling from the assassination of President Kennedy, the capital also had to absorb the significance of the civil rights marches led by Dr. Martin Luther King, Jr.; parse the stirrings of the women's movement for equal treatment; and respond to media revelations of the extent of poverty endured by a large proportion of Americans. How could such a prosperous society, founded upon beliefs in liberty and equality, fall short of those promises for millions of its people? The time was ripe for enduring historic change to mend those fault lines in what most had taken to be bedrock.

That year, I became assistant to the director of the Jobs Corps during President Lyndon B. Johnson's War on Poverty, but I am getting ahead of myself. That was not my first time in Washington on special assignment. I had spent a week in 1949 at Girls' Nation, representing North Carolina as its "governor." That's when I got Washington swamp fever!

Each year, the American Legion Auxiliary sponsored Girls' State in Raleigh, a summer program in civics and government for rising high-school seniors in each of the 48 states.

The governor and lieutenant governor, elected by their peers, represented their state at Girls' Nation. Having been elected Governor at Girls' State in North Carolina, I joined the similarly-elected Lieutenant Governor to participate in Girls' Nation, a week's workshop to practice civics and government at work among the executive and legislative branches of the federal government.

During the week at Girls' Nation, I was captivated by the hustle-bustle of the capital city and became fascinated with the art of politics. Until then, I had thought of Washington as a city of monuments for visiting tourists, and the home of the Senators baseball team for visitors like my dad who wanted to see a game every time we went up to the capital. And, of course, I always gazed admiringly at the Beaux Arts architecture of the stately Willard Hotel on Pennsylvania Avenue where Mom and Dad honeymooned in 1927, the spot as well of Abraham Lincoln's interim lodging before his first inauguration.

Upon arrival, our chaperone handed me an invitation. Addressed to Alice Joyner, "N.C. Governor," and Miriam Bryson, "N.C. Lieutenant Governor," the embossed card spelled out the date and time for us to join our senior Senator from North Carolina, Clyde Hoey, in the Senate dining room for lunch. I pinched myself, "Mimi, we have a chance to see and talk with a real live senator!" She seemed nonchalant but I could tell she was excited, too.

I had seen pictures of Senator Hoey in newspapers back home, dressed in his frock coat, high-collar shirt, and red carnation boutonniere. But when I saw him in living color with his long-flowing white hair, smooth complexion, royal-blue cutaway, with pocket handkerchief to match his carnation, I caught my breath in surprise and delight. He was known as a great orator, and he fit the part perfectly, as if he'd been sent directly from central casting.

His rhetorical skills were on display as well when he spoke to us in his office: "Young Ladies, welcome to the Senate, the great deliberating body of our federal government. I congratulate you ladies of North Carolina and am delighted you are here to represent The Old North State along with other young women from across the land. May I escort you to the dining room?"

We smiled, accepted his gracious invitation, and walked down the marble-lined hall with Senator Hoey as he spoke with colleagues along the way, exhibiting a fine flair and sophistication.

Ever the well-mannered Southern gentleman, he turned to us when seated and said, "Now, Ladies, you may order anything you wish, but I recommend the turtle soup with sherry. It is a specialty of the Senate dining room."

I had never had turtle soup—I did not even know human beings ate turtles. I knew sherry was liquor, but my family were teetotalers. Nevertheless, it would have been impolite to choose something else, given the Senator's recommendation. The soup was delicious, and I came home impressed that I had not only tasted liquor—learning years later that alcohol dissipated in cooking—but that I was the most sophisticated girl in Weldon's senior class.

By far, the most memorable event of that week, however, was meeting President Harry Truman. It was a strange feeling first to be on the grounds of the White House, then walking right in the front door! "How had this happened?" I wondered. "Am I Alice in a Wonderland that may evaporate the next instant?" All of us were looking in awe, turning our heads side to side and up and down, mouths open, eyes popping as we were escorted down the hallway to the Oval Office.

Along the walls were dozens of *New Yorker* and similar cartoons lambasting or poking fun at the President. He laughed about them, pointing out caricatures of Boss Tweed or John L. Lewis, just two of the famous American characters portrayed in the drawings. Once in the Oval Office, the President shook every girl's hand firmly as the 96 of us filed through his office into the Rose Garden. He struck me as a friendly, down-to-earth, and honorable man. No flourishes, no guile, but a candid and forthright man from Missouri, well grounded in history and secure in his personal identity, a man who had faced monumental decisions courageously during times of war and peace.

"Young Ladies, if you remember anything I say to you today, remember this," he said. "The President's duty is to *all* the people. I am the lobbyist for you and for *all* other Americans, whether Democrat, Republican, or neither. Congressmen and Senators represent districts or states; the President represents everyone."

That year of 1949 was the beginning of the Cold War with Russia. Clearly, the President must have had that on his mind as he spoke of America's responsibility as a world leader to protect Europe, Great Britain, and the U.S. from Communist dictators. He mentioned the sign he kept on his desk: "The Buck Stops Here," signaling that he knew his responsibilities and took them very seriously, not dodging them or passing them on to someone else to do.

I have always felt Harry Truman was my president because I became aware of and interested in politics during his presidency. I also reached voting age during his tenure in office. With other statesmen like General George C. Marshall and Dean Acheson, Truman led the United States in rehabilitating the defeated countries of Europe rather than imposing crippling reparations as the victorious powers did after WWI. We credit Churchill with *saving* Europe by his decisions in May 1940. However, Truman *restored* Europe with his decisions in June 1947 to undertake the Marshall Plan for reviving Europe's shattered economy. Simultaneously, he stationed General MacArthur in Tokyo to do the same thing in Japan.

President Truman also integrated the Armed Services in 1948, overcoming political opposition to sign an Executive Order that made right a long-standing wrong. At the same time, he faced head-on the Soviet threat and, with Dean Acheson as his Secretary of State, implemented Point Four, the world's first global technical-assistance program, and the Doctrine of Containment that shaped the foreign policy of the United States until the Iron Curtain came down in 1989.

I voted for the first time in 1952, wishing my vote could have been for Harry Truman. Deservedly, his stature has increased in recent years. He met his heavy burdens with determination, fidelity, bravery, and the courage of his convictions. Critics said of him that he was a little man trying to fill a big man's shoes. Little did they know then: history has confirmed that he more than beat expectations!

In 1964, more than a decade later, Henry Chauncey, president of Educational Testing Service (ETS), then my place of employment, gave me a year's leave of absence to work in President Lyndon B. Johnson's War on Poverty. ETS had never given a leave for such a purpose, but Henry thought my work with the Job Corps, an educational program for out-of-school and out-of-work youth from ages 16 to 22 was worthy of ETS's support.

Henry, a tall, stately man with silver hair and a broad smile, said to me in his genial voice: "Alice, I think you can benefit from involvement in the education of a population that ETS does not usually serve. So go. Then come back and educate us!"

President Kennedy, when elected in 1960, had sparked energy, promise, and hope among voters all over the country. Lyndon Johnson (LBJ), assuming the presidency following Kennedy's assassination in November 1963, had a big void to fill, but he, too, had a dream. He sensed the popular momentum building for government action to ensure the rights of all citizens; to attack gender and racial employment discrimination; to provide equal educational opportunity to all; and to restore debilitating lives mired in poverty. He was not blind to the Montgomery bus boycott or to Reverend Martin Luther King, Jr.'s August 28, 1963, march on Washington. He had followed the Sit-ins in 1960 in Greensboro. He had observed the all-too-slow progress following the Supreme Court's decision on *Brown v. Board of Education* in 1954. And, President Johnson had seen poverty close-up in Texas when, as a young man, he taught public-school children from all backgrounds. He knew we, as a country, could and must do better.

Immediately, he pushed forward Kennedy's New Frontier programs, many of which had foundered in the Congress at the hands of powerful committee chairmen opposed to change. Then he announced his own ambitious program.

Friend and foe alike acknowledged Johnson as the "Master of the Senate," where he had served from 1948 to 1960. His aides, one after another, marveled at his talent: "He knows power, knows how it works, and wants to use the levers of power to achieve great things." He knew how to form coalitions, to persuade the most reluctant of senators or to badger his opponents, to reassure his friends, to trade votes—in other words, to lobby senators ceaselessly on both sides of the aisle, and to pass worthy legislation with or over the heads of the opposition forces in the Congress.

The face of poverty in mid-century America was depicted, with vivid and disturbing images of hunger, desolation, and anguish in Southeastern Kentucky's Letcher

County. Harry M. Caudill (1922-1990), scion of a family originally from North Carolina that had crossed the Appalachian Mountains generations earlier, wrote a book/treatise, *Night Comes to The Cumberlands*, published by Little, Brown in 1963. Every day in his hometown of Whitesburg, Kentucky, Caudill lived among poverty, disease, and hunger. He saw children in rags and men maimed by injuries sustained in coal mines. Caudill's book came to the attention of the Kennedy Administration, and soon government staff flocked to Letcher County to see first-hand what Caudill was describing.

They saw real faces stamped with the diseases of poverty and hopelessness in Kentucky's rural mountains. President Johnson seized on evidence like that in his speech of May 1964 at the University of Michigan, as he outlined the goals of The Great Society: LBJ's focus would be on educational opportunity; on waging a war on poverty; on guaranteeing civil rights; and on constructing a safety net for the poor and elderly.

Action followed. Soon, I found myself present at the creation of that Great Society initiative LBJ had outlined in Ann Arbor. I was a mere soldier in his war, of course, recruited for the Job Corps while many others were marshalled from around the country to join one agency or another to get anti-poverty programs started.

Without taking even a deep breath, Johnson unleashed a tsunami of domestic proposals on the Congress. I watched with surprise, amazement, and wonder: "How can he expect to achieve what he asks?"

"You are not the only one amazed, Alice," Chris Weeks, a member of the advance team, told me. "The heads of committees' chairmen in the Congress are spinning, too! Daily, the Administration floods their offices with bills for new authorizations and funding. They are no match for him. He's like General Patton steaming across France to Bastogne in the Battle of the Bulge."

In two years, more legislation was passed that brought major changes in America than at any time before or since the time of FDR: The Civil Rights Bill of 1964, The Voting Rights legislation of 1965, the Elementary and Secondary Education Act of 1965, the Higher Education Act of 1965, Medicare and Medicaid, and The War on Poverty, to name a few.

The Office of Economic Opportunity (OEO), headed by a gifted and creative executive, Sargent Shriver ("Sarge" to all of us), was created to implement the War on Poverty. Sarge already had a solid reputation in Washington as the Director of the Peace Corps. Along with Vista, Head Start (moved subsequently to another agency), and the Community Action program, the Economic Opportunity Act created the Job Corps to offer basic education and training to youths 16-22, equipping them with employable skills.

I rented an apartment in Foggy Bottom about a mile from the office. Ready to report for work, I walked to the OEO office on 15th Street. When I saw the number on the building, I thought, "Where am I? Have I gone to the wrong place?"

Urban redevelopment had not yet reached that part of downtown. I faced an old, run-down hotel, then realized I was not far from a questionable part of town. I double-checked the address. It was correct. As I ascended the stairs to the front door, I looked back over my shoulder and pulled the collar of my coat up around my ears. Very much alone, I took a deep breath, pushed on the door, and entered the building.

"Don't worry, Alice," Paula, the Personnel Officer, assured me. "This location is temporary. For my part, it'd better be. I didn't come to spend my days in this part of town. No one wants to be mistaken for inhabitants farther south on these streets. We'll be out of here in a couple of months in our new quarters at 18th and M."

No one else seemed bothered by the surroundings. Instead, Job Corps staff were running here and there to one meeting after another trying to devise solutions to all the problems of starting a new federal program from ground zero. We were given no plans for identifying and enrolling the thousands of young people the program was to serve. Who was going to build the hundred or so centers, both urban and rural? How do you provide coverage 24/7 to young men who had lived all their lives in an urban jungle or in isolation far out in the countryside? Experts told us that students living in poverty needed a good residential environment and healthy diets to succeed in educational programs.

Soon, the outlines of the centers and the curriculum took shape: the Departments of Agriculture and Interior were assigned the construction of the rural centers, modeled on the Civilian Conservation Corps (CCC) camps of the 1930s, and the centers would offer both basic education and job training programs in skilled carpentry, mechanics, and outdoor conservation.

Contracts were also let for corporations to open centers on deactivated military bases. Job training in these centers would focus on industrial skills such as auto mechanics, welding, and metalworking. Centers for young women, placed in hotels or apartment buildings in urban areas, would offer entry-level jobs and training in cosmetology, health care, food service and nutrition, and commercial business skills.

A seemingly unsolvable puzzle was how to cast an organizational net large and wide enough to identify, recruit, and enlist thousands of applicants. I was assigned to that task force, given my background in admissions and testing.

"Obviously," I said to Lou Eigen, the director of recruitment, "public schools can't take up the gauntlet because potential enrollees are not in school. Colleges and universities don't have the reach or the expertise to identify out-of-school youth. And, community agencies don't have national networks or the necessary experience to identify and recruit our target population."

"We'll have to look around for another agency or network already in place, then," he said. "But there is a presumption among the idea men in the White House that old-line government agencies will stifle the program. So, don't plumb the bureaucracies for assistance," he advised me. "We need new approaches."

"I doubt that any of those guys has ever built a nationwide educational institution in less than six months," fumed the Job Corps Director, Otis Singletary. We concluded that the only agency with a chance of locating our enrollee population in both the numbers and characteristics we sought was the Bureau of Employment Security (BES). Even though it was a government agency within the Department of Labor, BES offices dealt with job applicants all over the country regardless of educational or employment background. The downside was that it served job-seekers who *approached* the agency, not the other way around. Our students had to be located, identified, screened, and persuaded to leave home to go to the centers. We would have to set very different expectations and goals for the BES offices, should we use them.

One day—unexpectedly—word came from the President through Sarge Shriver to our director: "Otis, the President has decided the Job Corps should be the initial public face of the War on Poverty."

We were flattered by that idea, but we were still in the middle of negotiations with BES: no applicant had been recruited, no center built. The President had told Sarge he thought nothing would demonstrate his commitment to breaking the back of poverty—and thus his ability to deliver on his promises—more than showing Job Corps enrollees in centers learning new trades.

"Let's get going, get this thing off the ground!" LBJ said.

"What specifically did the President expect?" Singletary asked Sarge.

"The impossible, as usual—enrollees living in centers very soon," Sarge replied, "but we have to make the effort, and somehow we will succeed." Sarge wasn't surprised by the President's command; he had worked with LBJ as Peace Corps Director. But we, unaccustomed to LBJ's mercurial ways, were shocked out of our seats.

Then the President himself called the Director of the Job Corps: "Hey, Otis, I think we ought to push hard and make a giant step forward to convince the public of the progress we're making. No reason we can't get 10,000 enrollees in the Job Corps by the end of the year."

"Mr. President," responded our shocked Director, "Once all the building blocks are in place and we push the start button on enrolling applicants, we can get a couple of thousand in centers by year-end. But 10,000? It's already late summer!"

Then, the other shoe dropped. The President, in his deep, compelling voice added, "And uh, Otis, while we need to roll out the program fast, keep in mind one thing. I can't let the War on Poverty be an issue in the upcoming presidential campaign. I need to be elected in November without the appearance of using poor kids as pawns to get votes; so you can't move any of the fellows into a center until after the election." His tone was folksy, his message lethal.

I watched the receiver drop back in its cradle and the Director's pale face sag as he sank down in his chair. After hanging up, he exclaimed, "What on Earth!? How do we get 10,000 enrollees, even if they can be recruited and screened, into centers that have not been built or only partially built—and do it between November 3 and the end of 1964? Eight weeks? Heaven help us!"

No point arguing or protesting, since no one wanted to feel the wrath of the President. Perhaps we novices should have figured into our thinking the political dimensions of what we were doing and given due consideration to the President's energetic "ways," his political proclivities, too. But we were going about things in a rushed yet focused way, not a "fire-the-torpedoes!" LBJ way.

So, the gears started grinding faster—and faster. The Forest Service poured resources into building the rural centers. Our Enrollment team worked day and night to develop publicity for BES to use in post offices, in newspapers, and on radio and TV to attract attention to the program. We needed a motto. And, we needed a uniform to distinguish the Corps from other groups and to enhance enrollees' self-respect, loyalty, and prestige.

"Let the young fellows decide," proposed Lou, a flexible guy who tackled every problem with gusto. "We'll get a group of potential enrollees from the D.C.-Baltimore area to look at the options. I'll have an artist draw several designs and we'll have a vote."

The young men came in and considered an array of designs, from khaki fatigues to dress-military to collegiate coat and tie. To our surprise, they chose the collegiate one: blue blazer, grey pants, white shirt, and striped tie. The Director of the Job Corps came up with the motto: "A Hand Up, not a Handout," a realistic, fresh, plain motto used many times by politicians since then.

Outside our halls, down Pennsylvania Avenue, were the Halls of Congress and the Capitol. Congressional committees controlled our authorization and our appropriations. Sarge Shriver was no stranger there. His was a face frequently gracing those halls, testifying to defend the War on Poverty before various committees, trying to persuade reluctant Congressmen who did not want centers in their districts to accept them, or to explain why every Congressional district could not have Community Action funds for their special projects.

I remember one encounter between Sarge and Adam Clayton Powell, Chairman of the powerful Education and Labor Committee. Chairman Powell occupied the most powerful position held by an African American in Congress. We knew that when Adam Clayton Powell, also the charismatic minister of the Abyssinian Baptist Church in Harlem, and Sarge Shriver were in the same room, there would be a show, two professional politicians sparring like the seasoned champions they were.

A tall, well-built man, with smoothed back hair and a delicate mustache, Chairman Powell was dressed in a fashionable suit and tie and seated in front of floor-to-ceiling cherry-paneled walls at the center of a semi-circle of Committee members. The members themselves were seated behind a polished wood-paneled skirting. The Chairman looked down at the audience and then at the other smartly-dressed man before him at the witness table. Mr. Shriver, whose eyes were dancing, his face lighting up in a broad smile, was that witness, and like the Chairman, he exuded confidence. You could feel the electricity in the air. Everything and everybody else, aides and all, were no more than props for the show.

"Welcome, Mr. Shriver. We are always glad to see you and hear from you. Tell us, in your usual engaging way, how you are going to get my people out of poverty—in fact, how you are going to get *all* God's children out of poverty? What new stories of progress do you have for us today? What's happening in the Job Corps? Are the young men getting jobs?

"And, what about the children?" he continued. "What good does it do to take young boys and girls three or four years old away from their mothers and put them in a school of some kind? Isn't Head Start just an expensive way to use taxpayer dollars for a babysitting service? And, what's going on with the Community Action program? Where's the action? Is the taxpayers' money just padding local politicians' pockets?"

"Thank you, Mr. Chairman. It's always a pleasure to be in your chambers," Sarge Shriver began in his clear baritone. "I am here to report to you, Mr. Chairman, on advances to-date in the country's War on Poverty. Every day, the President asks for detailed reports on what is happening. You can be sure he keeps tabs on us, much the way you do!"

When asked about specific projects in communities, Sarge used his opening to assure the Chairman that, "neighborhood organizations have been identified, and projects are being funded in your district, Harlem, as well as in other districts in New York and around the country. We are trying to reach local agencies that are close to the people we need to serve through our community-development projects. And we are using the Bureau of Employment Services to recruit young men and women for the Job Corps. They are employing every local office to locate and reach out-of-school youth."

The hearing went on for a couple of hours. During the dialogue, it seemed more a love feast than a confrontation, with Sarge praising Chairman Powell for his support and the Chairman nodding with acceptance as Sarge elaborated the need for authorization of all the programs and full funding of them as well.

But later, outside the room after the hearing, when the press's mikes were stuck in their faces, the demeanor of the two men changed. The Chairman attacked with rapid-fire questions and a frown on his face: "How will we know the programs are working? How will we know you are not spending us into the poorhouse? What are your criteria for success?"

Sarge answered in staccato rhythm, hurrying to make his points. Ever the pro, he explained the costs of the programs. He cited numbers of children being enrolled in Head Start. He cited plans for thousands of Job Corps enrollees in local centers within a year.

I couldn't believe the hundred-and-eighty-degree turn from their courtly behavior in the Committee Room. We'd witnessed sugar-coated testimony and genial conversation inside; only needling and drawn knives outside! Then it dawned on me; both men were putting on a show—a very lively and spirited show, to ensure an encounter spicy enough to be covered on the evening news and to please their constituencies. Conflict and high drama caught attention. Each man knew his part.

The authorization was never in doubt. We learned subsequently that the Committee authorized more funds than the President had requested, knowing, of course, that the Appropriations Committee would apply the axe down the line during the legislative process.

In the fall, with Christmas not far away, the first busloads of enrollees from the Baltimore area were taken to Camp Catoctin, an existing federal property, in the mountains of Maryland. It was a staging area used until centers were ready to receive occupants—after the election, of course.

"What? They are not eating the food?" exclaimed Lou after reviewing the first reports from the camp. "We prescribed hamburgers, steaks, chicken, fruits, and vegetables—healthy stuff. Haven't meals been prepared to teenagers' taste?"

"It isn't the food," the camp director said. "The young men have such poor teeth they can't chew the meat or eat the fruit. They are leaving everything on their plates but the mashed potatoes, applesauce, and ice cream."

Hastily, we employed dentists and doctors to repair their teeth and to strengthen their bodies before or as soon as they reached the centers. We hired an ex-Army sergeant, expert in physical training, to install equipment and begin body-strengthening programs in the rural centers.

For everyone in Washington, Christmas was normal that year. For us, it brought a miracle. By December 31, 10,000 young men had been enrolled in the Job Corps, even though they were on buses, trains, and planes, or waiting in camps to get to their new homes.

One large group was singled out for an emergency assignment. In California, wildfires were raging, and Jack Deventer of the Forest Service called our director, "We think we can help out in fighting the forest fires in California if you, Otis, will authorize our bringing Job Corps enrollees in to help. We can house them in tents and other shelters near the fire area."

Weighing the risks, the Director agreed, "Okay, but take extra care. They cannot be put at risk of harm. Have them back up the trained firefighters only and keep them behind the front lines." While their diversion was unplanned and unexpected, certainly by the enrollees themselves, their contribution to fighting the fires was significant, and the publicity put the Job Corps on the map nationally. Not only could the President point to thousands of enrollees, but he could praise their contribution to an important state and to a lifesaving endeavor.

We were surprised—but should not have been—that almost all the enrollees had never been away from home, not even away from their neighborhoods. Similarly, the rural students knew their farms but not much more—maybe a relative or two down the road. Now these young men were being shipped across the country on the theory that getting them out of the environment which had hampered their education was necessary to give them a second chance and a new start.

There was another reason for shipping them to places distant from home: to ensure racial and ethnic integration of the Corps. While this tactic may have broadened the youths' discovery of new places, meeting political and societal goals of the program as well, it did not take into account the homesickness many of the enrollees were feeling. Home is home, even if modest and simple. There was no way we could force the fellows to stay because the program was voluntary. We just worked hard to persuade them to hang in until the end of their employment training, nine months to a year. We lost some but, amazingly, the majority stuck it out.

The President made several trips to visit centers and was on the phone to us about once a week. "Someone is always after me," he fretted. "Of course, that is to be expected—but it's one request after another. A Southern Congressman needs hand-holding about kids from the North in his territory. A California businessman wants a contract for an urban center. A Senator from Indiana wants detailed information about a fight among enrollees at Atterbury. What does he expect among hundreds of young men, most of whom are strangers to one another? Saints?"

A New Jersey newspaper carried a story about enrollees in Camp Kilmer using narcotics. What was the real story, the full story? A few enrollees had sneaked in a handful of marijuana but the story was greatly overblown. The press feeds on sensational events. There were other problems, of course—fights in a center here and there, a missing enrollee now and then. They were always found and returned—just homesick. Some incidents hit the papers and reporters dogged us, exaggerating some of the situations and details. Even so, forward movement continued and even accelerated as procedures and rules were institutionalized and teaching and learning began in earnest. Things settled down.

In time, the high cost of the program led to opposition in Congress, especially among conservative budget hawks claiming, "It costs more to support a Job Corps enrollee than a year at Harvard! We can't afford it. Taxpayers won't take it."

"Our students have greater need than those at Harvard," countered Director Singletary. "Given the selection criteria, that's bound to be the case. The appropriate and fair comparison is to ask what unemployment costs society and, worst case, what crime and jail time costs. Moreover, the operating costs per enrollee—not counting construction and transportation costs—are less than Harvard's tuition, fees and living costs."

When he visited Job Corps centers, the President spoke with passion about the War on Poverty and his determination to attack poverty and reduce it, each time commanding the undivided attention and respect of the enrollees. It was easy to see why. President Johnson dominated the room when he spoke. He was a giant of a man, full of electrifying energy, tough-minded yet generous at times, even tender when he talked with the enrollees.

To an idealistic young woman, his words and commitment inspired me. For all of my adult life, my goal had been opening doors and extending opportunity to others, very much as I tried to do as Director of Admissions at the

Woman's College where I committed my energy to helping young women from all corners of North Carolina to enter college. What an exceptional opportunity for me now to be part of a national campaign to make lives better for all Americans by allowing them to gain work skills. I felt deeply that our 14-hour days were going to pay off.

Senator Orrin Hatch of Utah stepped forward to champion the cause of the Job Corps, and his words quelled some of the opposition. In the months and years ahead, Hatch was instrumental in defending it against attacks and negative press, assuring its continuation. Because he was a highly respected conservative Republican, his support was critical to the Job Corps' survival.

OEO, the Office of Economic Opportunity, continued for several years. President Nixon appointed Donald Rumsfeld, a Republican, as head of OEO in 1969. When the agency was dissolved, the Community Action program was discontinued and others were transferred to different departments. The Job Corps ended up in the Labor Department and survives today, continuing to offer opportunity to young people who don't qualify for other programs, yet need a new start.

A well-known statement by the late William F. Buckley, Jr., notes that a conservative is one who "stands athwart history yelling, 'Stop!'" In a different sense, it could be said that Lyndon Johnson stood against history to change its path, to give opportunity to those who had been left behind or overlooked. While far from perfect, ours is a better society today than had LBJ not waged his domestic wars.

Unintended consequences have caused policies and programs to be subverted from their original intent or skewed toward unworthy political ends. Some programs have died while others bear unsustainable long-term cost and should be modified. Programs designed as safety nets to help temporarily the down-and-out have morphed into lifetime entitlements for those up and down the income scale, often becoming bonanzas for special interests rather than improving fundamentally the circumstances of the target populations.

Without doubt, the Vietnam War overshadowed the President's domestic accomplishments, and the turmoil of violent protests in 1968 and afterward disrupted the political landscape. Yet, I believe that Lyndon Johnson's domestic achievements measurably improved chances for millions of Americans. I count myself among them, for women in those days still faced many kinds of discrimination, both overt and legal, until new laws forced change.

It was then and still is about dreams: the President's dream of a Great Society; our individual dreams of educational opportunity and worthy employment; and the dreams of those previously left out, those yearning for economic and personal security.

The death of Martin Luther King, Jr., 50 years ago on April 4, 1968, is remembered today with commentaries and special gatherings celebrating his life and his seminal contribution to the expansion of civil rights. His life reminds us that we must have dreams, too, and that one of our dreams should be to celebrate our oneness as Americans, not our fractional "tribe" or "identity group"; our individual humanity, not the color of our skin or social class *versus* some other color or social class; our worthiness in the eyes of God, not our mileage accrued wandering in a desert of cynicism. Pathways forged then and codified in legislation by the Johnson Administration remind us today of the importance of the "content of our character," of opening doors of opportunity to all, and of the importance of embracing unity in the celebration of our inheritance of individual freedom and liberty.*

Winter 2018

Langston Hughes and Martin Luther King, Jr., corresponded, and King was aware of Hughes' dream poetry. A famous line in one of his poems is "A dream deferred dries up like a raisin in the sun." King first gave his "Dream" speech in Eastern North Carolina, in Rocky Mount, on November 27, 1962—just thirty-five miles from my hometown. It became a call to moral and legislative action when he gave it nine months later, on the Mall in Washington.

Welcome to Rutgers

New ship, new long splice.

New job, to a campus again: Rutgers University, led by Edward Bloustein, a vigorous new president.

My first day was a lesson in confrontation and diplomacy. Dr. Bloustein called me, his new Vice President for Student Services, to his office on the first morning of my employment in 1972. Elated and eager, I pranced down the hall, excited to be meeting with the president first thing. Once there, though, I could hardly get in the door. A wave of students parted to let me through that hostile crowd. Undergraduates, two hundred strong, filled the reception area, the president's office, and every windowsill. A sit-in!

Dr. Bloustein introduced me, "Welcome Alice Irby, our new Vice President. She has charge of the areas that concern you, and I am sure she can solve your problems."

Suddenly the room grew silent. All eyes turned toward me. "Say something!" they were thinking. A student got up and let me have his seat. Questions flashed through my mind: "What are the problems? Why are they angry? Whose head do they want? What will calm them down? Why were more than two hundred students there, occupying all the chairs and sofas, sitting on the floor, and leaning against the walls?"

I paused—and took a deep breath, maybe two. Then, I said what was on my mind: "I don't know what concerns you. Tell me." And did they ever—many of them talking at the same time, their voices overlapping; some of them almost shouted.

"We can't get the classes we want! We get little or no academic counseling for our course selections and majors! We hate the registration system, which requires us to stand in long lines at the gym!" On and on.

Many of the students were dependent upon financial aid. They thought the Financial Aid Office was an unmanageable labyrinth of bureaucracy—and I found out later that it *was*. Everything about fall registration and the schedule of classes ticked them off, especially the arrogance of professors closing their classes before students could sign up for them. To request an exception, students had to travel to three geographic locations in New Brunswick and Piscataway searching for faculty offices, hoping to find their professors keeping office hours.

Their grievances seemed to be general, and they voiced no specific demands. That gave me an opening. I waited for a cue from the president, but he remained silent—relieved to have someone else there who could take some of the heat.

One of the students doing most of the talking seemed to be the leader. So I addressed him: "I sympathize with your frustration. I don't have answers. In fact, I don't even know all the questions to ask at this point. But I can listen and learn. Why don't we undertake a joint investigation?"

"What do you mean by 'investigation'? We want change, not just study," said Steve DeMicco, the leader.

"I can't change what I don't know. I'll name two or three administrators; you name two or three students. Together we can try to get to the root of the problem. Want to give it a try?"

How could they say No? There was a long pause, students checking with each other, mumbling among themselves, some signaling thumbs up, mouthing comments to Steve. They seemed surprised that I was inviting them to observe the internal workings of the university's offices and systems. But they accepted the offer.

Back in my office, I didn't know what to think. Were they interested in knowing what caused their difficulties? Or were they just interested in making noise and threatening the president and the vice president? Were they interested in solving the problem—or just *being* the problem?

It turned out that the students were onto something. There *were* real problems, but not in the process of registration, except that it was an antiquated system not yet adapted to the computer age. It worked, even if it was cumbersome.

After several months of study, it became apparent that the problems were in the deans' offices. In some instances, classes were closed by the deans of the colleges before students receiving the last registration tickets could sign up. Worse still, deans applied unwritten and unannounced quotas against students of other colleges.

There were four separate undergraduate colleges in the New Brunswick area, not counting the professional schools and the evening college. This meant that even though the undergraduate offerings of Rutgers University were abundant, high-quality, and varied, many students had limited access to offerings other than those in their home colleges, thereby severely restricting their choices. I likened the university, especially its undergraduate liberal arts and sciences colleges, to the Balkan States in Eastern Europe before WWI.

It took years to eliminate the restrictive practices completely, but merely exposing the protectionist policies resulted in a few barriers being relaxed right away. Only years later, when the faculties of the undergraduate colleges were combined, did the walls come all the way down, but we made a good start that year. Steve DeMicco and I became friends. After college, he went into politics and became a member of the N.J. Legislature. I know he was successful; it would be nice to see him again.

My introduction to the students was just a warm-up for my engagements with the faculties—all 22 of them: those of the liberal arts colleges; professional schools; and two law schools. The colleges spread across four locations in Camden, Newark, New Brunswick, and Piscataway. Each school had its own dean and faculty. In earlier years, a couple of the colleges sought their state funding directly from the legislature, bypassing the university administration entirely. Because the colleges controlled their own admissions and sizes of entering classes, the university administration could not predict the number of enrolled students for any given semester, yet its state appropriation was based on an enrollment-driven budget. Additionally, faculties had great autonomy regarding course offerings, geographic location, and scheduling of classes, their focus being more on the convenience of faculty members rather than on that of students. In fact, the university administration controlled very little.

My first major assignment was to consolidate the academic support functions of admissions, financial aid, scheduling of classes, registration, facilities usage, and student health services, transferring those functions from the colleges to the university administration.

"Start with something simple and easy," I said to myself, "maybe recruiting materials or a catalog of course offerings across colleges." I was eager to avoid a confrontation with deans. Yet, when I tried to create a university catalog, howls went up.

"What's so threatening about that?" I asked. "Each college will be equally represented."

The deans didn't like it at all. Each college wanted to put its own stamp and spin on its separate publications. Only by getting the representatives from the colleges in a room together, closing the doors and opening the windows, and offering to stay all night—if it took that—did I get agreement to work together on a single catalog. Each school continued to print its own recruitment brochure, but at least there was only *one* university catalog containing *all* the course listings.

Things went downhill from there. The president expected me to plan a reorganization, to present the plan to the officers, and then to present it to each college faculty.

The plan transferred staff then reporting to deans to a central office of Student Services under my aegis. I should have expected that when I stood before each faculty to explain the changes, I would get stares, growls, and endless criticism and questions.

I didn't have to dodge tomatoes, shoes, or water balloons, but I was the target of a heavy dose of vituperation. The deans and faculties couldn't prevent the president's reorganization, but they could create a lot of noise and trouble. And they did. More than one dean mobilized alumni to oppose the effort and to attempt my ouster. I became known as the ogre of Old Queens, the building housing Central Administration.

Having survived the faculty inquisitions, I readied myself to unveil the plan in a presentation to the entire faculty council. Prepared with organizational charts of BEFORE (chaotic) and AFTER (orderly and straightforward), I spoke before the council for about 30 minutes in a crowded hall with all lights turned on me.

At the end of my speech, there was not a question or a comment: SILENCE. ABSOLUTE SILENCE. My heart sank. My knees weakened. Then, loud clapping came from the back of the room. Once that clapping started, other people joined in. Soon, almost all the faculty were clapping, some more enthusiastically than others. Standing at the back of the room, smiling, was Dr. Sam Proctor, former president of A & T University in Greensboro, N.C. He was at A & T when I was at the Woman's College. He was at A & T when the sit-ins occurred in 1960, and I was then the Admissions Director of the Woman's College. I knew Dr. Proctor, not well, but we had met on several occasions. He saved my career that day, and my reputation. I dashed to the back of the room and gave him a hug, thanking him. We renewed our acquaintance of years before.

He had taken a position as a University professor at Rutgers and had also assumed the pulpit of Abyssinian Church in New York City, succeeding Adam Clayton Powell. He came to New Brunswick several days a week to teach, and that Tuesday was one of his days. I don't know what made him drop in on that faculty meeting. I am sure he had no interest in faculty meetings, but that day he kept my blood from running in the streets of New Brunswick!

The reorganization was implemented with a few bumps and continual griping by three of the deans, but most were quietly cooperative. Working with my staff, faculty admissions committees continued to function within each college, setting their local policies *within* the context of university-wide policies. The central administration was then able to set enrollment targets for each college and manage the registration of students, thereby gaining control of its requests for state funding. Both the Higher Education Coordinating Board and the University's Board of Governors held the president, not the college deans, accountable for enrollments, the budget, and the operation of the university.

Shortly after I arrived that first year, the U.S. Congress passed Title IX, a civil rights law relating to women in higher education, part of the Education Amendments of 1972.

President Bloustein called a meeting of his cabinet. "What should we do about Rutgers College?" he asked his officers. Founded in 1766, this all-male College was the oldest and most prestigious in the University system. Under the new federal law, public institutions had six years to turn all-male colleges into co-educational institutions.

"What's the advantage in waiting?" asked John Martin, a vice president. "We might as well get it over with. Otherwise, opposition has a chance to build up and interfere with other goals we want to achieve."

"An abrupt change might be very disruptive to the faculty and especially to the alumni. And the College has a vocal alumni group. We will get a lot of pushback from them," said Henry Winkler, Executive Vice President. Henry had been a faculty member in Rutgers College and knew the environment there well.

"We have plans to increase the size of Rutgers College," said the president. "We can no longer justify an all-male college of 5,000 to the Board of Higher Education and the legislature, especially when New Jersey needs to provide space for more in-state students in its colleges."

"Expanding the size of the college will enable us to add women without decreasing the number of men, if we increase total enrollment at the same time," I added.

President Bloustein concluded, "We might as well make the change now because we will get pushback anytime we do it. This way, we won't have to reduce the number of men at the outset."

"Alice," the president said to me, "you are the designated Title IX compliance officer, and you also direct the admission of students. So, you have the lead on this."

Once again, I had visions of an uprising of faculty and alumni as the thought and later the plan for admitting women to the student body of Rutgers College reached the dean and faculty—and alumni! I asked myself, "What did I do to deserve this—another opportunity for faculty and deans to call for my resignation and portray me in the student press as the ogre of Old Queens?"

Like Daniel in the lion's den, I found myself standing before an angry crowd of Rutgers College alumni on Alumni Day at Commencement time, trying to assure them that female students would not rupture or spoil the quality of the College—or its fine heritage. "We plan to expand the enrollment by four thousand students over the next several years," I told them, "which will also give the College additional faculty and resources. The number of men can remain the same or perhaps increase."

That did not pacify them. They wanted to continue their historical role as a men's college. "After all," the dean said proudly, "it was originally Queen's College chartered in 1766, eighth of nine chartered during the Colonial period. Besides, the new law provides a grace period of several years."

When women were admitted the following year, I relaxed when we faced no censure votes or student protests. Most likely, the dean liked having more resources to hire new faculty, and professors were already accustomed to teaching the few women who were able to cross-register from other colleges. Yearly, as the women enrolled in Rutgers College, they demonstrated that they were as intelligent and as well prepared as the young male students. In a few years, the freshman class was more than half female! They did not need preferential treatment, just equal opportunity.

In a couple of years, the Student Services departments were chugging along without major conflict or complaint. University administration was gaining unity and strength and could present its case to the legislature effectively. Funding increased. Faculty were productive and well paid. Students were settling down and concentrating on their coursework and plans for graduation. I measured my success by the *in*frequency with which my face or name appeared in the *Daily Targum,* the student newspaper. I felt I was making progress.

But new issues always pop up on a university campus. A contentious one soon came my way: the admission of athletes. A member of the Board of Governors, Sonny Werblin, wanted Rutgers to have nationally ranked intercollegiate football and basketball teams. He encouraged Rutgers to "go Big Time."

Mr. Werblin, a creative disruptor in the media world as well as in the sports world, owned the Jets football team, had been an initiator of the AFL, and a key executive in setting up the first Super Bowl. He also developed the Meadowlands sports complex. A Rutgers graduate, he felt that having a major Division I athletics program would enhance Rutgers' reputation both in New Jersey and nationally. Competitive teams would generate pride in the state, he reasoned, and members of the board, the legislature, and loyal alumni could enjoy the games. The pipeline of state funding might open wider, and talent would be easier to recruit. All we had to do, advocates claimed, was to relax the admissions standards, as had been done in some big-time colleges.

The athletics director and the coaches had never made admissions decisions at Rutgers. The admissions officers did so, based on policies of the colleges within university guidelines. At that time, the NCAA had no minimum eligibility requirements for recipients of athletic scholarships other than being "in good standing," which meant any definition an institution chose. Rutgers' standards for admission were, in any case, not likely to draw the kinds of athletes that dominated Big-Time football and basketball.

Everybody entered the fray and the debate: the president, the executive vice president, the provost, the vice-presidential liaison with our athletic conference, deans and faculty, and the athletic director. Going Big Time meant not only recruiting student athletes aggressively but admitting them and then keeping them eligible to play. It also meant raising money for modern facilities. Our football field was attractive, nestled in a small natural bowl, but it did not approach the size or looks of the Big-Time football fields. The basketball court was in an aging gym, with limited parking, in the middle of the campus. The locker rooms were clean but old. The subject became a matter of public conversation, and speculation filled discussion around tables in the Faculty Club and along College Avenue. Soon, the board acted and came down on the side of growing the athletic program but taking care not to compromise the academic core of the university. The president made a carefully crafted public announcement in a press conference that Rutgers was setting a course to expand its major intercollegiate sports programs and that we intended to be a major force in our conference. He was careful not to promise too much but savvy enough to announce changes that would satisfy the members of the board advocating change.

Where did that leave admissions standards and eligibility requirements once athletes were matriculating? The hope was that with more aggressive recruiting and availability of scholarships, the coaches could attract stronger recruits. The athletics director agreed that he, on behalf of the coaches, would not try to force the admissions of students that did not meet minimum standards. We agreed to review doubtful cases they called to our attention. We insisted that any candidate admitted must, in the judgment of the admissions officer, be able to meet the academic course requirements of the freshman year. Their SAT scores had to be acceptable, as well as their high-school transcripts. This arrangement worked. High-profile athletes were reviewed on an individual basis by an admissions officer. The coaches dialed up their recruiting. The university's football and basketball teams improved their win-loss records.

Then, well into the fall semester, an unexpected problem brought us up short. Word came that the star recruit of the basketball team was not likely to complete his first semester with the passing grades he needed to stay in school and to play. Harold Hirshman, our registrar, pointed out that the university did not have a uniform policy for determining "good standing." Each college had its own. No uniform university policy for athletes? Neither did the NCAA have such a rule at that time.

Quickly, the president called together academic officers and deans, as well as selected faculty members. My staff offered options and possible solutions.

Finally, with unanimous support, Executive Vice President Henry Winkler issued what became known as the Winkler Rule: any student playing intercollegiate athletics would need a 2.0 average for the semester preceding participation and must have completed a specified number of courses necessary to continue in good standing.

We were set... until the beginning of second semester when basketball would be in full gear. It was time to check the eligibility of the members of the basketball team. Would the new recruits make the team? What about the star recruit? Let's call him Frank. My heart sank as I learned he was having difficulty with one course and barely passing another. He needed Cs in both courses to be able to play. The team needed him if the university was going to field its new, high-powered basketball team.

The day of the first game after fall semester, final grades were due in the registrar's office. I badgered Harold to get Frank's grades. He called the professors to get them. The grade for Frank's last course was not in as of 6 p.m. The president, the vice president, the registrar, and I were standing by, waiting for the grades and the GPA to be calculated. Frank was suited-up but still in the locker room. The game was to start at 8:00 p.m.

At 7:00 p.m. the call came in from the Registrar. Frank was eligible. You could hear the sighs and shouts echo down the hall of Old Queens as well as in the locker room at the gym. Relieved, we put on our overcoats, walked the several blocks down College Avenue to the gym, and watched the game. Frank played well but did not excel—no wonder; he probably had the jitters for the whole first half. But Rutgers won....and went on winning!

In 1976, the team got to the Final Four in the NCAA basketball tournament. Rutgers became competitive in its conference though not a national powerhouse. Mr. Werblin remained a fan. The Werblin Sports Center on the Rutgers campus was made possible by his generosity.

My life at Rutgers was not all conflict, crises, or overcoming obstacles. Services for students improved significantly, and I thought of myself as the students' advocate, frequently speaking out on their behalf. There were students, however, who felt differently. One day Chief Bob Oakes of Campus Police came to my office to tell me to close the door and stay inside. He stood outside my door to meet the students from one of the campuses who came to "take me to meet some other students." He had received word that they planned to kidnap me. They were angry because I had closed a sub-standard health clinic on their campus and consolidated it with the one that was eligible for insurance reimbursement. To them I was the university's central administration tyrant who was destroying the individuality of their college.

But there was also the time that I attended a Commencement luncheon at the president's residence and sat beside Eudora Welty, the well-known Mississippi writer. She spoke like the ladies in my hometown—with a soft, almost confidential voice that made me feel she was telling me her secrets. She was to receive an honorary degree, though she was not required to make a long speech—her presence was enough. Naturally, everyone in the room wanted to engage her in conversation, but the president gave me the honor of sitting by her. He said the two Southern ladies should sit together. I felt special. Seated at the round lunch table I had her rather to myself. She spoke almost in the dialog of characters in her short stories. I could see the story-book ladies in the beauty salon gossiping with each other. Or the guests at the *Delta Wedding*. Her humor was sharp, her conversation engaging, and her smile seductive. I drove home on Cloud 9.

For all the ups and downs, my years at Rutgers were good ones, in large part because several members of my staff became lifelong friends. They were talented, competent leaders in making possible the changes I was hired to bring about. My right-hand assistant was David Burns. Among those I considered for the role, David was clearly the most engaging, well-informed, and articulate. An easy rapport developed between us early, probably because of the way I offered him the job.

"Mr. Burns, I've chosen you to be my assistant. You may be interested in knowing why." He nodded. "It was quite simple. Your name, William David Burns, is an easy one for a Southerner to pronounce and remember." David was speechless, uncharacteristic of him. Surprise written all over his face, he took a step back, paused, and broke out laughing—as did I.

"Now," I continued, "each of your three names rolls easily off my tongue. By which one do you want to be addressed?"

"David," he said, "because I was known as William during my undergraduate days here, and I think I need to make a fresh start."

He had been among the avant-garde of the student movement at Rutgers in the 1960s—not a rock thrower but a persuasive spokesman for change. Some of my colleagues who knew him were surprised when I hired him, especially the Associate Dean of Rutgers College who had dealt with him during his undergraduate days. "What is that innocent, prim little lady getting herself into?" they may have wondered. But the deans and other administrators kept mum. David surprised them by his effectiveness in his new role. In every way, he more than lived up to my expectations.

Truthfully, he was one of those rare individuals—an articulate, creative generalist who could be effective in a myriad of situations, from counseling students to negotiating with deans, or from reducing conflict among opposing student factions to speaking publicly as a representative of the university in the Halls of State at Trenton. He was a quick study and could handle multiple projects simultaneously.

He was so facile and swift on his feet in argument and presentation that I thought David could represent me in Trenton when I was unable to appear. It would be helpful if I could find a person to substitute for me who could command respect at the outset from members of the Board of Higher Education. In those days, I seemed to be spending more time in Trenton than I was on the campus, but I wasn't yet in dire need of assistance. The more I reflected on the possibility, the more I thought that David, with his youth, his loyalty to the university, his non-threatening temperament and his ability to engage effectively in policy discussions, would be a good ambassador for us with state higher-education administrators.

"David," I said one day, "I have been thinking about identifying someone who can assist me in dealing with matters the university faces in Trenton. The web of interconnected budget and policy concerns I am trying to juggle is taking so much time and energy I don't have enough time to focus on our reorganization and services here." I was watching, trying to get an idea of whether he was interested.

"Well, I'm under that impression that Trenton is a BIG problem, always coming up with new demands and regulations, but I suppose using friendly persuasion is the best approach."

A few days later, David came to work dressed in jacket and dress shirt, hair combed attractively. That was the signal I hoped to see. He was ready; I was, too. From that day on, David became a successful diplomat not just for me but for the president and others in the administration. Since the 1990s, David has employed his energy and intellect in forming a new organization, *SENCER*, a creative, multi-disciplinary network of collaborative educators dedicated to integrated learning in the teaching of science. It was established in 2001 and its resource materials, seminars, and awards are used effectively in universities and consortia today. David is a twenty-first century Renaissance humanist and trailblazer. Last I heard from David, he had just reread all of Herman Melville's prose works and was reading Pliny the Elder's *Natural History*.

Ellen Mappen, a colleague and now a close friend, started in Student Services as Special Assistant for Title IX Compliance, then worked as my assistant until she took the reins of graduate admissions as Associate Director. Like David, she was competent in handling multiple issues simultaneously. Her dissertation in British history was a study of women workers and unemployment polity in Late Victorian and Edwardian London, which led to further work about women in higher education, technology, and science. She directed projects for women in math, science, engineering, and science at Douglass College, and later became active in *SENCER*. Graduate deans were comfortable having one of their own handling the admission of their students.

In contrast to David, who was flamboyant and outgoing, never having met a stranger, Ellen was cautious, quietly persuasive, and always prepared with facts and good arguments. They made a good team. I got to know them, their families and their children, and cherish their friendship today. I don't see them often, but it is comforting to know they are there—just their *act of being* is important, reassuring and comforting to me.

There are many more I can name and describe: Katheryne McCormick, mathematician, former instructor in

Douglass College, was a most efficient manager in dealing with faculty and students in scheduling classes. She overcame their objections, all the while increasing the utilization of classroom buildings. Until Katheryne came along, the Chancellor of Higher Education badgered us over "excess" capacity, threatening to deny requests for new buildings to accommodate a growing student body. She demonstrated to him and the board that our utilization statistics more than met the State's guidelines. The result? We got approval for new buildings.

During my time at Rutgers, Richard Nurse (Dick) was the administrator responsible for overseeing university-wide programs, such as the Educational Opportunity Fund and Veterans Affairs. Informally, Dick served as an ombudsman for students and others on campus who wanted to express concerns. He had a non-threatening manner that invited students of all backgrounds and administrators alike to approach him for advice and help in troubleshooting problems.

In the decade following my tenure, Dick became Assistant Vice President of Academic Affairs in 1986 and, later, under President Francis Lawrence, he was promoted to Assistant Vice President for Undergraduate Education. His multiple skills and quiet diplomacy made him an effective troubleshooter of the administration in implementing educational policy and coping with sensitive student issues. He was a valuable resource to students and a proven asset to administrators in any role he assumed.

Registrar Harold Hirschman handled with tact and politeness every big and little crisis that erupted in his area, and there were many. Ken Iuso, also an even-tempered, capable administrator, assumed Harold's role when I promoted Harold to Assistant Vice President. Harold never raised his voice, never spoke harshly of anyone, even those students and faculty who sometimes made his life difficult. He was genuine in his desire to help students and always able to deal forthrightly with tasks and provocations.

Saka Hata, my faithful secretary, kept my office humming efficiently and knew where everything and everybody was at any given time of day. And there are more! Don Oppenheim headed Institutional Research, and Natalie Ahronian, Director of Admissions, persevered in handling a severe statewide-budget crisis jeopardizing the admission of an entire freshman class. With an indomitable spirit, she led her staff through weeks of uncertainty and constantly changing admissions targets.

In 2012, David Burns and Valerie LaPorte, his wife, organized a reunion of some of us at their home. David is a gourmet chef in addition to a gardener, home builder, literary and music critic, and academic entrepreneur.

Our reunion transported me to earlier times: times that demanded boundless energy, that tested my fortitude and courage, and that challenged my problem-solving skills. But they were also happy times, as revealed in the stories we told each other that evening. Would that I could see their faces often! Photographs take me back but not close enough.

HAROLD HIRSCHMAN, ELLEN MAPPEN, ALICE IRBY, VALERIE LAPORTE (DAVID'S WIFE), DAVID BURNS, DICK NURSE, MARC MAPPEN (ELLEN'S HUSBAND), EDNA MAY HIRSHMAN (HAROLD'S WIFE), AND DICK NURSE'S WIFE, NINFA MUELLER

These friends do live still in my rich, lasting memories of those years at Rutgers. That's why my years there were good ones, some of the best of my life. I thought I was grown up: 39 years old, with a daughter and a useful, professional role in a national organization, ETS. But unanticipated crises landed on my dance card when I became the first female vice president of a major American university in 1972.

In the span of a half-dozen years, I lived a life full of ups and downs, much like others who get thrown into an overwhelming role, one carrying unanticipated responsibilities. I learned to cope with people who aimed their anger and hate at me—not for who I was but for doing my job—and I had to absorb harsh criticism from many quarters simultaneously. Recalling that Harry Truman had entered the Presidency uninformed about the threats facing the nation and, thus, was subjected to ridicule and doubt, gave me strength and resolve to meet crises I faced.

And the legacy of Granny—a widow operating a boarding-house business in the early 1900s and sending her children to college—stiffened my courage to fulfill my promises and to pursue my goals. "Backbone," my mother called it.

Like Zorba, the fictionalized character who captivated my fancy when I had to make decisions about my career after graduate school, I loved life, and especially my daughter, Andrea, who was my daily joy. Sustained by the power and good will of my staff and colleagues, I absorbed life's arrows and ran its marathons as I tried to overcome my misjudgments and stumbles.

I was inspired by role models like my boss and friend, Dean Mereb Mossman, a child polio victim and adult breast-cancer survivor, who in her role as Vice Chancellor at the Woman's College, was optimistic about students and their future. Every day, she was excited about life's possibilities, and she had no time for doubt or cynicism.

I am thankful for my heroes, living and dead. From them, I learned what it meant to be fearless in pursuit of making a difference in the lives of young people. I learned how hard it was to be useful. I learned that friendship shielded me from despair, strengthened me for the next struggle, and contributed to my successes. And I learned never to be afraid of an administrative job again. After that, my jobs seemed doable—challenging, but doable.

The life lesson I learned at Rutgers is how immersion in a job, a task, a campaign for change can stretch but also threaten one's self-confidence and values in ways unforeseen and, often, in ways for which one is not prepared. It really was "sink or swim." I was able to swim, with help from lots of people. It was very painful at times, but it made me better—more confident, but also humbler and more tolerant of others' mistakes—than I was before that experience.

I dug down deep, pulled myself up, and moved forward, embracing life with exuberance and determination—all the better for having survived my immersion in university life at Rutgers.

Summer 2018

Second Time Around

I had not thought of leaving. Times were good: no deans demanding my scalp; no sharp blades aimed at my back; no sit-ins; no battlegrounds aflame. My friends were fast in support and colleagues were congenial in conversation. The new administrative structure was in place and students were not complaining. Deans had the information they needed to counsel students and set course schedules. I enjoyed the intellectual and social life of the university, and being at Rutgers seemed like home, reminding me of my campus days at UNCG in the early 1960s. I liked being among students, listening to their accounts of campus politics.

But then in the spring of 1978, disrupting the calm and forcing me to think about reopening doors I had closed, an unexpected call came in from Bill Turnbull, President of Educational Testing Service (ETS): "Alice, would you be interested in talking to Robert Solomon, Executive Vice President, and me about coming back to ETS?"

Why would I do that? I enjoyed my relationship with Ed Bloustein, the President of Rutgers, and projects I had in motion with my peers and colleagues were working well. I was especially fond of the staff in Student Services, my area of responsibility. Together, we had streamlined the admissions process, relocated offices to be accessible to students, and improved communication with deans in the colleges.

Andrea was prospering in her junior year of high school in Princeton, where we lived, and she looked forward to graduating there before heading south to attend the University of Virginia. She was doing well in her studies, working at a stable to finance upkeep for her horse, Chipper, taking lessons from a New York ballet teacher, and attending parties and dances with her friends. She was happy. I was happy.

At the same time, I couldn't say *No* to Bill or anyone at Educational Testing Service. ETS is the organization students love to hate because its high-stakes exams are required of millions of students to get into college, or into graduate school, or to become teachers. Many students get uptight about taking the SAT—then known as the Scholastic Aptitude Test—or the Graduate Record Exam (GRE)—because their parents overemphasize the tests' importance.

To me, ETS is simply a place filled with top-notch people: competent, helpful, articulate, knowledgeable, and engaged in useful work and research—not at all intimidating. At the outset in 1947, Henry Chauncey, its founder, set a high standard of excellence when it first opened its doors. Employees, regardless of level or gender, were treated fairly in both compensation and opportunity. Supervisors were, first and foremost, helpful.

Ready to spread my wings beyond North Carolina, I had originally accepted a position in New Jersey at ETS in 1962.

Being on the inside of making the tests I had used in admitting students to the Woman's College would be appealing and demanding.

I packed my car with Andrea, her toys, and some clothes, and headed to Princeton. A year after I began my job there, I entered Andrea in nursery school and soon realized I needed to start the workday at 9:00 a.m., 30 minutes after ETS opened. I asked Henry Dyer, my vice president, for permission to take Andrea to nursery school when it opened at 8:30 a.m. and then come directly to work. Immediately he responded, "Sure, Alice, we can arrange that. Just make up the time as you can. As a matter of fact, a woman in the Test Development division has a similar arrangement. We try to accommodate working mothers."

Margaret Nevin, head of Human Resources, called me upon hearing of a housing problem I had: "Come stay with me for a month, Alice, while you get the problems with your housing worked out." (We became fast friends until she retired and left for San Miguel, Mexico, to become a full-time artist.)

Such gifts of reason, grace, and hospitality as Henry's and Margaret's were examples of life at ETS that made me feel accepted and worthy. No wonder I could not refuse Bill's invitation to talk. ETS had been my career home for a decade until 1972.

Unless you have taken an exam to get into college or graduate school, you may not recognize the name, Educational Testing Service (ETS). Before ETS came along, colleges evaluated an applicant's skills for college work by administering their own tests or tests written by another organization; some did not use tests at all. Students often had to take more than one test. With the creation of ETS three organizations consolidated their testing programs into one, and colleges across the country started using the Scholastic Aptitude Test (SAT), sponsored by the College Board, for undergraduate admissions, and the Graduate Record Exam (GRE), sponsored by ETS, for graduate school admissions.

The exams provided a yardstick for college entrance that nothing else, neither grades, recommendations, activities, nor work performance—all of which vary by high school or region—could provide: a way to compare the scores earned by groups of students regardless of who took the test or when and where they took it. In other words, one student's score could easily be compared with a student's score from another school or state, or even country. To make this comparability possible—and fair—questions and answers had to be "secure," i.e., held under lock and key.

Did I want to reenter the testing world? We used the SAT at Rutgers, but I did not spend my waking hours thinking about writing, disseminating, and securing high-stakes tests. I had my doubts, but I met with Bill and Bob Solomon the following week. The role they outlined was a complete surprise.

Bob started out by saying, "We want you to go to Washington, Alice, and establish a government affairs office for ETS."

My first thought was, "Why does ETS need a presence in Washington, other than to provide information to test candidates, which it already does?"

Puzzled, I asked, "Why there?"

"We need eyes and ears on the ground to keep up with what is becoming an intrusive federal involvement in education," said Bob. "Just a couple of examples: as you know, we process thousands of financial aid forms for the College Board, but the Feds make the rules. And more and more research is sponsored by federal agencies, much of it related to research we do on student performance."

Bill chimed in, "We also need to be where our clients are, and many are in Washington, such as the Council of Graduate Schools."

Just as for Rutgers and other universities, the political world was changing for ETS. The change began in 1964 when Congress passed the Elementary and Secondary Education Act (ESEA) and the next year the Higher Education Act. The initial appropriation of $1 billion to ESEA seems small now but was groundbreaking then. Like Topsy, spending and the bureaucracy grew and grew. Expanded federal financial aid, research projects funded by the National Science Foundation, federal studies of student performance, desegregation orders for public schools, and other initiatives reached every layer of educational practice.

The more I thought about going back to work in Washington for the second time, the more I warmed to the idea.

Familiar with the legislative world from my work with the Job Corps and the New Jersey state government, I felt suited to the task Bob and Bill laid out. So I worked out a way for Andrea to stay in Princeton for her senior year, moving her into our upstairs apartment that had been used by *au pairs* during her childhood, and renting the rest of the house to a woman with two high-school boys. I rented an apartment not far from Capitol Hill for a year until I could buy a home and get Andrea into college.

When my colleagues in Princeton asked, "Alice, why on earth would you ever want to go live in Washington when you can continue to live in Princeton?"

My immediate response was, "Because it's halfway toward home in North Carolina. You know what they say about Southerners…they always go home!"

What a difference a decade makes. Washington had changed in the fourteen years since my time there in 1964–65 when I was involved in the Johnson Administration's efforts to stamp out poverty. A new Metro was in operation. Sunday blue laws were a thing of the past, resulting in new, high-quality restaurants sprinkled across town. The Kennedy Center had opened, providing a home for orchestras, operas, and the dramatic arts. New theaters, such as Arena Stage, attracted artists-in-residence. No longer merely a Government town, the city became a mecca for the arts and offered careers in educational and scientific research, in museum administration, in university administration, and more.

What else had mushroomed? Congressional staff and the bureaucracy, of course! I found that with rapid growth, collegiality and informal collaboration among people seemed diminished from that of earlier years. The neighborhood around Capitol Hill had been gentrified, attracting young staff to the Senate and House offices. Fast-walking legislative aides jammed the halls of the capitol. Elevators were in motion all day.

By 1978, everyone seemed busier than before, but not with a sense of purpose and excitement that had driven me in 1964. For all the growth and apparent sophistication, the expectation of slow but continuous societal improvement and progress had vanished. Back then, every day had started with promise and hope for a better country.

I still felt the familiarity of the City and knew my way around the downtown traffic circles, along the avenues crisscrossing the streets, and along the curves weaving under the cragged rocks of the Parkway. But a decade earlier, I felt as if I were laying bricks for the castles of the future. This time, it turned out I had an altogether different kind of foundation to lay.

By the summer of 1979, I had settled into my new ETS role, made friends with executives in the educational associations, and found my way around the halls of agencies and Congress. But I missed the students. At Rutgers, and before that at the Woman's College, I spent a lot of time thinking about students, designing services for them, and talking with them. In Washington, all I saw were adults, and the workday was filled with observing politicians and bureaucrats advocating their special interests. What a difference! I felt at loose ends—and sometimes quite bored.

Then came something out of the ordinary—a serendipity! A Chinese delegation visited town and our office was their destination. President Nixon had established government-to-government relationships with the People's Republic of China (PRC) in 1972, but it fell to the Carter Administration to normalize relations with China through a *Joint Communique* by establishing accredited embassies as of January 1979, and encouraging travel, business, and academic exchange programs.

That opened the door for an arrangement between ETS and the Chinese Ministry of Education to facilitate China's sending students to U.S. universities.

All of us remember with sadness the plight of teachers and professors during the decade of the Maoist Cultural Revolution that began in 1966. University libraries were destroyed, books were burned, professors were fired, killed, and/or exiled to distant provinces, and scholars were no longer permitted to engage in their teaching or research.

Under Deng Xiaoping, order was restored and exiled educators found favor within the Party. They became part of an effort to increase communication and commerce with the outside world. A priority of the new Chinese leaders was teaching and learning English and sending graduate students to the U.S. to study. That meant students had to sit for ETS exams before they could be enrolled in American universities.

First to ETS in Princeton, then to Washington, the Chinese diplomats from the PRC Ministry of Education gathered excitedly around staff in our office, eager to know about the Department of Education and the Congress. They also visited educational associations to learn about American higher education. Uninhibited, they cheerfully peppered us with questions about American education and life in Washington.

Presiding at a formal ceremony and reception, Bob Solomon, ETS Executive Vice President, greeted the Chinese delegates and announced the ETS-China Agreement: "We welcome our visitors and their colleagues from the Chinese Embassy. We are happy to have with us today scholars from the Asia Society, executives from educational associations, officials of local universities, and Congressional staff.

"After extensive negotiations, ETS is pleased to make available the Graduate Record Examination and a standardized test of English for applicants to United States graduate schools in exchange for the People's Republic Ministry of Education guaranteeing secure administrations of the examinations according to ETS standards and procedures."

The two parties cemented the relationship by signing and sealing an agreement in the presence of witnesses from both ETS and the Ministry of Education.

At the end of the visitors' stay in the Capital, we held a small dinner at the International Club. Until then, social events had offered hors d'oeuvres and drinks, not sit-down dinners. This venue offered a more intimate setting for our staff and the Chinese delegation.

The International Club, site of the dinner, was a fitting location because of the international diversity of its members. I joined the Club when I moved to Washington on the recommendation of partners in our local law firm, Wilmer Cutler and Pickering. Because the Cosmos Club did not admit women—as the University Club and the Metropolitan Club did not, either—they had transferred their membership from the Cosmos Club to the International Club so that their female partners could enjoy the same benefits as the men.

Soon after I arrived in Washington, a friend asked me to apply to the University Club for entry, creating a test case for the admission of women. I couldn't do so, given my schedule, but by the mid-1990s I was recommended for and granted membership in the Cosmos Club. To walk into the dining room of the Cosmos Club one day and see Betty Friedan eating alone was recognition enough that one more mountain-size barrier had fallen. It is noteworthy that men of all racial and ethnic backgrounds had been members for years before women were given the chance to join.

Conventional wisdom has it that not until the Mayor of Washington threatened to take the liquor licenses away from the three clubs would they change their policies.

Maybe a myth; maybe not?

Our dinner for the Chinese delegation was held in the spacious, formal dining room of the Club, several stories above the glistening, well-lighted avenues of the Capital City. All of us, the Chinese visitors, their translators, and ETS staff could be seated at an oversized square table covered with a white cloth and silver place settings.

"We've chosen flavorful dishes that will give you a good sampling of American cuisine. There are a variety of entrees," I explained, speaking slowly and distinctly to insure accurate translation. No sooner had the waiters served the main course than our Chinese visitors started passing their plates around to each other.

"What's going on?" I wondered. "Don't they like what we ordered?" I asked the translator. The scene mimicked a revolving Lazy Susan with each Chinese diner picking up something from another's plate, tasting a little bite of every dish. Then I realized they had created a family-style meal. Why not? They wanted to taste everything, and that was the best way they saw to do it.

Dessert, the climax of the evening, turned into a show. Crêpes Suzettes were served at the table. Attired in his usual formal uniform, the waiter walked slowly to the table, careful not to disturb the ingredients on his cart. He appeared to know he was on stage. Using the bowls, bottles, and utensils on his tray, he made the crêpes tableside, piling them up one by one in a giant-size stack. Our guests gasped, wondering if the tall tower of thin crêpes would collapse momentarily.

"Now," explained the waiter with a flair, "I will set the flame! Watch carefully." In a giant-sized sauté pan, he lighted the *liqueur*, throwing a flame at least five feet high. Our visitors jumped out of their seats, amazed and shocked, and ran around the table, exclaiming their surprise and waving their hands, encircling the waiter. The waiter, firmly holding his position, was all smiles. In unison, our visitors started clapping and cheering. We, too, started clapping and cheering, and other dinner guests in the room joined in.

"Please, Sir, can you do it again?" asked the Chinese guests through their interpreter.

"Of course! Just stand back a little so the flame won't hit you." Again the delegates clapped and cheered, moving around the table, shoving each other aside to get close to the waiter.

The crêpes were a lively way to end the delegates' visit, but we also knew then that this trip marked the beginning of years of cooperation between staff at ETS and the Chinese Ministry of Education. They came here; we went there on various projects—we, in turn, learned to dine comfortably with chopsticks rather than forks.

Abruptly, the fun stopped a few weeks later upon my return from a trip to Europe and England with my daughter and mother to celebrate Andrea's graduation from high school.

A telephone call the day I got back in the office caught me by such surprise that I thought about turning around and heading back to France. Out of the blue, New York Congressman Ted Weiss had introduced a bill to regulate the SAT and other admissions tests. Carl Perkins, the longtime Congressman from Kentucky and Chairman of the powerful Education and Labor Committee, had agreed to mark it up—meaning that language drafted and passed in committee would sail through both houses of Congress.

The proposed legislation required the publication of the actual questions and answers on college entrance examinations, e.g., the SAT and ACT that students took on Saturdays several times a year.

The bill required the release of the *real thing*, not just sample questions and answers used for study, which were already publicly available free of charge. The proposal would enable students to get their test questions and answers, and anyone could purchase current, operational forms of the tests. Sponsors of the bill claimed that free sample tests were insufficient.

Why did it matter? High-stakes tests—those used for selecting candidates for college, graduate school, or the professions—were not made public or released to the test takers because questions needed to be used more than once. A few questions were repeated in multiple versions of the exams in order to link one test to another. Otherwise a score of 500 would not mean the same thing from one test taker to another or one test date to the next. Admissions officers needed to be confident they were being fair to students in comparing their test performance.

So... why have admissions tests, anyway? Why do colleges need them? The absence of a standardized exam would result in admissions decisions being based solely on grades, recommendations, and activities, none of which are comparable or valid across high school classes, parts of the country, states, or years.

But eliminating the test was exactly what the sponsors of the bill wanted to do. The proposal did not suddenly appear on the committee docket. It came about as a result of extensive lobbying by a nascent, fledging organization called Fair Test, with general assistance from Ralph Nader and his affiliated interest groups.

"Why would anyone want the Congress to meddle in the technical aspects of admissions testing?" I asked Bob Solomon, returning his call. "What have we done that is so damaging that we need to be regulated? We try to identify talent, not suppress it—to give candidates a fair chance, not a favor."

Bob knew little more than I did. We were aware of anti-testing groups that, from time to time, leveled their fire at ETS and the College Board, complaining that the tests were biased, that tests determined and limited the curriculum in high schools, and that tests took time away from teaching.

Now, instead of the usual complaints, which in the past had gone nowhere, this bill, on its face, seemed to a lay person like a reasonable proposal. At least, that is what the young, first-term Congressman Weiss may have thought: "Passing an innocuous bill will get my name on a piece of legislation as sponsor and give me bragging rights back home among teachers and parents."

The proponents claimed to have the interests of students at heart. They called it "Truth in Testing" legislation. Lois Rice of the College Board called me to discuss strategy: "Alice, you know as well as I that these folks are not so much interested in the students as in regulating ETS and the College Board. It's far from 'truth in testing' to help students. They really want to eliminate the use of tests in college admissions. We need to get the facts out to people on the Hill."

"And they are pretending to a kind of innocence," I added, "by claiming to want a simple thing, i.e., for students to see their tests as they might after taking teacher exams. But they know the bill is a means of destroying the tests. Their publicity accuses us of being gatekeepers—and of operating in secrecy. As we both know, we are not the gatekeepers; the universities are, and rightly so. These folks know we are only the messengers, but they are after us because we are easy targets. Helping students is not what they are after. It's the colleges and universities they are really after but know they cannot succeed with a frontal attack on them."

Caught by surprise, we and staff in other educational organizations met quickly to review developments. Each of us requested a hearing. We contacted experts in psychology and testing to offer to appear before the committee. Each person took responsibility for a specific task: contacting university presidents who would testify or who would contact congressmen on the committee; finding admissions officers to testify about the importance of keeping exams secure; providing information to staff of the Minority and Majority offices of the committee; approaching leaders of the educational associations and teachers' unions; and writing news releases to blunt opponents' claims in the press.

The shock was not just that someone did not like us. Our pride was hurt. Since its founding, ETS had prided itself on being on the side of students, identifying talent that would not be obvious were it not for the tests, assisting them in their search for colleges, publishing materials that would familiarize them with the tests, offering the tests multiple times a year, including Braille and Sabbath editions, to facilitate access and accommodate special needs.

"Where are the students in all of this? I haven't heard any outcry. What do they think?" I asked Bob Solomon. "Are they part of the push to regulate? Had we received demands to see secure questions and answers? Were there student protests?" Bob said neither the College Board nor ETS had received any inquiry favoring publishing the tests.

Early in my career at ETS when I was involved in the administration of the SAT, I had answered students' requests to confirm their test answers, a service we provided free to any student who questioned the score. There were about a dozen requests a year to check scores, and, to my knowledge, there had never been a request to see the questions. Clearly, all this bluster was not initiated by students applying to college.

My UNCG and Rutgers experiences had been similar. I had never heard a complaint about the test questions not being released. In fact, when I talked with applicants about their testing experience, they had never raised the issue of wanting to see the questions.

"Why look back at a test?" a high-school senior said to me. "The test is never the same the second time. Besides, the score is not like a test score in high school. We are too busy studying and preparing to do well on the next test to waste time lobbying to see answers on the previous one."

"Yes," I concurred, "and to make sure everyone is treated equitably, a small number of questions are the same in various tests so the tests can be linked to each other—like braiding rope or hair. Without using questions more than once means a score of 600 at one time—say, November—will not be comparable to a score of 600 next time—say, February. That would be unfair to you and to admissions officers."

The only way to stop the bill from becoming law was to defeat it in committee. Congressman Weiss seemed confident that the members would go along with the bill because, for them, it was not controversial but rather a simple matter of collegial courtesy.

A request for hearings gave us three to four weeks to assemble opponents to present arguments to members of the committee.

As we were strategizing, we had an idea. Since Ralph Nader's affiliates were supporting the bill, why not invite Mr. Nader to present his arguments in a public forum, with Mr. Turnbull, president of ETS, presenting the other side? It was just the kind of thing Mr. Nader relished—and a good way for us to get our arguments in the press.

The crowd gathered in the first-floor auditorium of our office building on DuPont Circle. The tension in the air was palpable: floodlights bore down on the podium and stage; Messrs. Nader and Turnbull were seated side by side; and the auditorium was filled with educators, testing officials, supporters of the proposed legislation, association leaders, our staff, and the press.

Briefed well by his supporters, Mr. Nader positioned himself as the savior of students. Speaking with vigor and zeal, he staked his claim: "We all know the impact that large corporations and monopolies can have on people. In this case, students are disadvantaged by the giant testing organizations that control access to higher education. Secrecy is never good, especially when information is kept from students and their parents. The public has a *right to know* and to regulate monopolies that govern the lives of young people. They must be held accountable. There must be truth, not secrecy, in testing."

The cannonball landed right in Bill Turnbull's lap, but he rose to the occasion in a calm, deliberate voice, setting the record straight: "First, we are not a monopoly. There are other testing companies, and those institutions who use our services do so voluntarily. We are accountable in numerous ways: to the College Board, a membership organization of thousands of schools and colleges; to the clients for whom we develop examinations; to the professional community in which we work; and to external committees that oversee our policies and procedures.

"Now, as to students, we treat everyone fairly by making sure no one test-taker sees the examination ahead of time; that the examinations are comparable from one administration to the next; that the integrity of the score scale is preserved through careful use and reuse of secure questions; and that tests worldwide are monitored closely to discourage and prevent cheating. That way admissions officers can have confidence in the validity of the scores reported to them."

"That's the point, Mr. Turnbull!" interrupted Mr. Nader. "The tests are not good predictors of what students can do and are given much too much emphasis—far beyond their value, in fact. Students could be spending their time on other things."

"I beg to differ, Mr. Nader. Research over the years has substantiated the predictive value of the tests and their practical use in offsetting the variability of high-school grading systems. You are impugning the wisdom of college admissions officers by questioning their choice as to which factors they consider in selecting students to attend their institutions."

The heated exchange continued for an hour, after which supporters of each position gathered around each speaker as the press pushed to interview the men. As expected, Mr. Nader painted ETS as the spoiler of every student's dream. He characterized it as a massive behind-the-scenes invisible hand selecting students admitted to college.

Bill spoke so calmly and precisely that he was visibly overshadowed by Mr. Nader's assertive style. Yet, his defense of ETS was cogent: "ETS does not select students for college. I think you know that, Mr. Nader. You just find it easier to attack ETS than to criticize the selection practices of colleges and universities."

After the press and a good part of the audience had disappeared, Mr. Nader approached Bill in a most cordial manner, almost apologetically, claiming that he did not intend harm. He recognized the need for tests, he said, but felt that ETS was too secretive about what it did. Again, Bill explained, to no avail, the basic principles of secure exams. However, had Mr. Nader acceded to Bill's explanation, he would have undercut his own claims, and he was too shrewd a politician to do that.

The debate set the stage for the hearings. Our strategy group, composed of educators and College Board, ACT, and ETS staff, focused on selecting witnesses and identifying topics for testimony. Calls went out to university presidents, to members of associations, to admissions directors, to psychometricians, asking them to write, call congressmen, or offer to testify.

They answered the call of our full-court press. High school guidance counselors described the importance of the examinations to parents as well as to them. Admissions officers from small, large, private, and state-supported colleges explained the use of tests in their decisions. Professors of psychology gave testimony about the properties of high-stakes, secure exams and how they differed from teacher-made tests in schools. Behind the scenes, university presidents and deans visited the Hill and spoke to members of the committee.

While some who became involved did not have a direct stake in the outcome, they feared what regulation of educational policy might mean for colleges and universities in the long run. The crux of their message was, "The federal government should not assume an intrusive role of influencing or controlling academic policies of independent institutions." They drew an imaginary line in the sand, same as ours.

Their testimony and visits were effective. We garnered the support of several congressmen on the committee. Congressman Goodling, the ranking minority member of the committee, and his staff had been helpful in persuading his Republican colleagues that the Government should not be in the business of regulating admissions and testing. All of them were prepared to vote NO. But the Democrats were in the majority, and many of them were supporting their colleague, Congressman Weiss.

Time was running out. Two days before the scheduled mark-up, I got a call from a colleague close to committee staff and was made aware of the head count. "Alice, they've made a count of the votes and there's a tie. Can you find one more vote? A tie puts the Chairman in an awkward position."

I called Bob Solomon. "What can we do, Bob? Any ideas? All our friends here have reached the people who could help. Do you know of anyone in the district of one of the Democratic congressmen?" I asked.

As we talked, we suddenly remembered that the committee was the Education and *Labor* Committee and that many of the Democratic congressmen were close to national labor leaders. "Maybe," Bob said, "there are union leaders in education who might understand the issue and realize the risk. Let me put out some feelers and see what happens. I'll get back to you in a few hours."

We remembered that a high-level official of a national union had commented favorably on the bill. Bob knew him personally—well enough to call him and sound him out as to why he seemed to favor the bill. Maybe he did not understand fully the implications. "He's a reasonable man," Bob said, "and an independent thinker. He might change his mind if he understands the facts of the situation."

Bob's call went well, and the gentleman said he would make a call to the committee. We continued our activity in mobilizing college administrators to call congressmen. The gears ground faster with hope that we could garner additional votes by the time of the committee meeting.

On the day of the vote, we held our breath, waiting for a call from a staff person in the Chairman's office. Finally, late in the day, we learned that the only affirmative vote was that of Congressman Weiss. The testing organizations had dodged a bullet, and by implication, the educational community had done so as well.

About the time we started popping the champagne corks, another message reached us and put a damper on our party. While the encounter in the Congress was over, Fair Test and the Nader-initiated interest groups turned to state legislatures and, within months, similar "Truth in Testing" bills popped up in 22 state legislatures across the country. It seemed that as soon as we cleared one fence, another one appeared on the horizon.

Fortunately, both ETS and the College Board had field offices spread geographically around the country. While ETS staff had not been politically active, they were familiar with state educational policy and knew people in administrative offices as well as a few legislators. They certainly knew the issues and could present sound arguments for defeating the proposed legislation. In states where we didn't have contacts, we hired lobbyists who knew the ropes and could assist our staff in reaching legislators.

Time after time, as we cleared one hurdle, another would appear. Defeating proposals one year didn't carry over to the next; they appeared in the hopper a second or third time. It took several more years, fighting each bill state by state, year after year, before the multi-state campaign to destroy admissions tests faded into history.

The Congressional legislative battle, while over, spurred internal debates at ETS about the feasibility of releasing test questions and their answers. We had never objected in principle to letting students see their questions and answers, but test design and operational necessity prevented it. ETS had always sought to be as transparent as possible; at the same time it was absolutely committed to protecting the integrity and validity of the exams, which meant keeping the questions and answers under lock and key.

Psychologists and statisticians at ETS saw the issue as a puzzle to solve. My creative colleagues were always researching new approaches to old conventions. Technicians went to work and devised ways to release some sections of the tests—not all parts—without damaging the comparability of the tests and the validity of the score scale. This enabled the College Board to announce that students could request copies of actual questions and answers to the sections of the test that composed their scores. Eventually, the College Board published "real" test questions and answers for the public.

In the long run, students gained access to hundreds of test questions—better than what the coaching schools had produced for them to use in practice.

The testing organizations and higher education more broadly were not burdened by the regulatory hand of the federal or state governments.

And supporters of regulations could claim that, even though they were defeated in their attempts at legislation, they had created an impetus for change in the testing industry.

Everybody could claim victory. And, with that victory, I decided my second time working in Washington was enough. I didn't need a third time around the circles—physical, legislative, and emotional—of our Capital city. In 1990 I moved my office back to Princeton and assumed a different role at ETS.

I still love the nation's capital: its museums, parks, cultural events—but not so much Capitol Hill—so I camp out there upon occasion in my *pied á terre* in Foggy Bottom close to The Kennedy Center. With no more legislative fences in my path, I enjoy Washington as a great "walking" city, with low-rise buildings, the elegant Mall, tree-covered sidewalks, rambling parks and gardens, marble monuments enhanced by cherry trees—many places to roam and discover. Of course, I insisted that my apartment be close to the water, in this case the Potomac River with its walkways and park benches.

The Potomac's flowing waters—always calming, soothing, ever-changing, and life-sustaining—took me back in time to my early life on that other river, the Roanoke River in my hometown. Thus, for a few years in mighty Washington, I really was halfway toward home and imagined myself making it all the way to North Carolina one day.

March 2018

MY CELEBRITIES AND MY FRIENDS

Clearing Fences

From my time in high school when I sat on the fence in my Weldon backyard, watching Little Joe move surefooted around the ring, until now in Raleigh at the Fairgrounds, I have watched horses and their riders walk, canter, trot, jump, and hunt. I have cheered for my brother, my sister, and now my daughter, Andrea. I have worried about her and congratulated her. But I've always been on the sidelines, never on a horse inside the show ring. I've been so near, yet so far.

Like her Poppa, my dad, Andrea fell in love early with horses. My dad entered shows of gaited horses with George and Margaret (Monk) as his star riders. I was the jockey for practices but was never allowed to do more than support my siblings at the show. I cheered them on when they high-stepped around the show ring, their three- and five-gaited horses majestic, especially when working.

When George and I began our days as novice equestrians, Dad believed that George should be the showman. Riding in strenuous competitions was not for young women, he felt. I could ride but, somehow, it was unseemly for a lady to ride English saddle and enter all-male classes. Several years later, when George left home for college, Monk took over. She became the equestrian sitting astride Dad's horses. She was the only child left in the family—all Dad had. But she was more than enough.

Mounted on Dad's elegant chestnut mare, Sweet Sensation, Monk won handily in competitions when she was only eleven years old. She was petite and the mare was *so* large that Monk looked like a doll on a giant rocking-horse. Crowds cheered her with shouts and applause.

Monk was a terrific rider, shorter than five feet but with nerves of steel—and determined to control her horse by reins, by crop, or by a nudge of her heel. By that time, young women riding in competitive shows was permissible. That was all right with me. I didn't feel left out or treated unfairly. I was away in college, studying, making friends, and enjoying an active social life.

Fast-forward twenty years, when Andrea, aged ten, and I were living in Princeton, New Jersey. Jan Flaugher, a friend, came by the house one day and changed Andrea's life—and mine, too. I went back to having horses in my life and Andrea began her life with them. Jan had invited Andrea to join her two daughters one afternoon in riding horses in a big, open pasture just outside town. From then until now, forty-seven years later, horses have been Andrea's passion and support.

She rode at Hasty Acres in Kingston, New Jersey, a stone's throw across the creek from Princeton. The YWCA in Princeton sponsored a horseback-riding program there, and fees were something that I, a single mom, could afford.

With that decision, her avocation of a lifetime, taking lessons, competing in riding-school shows, and mucking out stalls to pay for her riding lessons, was born.

ANDREA, AGE 11, ON FROSTY, AT HASTY ACRES, 1972
HER SECOND HORSE SHOW

Most children Andrea's age went to camp in the summer. I thought Andrea, an only child, should go as well but didn't have the resources for a lengthy residential camp. Her first camp experience was in North Carolina under the watchful eye of my parents. Camp Triton was a two-week overnight camp only twenty miles from Weldon, my folks' home. They could visit Andrea as allowed and rescue her if needed. No rescue was required, though Andrea did not want to return the following year. She rode horses but Camp Triton's teaching method was different from that of Hasty Acres', so Andrea believed the camp had retarded her progress.

The next year, 1973, I learned about a six-weeks summer camp on Deer Isle, Maine. It offered two things Andrea loved: riding horses and learning French. It was much more expensive than the two-week camp in North Carolina, so I was apprehensive about my ability to swing it. The camp, Les Chalets Français, near Blue Hill, was owned and operated by two rather eccentric but charming sisters, one of whom, Helma Nitzsche Bush, lived in Princeton in a large grey-shingled home with a majestic mahogany staircase right out of the nineteenth century. Several families in the Princeton area sent their daughters to the camp. I was introduced to Helma, who was sympathetic to my single-mom status and assured me they would help me economize on costs while giving Andrea all the advantages the camp had to offer.

In talking with the sisters, I discovered that the horses used at the camp were the very same horses owned by Hasty Acres and used in the YWCA riding program. When a good family friend, Sue Fremon, learned of Andrea's plans, she asked, "Andrea, do you know any of the other girls from here who are going?"

"No," she answered, "but I know the horses and Beaver."

David Lee Johnson, affectionately known as "Beaver," worked at Hasty Acres assisting in lessons and managing the stables. He handled the horses, trailered them to Maine, and stayed at the camp coaching the girls, helping them with their tack, and putting on stunt shows for them using the school horses. He rode bareback, making the horses who would hardly move under the girls' reins look like prancing ponies. He thrilled his audience by standing barefoot on the horses' backs as they performed their routines. The girls adored Beaver. He was their friend, their teacher, and a fellow with a big shoulder for their tears when they were disappointed.

Mothers hate to let go, and I was uneasy about letting Andrea go alone to a camp in far-away Maine. To soften that anxiety, Mother and I took Andrea to camp by way of Boston and Chatham on Cape Cod. Mother always liked to explore the history of an area, so we took the historical walking tour of Boston. Mother liked Faneuil Hall; Andrea liked the Quincy Market. Exploring the town of Chatham in the elbow of the Cape and also the national park north of it impressed us as we came to appreciate the topographical and geological variety of the shoreline along the Atlantic Ocean.

Once we deposited Andrea at Les Chalets Français, Mother and I drove to Fredericton, Canada, to see Weldon friends, Steve and Glenda Turner. They had emigrated there when Steve joined the faculty of the University of New Brunswick, founded in 1785 and thus one of the oldest universities in North America. For ten days in June, it rained and rained and was quite cold. I had sent Andrea off with summer clothes—in late June, doesn't every Southern mother do that?—and without a sweater. I bought sweaters for her, shipped them to her, called the camp to alert them to their arrival, and inquired about Andrea's welfare.

"Andrea? You wonder how she is coping? She's having a great time. I will have her call you," the camp director told me.

"Hi, Mom. What's up?" she asked when I picked up a few minutes later.

"How are you getting along in all this rain and cold? Aren't you freezing? And soaked?"

"Oh, no, Mom. I'm doing fine. I love it here and we ride rain or shine."

For several years the camp became a magic summer place for her. The French lessons were incidental to Andrea's horseback riding. The horse show at the end of the season celebrated the girls' achievements, and proud parents were there to watch from all over the eastern third of the United States. Andrea developed friendships with girls in Cleveland, Ohio; in Yardley, Pennsylvania; as well as in New Jersey. And I enjoyed the association with their parents.

Again in my life, though, I was on the sidelines, this time watching and cheering on Andrea and her newfound friends to their successes.

When Andrea was growing up, graduate students at Princeton lived with us to make sure someone was home when Andrea came home from school and to care for her when I traveled for my work. One of them, Sandy McCardell, had gone on the Experiment in International Living and recommended strongly that Andrea go, too, even though Andrea was not yet a high-school junior. Both Sandy and her mother persuaded me that Andrea was mature enough to go to Europe for a summer and that, while there, she would be able to develop further her skills in French.

By that time, I was a vice president at Rutgers University and, with careful budgeting, could afford for her to go. But talk about apprehensive?! I was weak in my knees and verging on nausea when I left her at a midtown hotel in New York City to join the rest of the students headed for Europe. I cried as I turned the car toward the Lincoln Tunnel headed back to Princeton. I fretted that I had done the wrong thing—turning her loose at such a young age—or worried that something would happen and I could not get to her. I didn't know where she would be and had no idea how to contact her. I had only the headquarters address of the Experiment in Middlebury, Connecticut.

For two weeks, I did not even know what country she was in. Finally word came that she was in Switzerland living on a farm with a French-speaking German family. Only the father spoke English, and he traveled during the work week. Andrea learned colloquial French fast. But, the language deficiency was no barrier when she discovered horses on the farm. One of the horses was registered with the Swiss National Defense Agency. Who would have even guessed there was such a thing in Switzerland?

The children on the farm treated Andrea like a sister. She helped them with their chores, and the whole family went sightseeing. She met others in her group occasionally; one time on an outing with them, she ended up on the wrong side of Lake Geneva, in France without a passport!

All alone, she tried to explain her plight to the border patrol, asking for their help. She did not know which ferry to take back to the Swiss side of the lake. Lucky for her, by that time she had learned to speak French fluently and was able to negotiate her return on the appropriate ferry, then find her way to the town of Arzier and the family's farm.

In Princeton the next fall, Andrea came home from the movies one night excited about a foreign film she had just seen. "Mom, guess what?!" she exclaimed. "I saw Zola."

"Who?"

"You know, the horse on the farm in Switzerland! She was in the movie. Part of the movie was filmed in Arzier, and Zola was walking down the street in a parade."

"Really? What was the movie about?"

Andrea didn't remember much about the film's characters, but she knew the horse!

By her senior year in high school, Andrea was proficient enough in handling horses to merit a horse of her own. She wanted one in the worst way.

"Mom, I will get an after-school job. Please," she promised as we investigated the cost.

"I suppose that since you don't have a brother, the least I can do is try to give you a horse for companionship and pleasure," I said, relenting. When I thought about it, the monthly costs were probably about equal—a brother or a horse, at least until the college years. However, having a horse meant no more summer camp.

Mr. Diamond Chips (Chipper), was a strong, handsome, sorrel-red quarter-horse. Andrea was able to control him in the ring most of the time, and she set about entering local shows. Hasty Acres was not a boarding stable, though, which meant we had to find another stable for Chipper. It also meant Andrea's leaving Beaver, a downer for her.

ANDREA ON CHIPPER, WILMAR FARM
SENIOR YEAR AT PRINCETON HIGH, SPRING 1979

Andrea ended up at Wilmar Farm outside Princeton, near Rocky Hill, New Jersey. By that time, she had her driver's license and could get there on her own after school. The property was an expansive, lush horse farm with good show rings and indoor facilities, run by a high-strung woman whose behavior, thank goodness, was tempered by her small, gentle, friendly husband. The stables were spacious and well-maintained, and the daily care was first class. Chipper and Andrea did well there. The bond between them was so strong that she didn't want to leave him behind when she went to college. I hadn't fully anticipated that, but she offered to work to help support him.

For college, she didn't intentionally choose the University of Virginia (UVA) because of its equestrian program, but she found it to be a good one when she landed there as a freshman. UVA had an active riding program with an equestrian team that competed with other colleges in Virginia and North Carolina. Chipper was at home in The Barracks, a horse farm with rolling hills and green pastures, nestled at the foothills of mountains just outside Charlottesville. Andrea worked there, mucking stalls as she had at Hasty Acres, and joined the UVA Equestrian Team.

The owner of the barn referred to Chipper as a "hotspur." He was sometimes difficult to control, but Andrea kept the reins tight with firm hands. Together, they contributed to the team's success. The team won often against opponents, but Sweet Briar was the champion most years.

Much of her activity there is unknown to me because I was no longer on the sidelines at her shows or visiting the barn to check on things. I was away in Washington or Princeton working at Educational Testing Service. Even so, Andrea seemed to thrive, enjoying being on her own.

Andrea and Chipper did more than compete with the team. Once Chipper was under control and responding to Andrea's guidance, they ventured out alone to a regional show. The three-day event, located in Orange, Virginia, required the horse and rider to perform in dressage, in jumping over fences in a ring, and in galloping across country in something like a steeplechase. Watching Andrea in the ring was familiar to me. I had also seen her compete in dressage. But I had never witnessed a cross-country event, much less one that involved my daughter. Seeing her make her way independently made my heart swell with pride, though several times my knees almost buckled from fear of an accident.

She had been introduced to Eventing—as it is called—a competition that involves dressage, stadium jumping, and cross-country, by Deri Cupas, the daughter of one of the women who owned Les Chalets Français. She had competed in several events in Maine, but nowhere else and always with Deri and Beaver to guide her.

Again, I was on the sidelines. I couldn't believe that, by herself, Andrea would dare take Chipper to a three-day event. It is not only a grind. It can be very dangerous, especially the cross-country component. Christopher Reeves, also from Princeton, broke his neck in such an event. Thank Goodness, that accident had not yet occurred when Andrea went to Orange; otherwise, I would have been lobbying for a No-Show.

She did very well until late in the competition when Chipper landed hard on the other side of a steep, banked fence. He pulled up lame and was unable to continue in the dressage, but she achieved one of her goals: to go clean, i.e., zero mistakes, on cross-country, which is difficult to do. *She did it!* The entire experience was exhilarating, given that it was her first attempt in a recognized regional event, one that many seasoned riders did not finish, especially the cross-country phase. I left our hotel that weekend with my chest puffed up, anxious to tell my colleagues back in Princeton about my courageous and accomplished daughter.

Graduation meant that Andrea had to land a job to support herself. She got a good one, but it was in New York City with Macy's. There were no stables there, at least none that she could afford. She couldn't afford the upkeep for Chipper anywhere, in fact. A half-hearted attempt to sell Chipper was unsuccessful, so she decided to give the horse to the daughter of a friend of her grandmother in Halifax, North Carolina. Chipper made the trip from Charlottesville to Halifax on Christmas Eve. Normally December 25th does not bring a White Christmas and temperatures are well above freezing in Eastern North Carolina. That year, there was no snow on the ground, but the temperature was well below freezing, close to zero. Andrea went to Halifax to check on Chipper and found him without blankets in a barn with no light, no windows, and big cracks in the walls between the slats of wood. She blanketed him, realizing that the new owner did not know how to care for such an animal.

All during the holiday, we worried about the horse. The young girl was excited about her Christmas present, so Andrea coached her dad on Chipper's needs and proper care. The horse was probably too lively and high-strung for the young girl to handle, and he did not stay long at that farm. He found a good home eventually, but I never knew what happened to Chipper after that first winter. I was afraid to ask and chose not to know.

Horses vanished from Andrea's life, but not from her mind. A tour of duty for Macy's in Texas, graduate school in Washington, D.C., romance and later a new baby, James, occupied Andrea's time for years. Things did not work out with James's father, however. Cast in the role of a single mom, she worked hard at American University in academic advising and admissions so she could support James. When expenses began to exceed income, she sought a less expensive location south of D.C.

Through a friend, she learned of a job opportunity at North Carolina State University (NCSU) in the College of Management, again advising students, a role which played to her strengths. Soon her skills were noticed by others, and she became the developer and director of Advising Central, a virtual (online) advising program for students throughout the university. After fifteen years there, she moved down the road to Meredith College, also in Raleigh. Occasionally, she was able to afford the time and money to ride a horse at a nearby stable, but riding then was neither routine nor regular for her. Andrea's passion for horses was still there but not the financial means or time to get involved.

When James, her son, entered LSU, greater demands were made on the family treasury. But the empty nest provided an opportunity for social activity, culminating eventually in her marriage. In January 2010, Andrea married Cecil Bozarth, a professor in the Poole College of Management at N.C. State. But then, even before they married, breast cancer knocked the balance out of their new life together. Cecil, having lost his first wife to cancer, was attentive in his support and fidelity. As a man who took pride in caring for his family, he was sensitive to Andrea's turmoil and pain. He knew that Andrea loved horses—just as he loved to acquire and restore antique cars—and was sympathetic to her sadness and low self-esteem caused by the disease.

ANDREA WITH PARKER, CHRISTMAS 2012, BUCKHORN FARM, APEX, N.C.

A thoughtful and generous man, he gave Andrea "half a horse" for Christmas—said he did not know which half, head or tail! That meant he leased the horse half-time. The horse, named Parker, was stabled at Buckhorn Farm, about twenty minutes from their home. Parker's absentee owner benefitted from Andrea's care of and attention to the horse. Andrea was in a dream world, finally: good home, caring husband, a son and stepson she enjoyed loving, a dog, a cat, and now a horse—a big love in her life! The horse provided things she needed: companionship, strength, psychological and physical therapy, solitude, and pleasure. I felt relief, gratitude, and pure joy for her.

How many ups and downs can a young woman bear? Breast cancer struck again, four years later. This time it meant chemo, the dreaded cocktail that almost kills in curing, and a mastectomy with reconstruction. With Andrea's loss of hair, the nausea, and stress on her nails and teeth and throat, it was not a good time. It was made worse by Parker's owner's moving him to another barn away from Andrea and discontinuing Andrea's lease. It was a crushing blow to lose Parker just when she was at her weakest point, physically and mentally.

At the end of her chemo treatments, the doctors said Andrea could ride again. It would strengthen her legs, boost her morale, and give her confidence in herself again.

She had been knocked down; but she got back up. Now she is back, healthy and active! She refused to be defeated by adversity, remaining strong in her faith and in her unshakable spirit.

Cecil decided "No more half-horses." No more horses that can be taken away, then break Andrea's heart. He bought her a horse all her own: a tall, 17½-hand Chestnut thoroughbred with blaze face and two white front leggings.

He is a robust and high-strung horse with a long stride and good leg/foot action. Jet—Cyberjet, to be exact. A fitting name because he likes to fly.

ANDREA ON CYBERJET, RALEIGH HORSE SHOW 2016

Cyberjet is trained for dressage, hunter jumping, and cross-country, but Andrea concentrates on hunter classes in shows because her trainer specializes in hunter classes. With the boys away in college and graduate school, she now has a new "somebody" to take care of—Jet. Andrea and Jet make a good team. Each is learning from the other. Andrea not only goes into shows again, she wins ribbons from time to time. While the ribbons are not in themselves important, they serve to encourage her to keep learning and growing.

Once again, I am sitting on the sidelines at the Fairgrounds in Raleigh watching her ride in a local show. She is gaining confidence as she gains experience. Her concentration is totally in the present as she guides Jet to jump fences in the ring. Andrea is whole again, not just in her equestrian endeavors but in her personal life as well.

She goes with Cecil to compete in antique-car shows with Rita, his 1937 Lincoln Zephyr Coupe, and he stands by the rail at the horseshow ring, cheering Andrea on in her hunter classes.

A perfectionist, Cecil wins first place each time he competes because his car is in pristine condition and one-hundred percent compliant with the car's original specifications. At horseshows, she wins more ribbons than she ever expected, increasing her confidence and love of the sport with every outing. They support each other, she with her generous spirit and enduring thoughtfulness, Cecil with his strength and devotion to his home and to her.

She also stays in touch with her "boys," James and Philip. Nothing escapes her eye when one of them is in need, whether for advice about a career choice or for a dish of ice cream. At fifty-five, she is again as generous, joyful, and playful as the child I remember. My eyes are filled with tears of joy, and my heart is filled with love for the woman Andrea has become, an accomplished woman of stature with a caring heart.

October 1, 2016

I Know Who You Are!

Pinehurst attracts golfers—young and old, good putters, poor duffers, scratch handicappers. Visitors come to play; retirees come to stay and to play, sometimes playing six days a week. Visitors liken the town to a New England village; townspeople call it The Village. That's an apt description except that the town is dominated by longleaf pines and the imposing, historic Carolina Hotel, standing in the center of town—not landscape items most New England towns possess.

Picture a rambling, white-clapboard hotel, built early in the twentieth century at the center of a town surrounded by named twentieth-century cottages separating it from several short blocks of shops, restaurants, a library, and a Village Green backing up to another historic landmark, The Village Chapel.

The Carolina Hotel's lobby and halls display descriptive scenes of early buildings; of celebrity-visitor Annie Oakley and her sharpshooter exhibits; of former champions; and of Mr. Tufts, Pinehurst's founder, and of his companion Mr. Ross, the Donald who designed the courses. Attached to one side of the building is a full-service spa with pool, sauna, and associated services to complement the conference facilities of the hotel.

The Pinehurst Resort clubhouses, accommodating two golf clubs, one for members and another for the public, balance the position of the hotel at the opposite end of a quarter-mile drive shaded by trees, beds of colorful seasonal flowers, and dotted by tennis courts with an adjacent clubhouse. From this one facility, five golf courses branch off, circling through the residential areas of the town. Add a lawn-bowling court, two croquet courts, and an aquatic center and you have at your fingertips a full-vacation pack!

Walking the halls of the public Pinehurst Resort Club, a visitor is carried back through golf history in the Hall of Champions by displays in glass cases of pictures, trophies, and biographies of golf celebrities.

The shops in the Village offer abundant memorabilia of Pinehurst's glorious past and books about champions of an earlier era, as well as many upscale, delicately arranged artifacts available for sale to collectors. Other shops sell fashionable golfing outfits and accessories to those who come to look chic on the golf course, even if they cannot lower their handicaps during their Pinehurst visit.

On another side of town, about a mile away from the center of the Village, is the medical complex serving the Sandhills region with specialists in cardiology, orthopedics, and cancer. The hospital ranks among the top 100 of community hospitals in the country, and 56th among cardiac centers. Availability of excellent medical care is another reason retirees settle in Pinehurst.

Works of local potters from nearby Seagrove, beautiful in their artistry and functional in their use, line the shelves of potpourri shops along one or two of the other streets downtown. A rich history envelops the visitor in some way every day.

Something is always going on—a tournament of some kind; a charity game; a corporate retreat; a family vacation of golf, tennis, swimming, and boating on the lake. Pinehurst is the site of numerous regional or national tournaments, including the USGA Open for men and for women, the U.S. Amateur Open, the North-South competition, and tournaments for young, aspiring golfers. Organizations promoting the development of golf for both young and old host events and tournaments on the Resort's famous courses, including course No. 2, as well as other courses throughout the area.

Moore County (with Pinehurst, population 15,000, in its southeast corner) offers enough golf holes to accommodate small and large events—about one hole for every square mile in this county. Between 40 and 50 golf courses, some serving as the core of residential communities, some dotting the hills and valleys of the nine courses of Pinehurst Resorts, and others offering courses open to the general public, make good use of the sandy soil that also nourishes the roots of longleaf pines dominating Moore County's landscape.

Believe it or not, there is something in the area that is as important as golf—at least for conservationists: designated pine trees. These trees take precedence over the construction of homes or golf courses if they house the cockaded woodpecker, an endangered species in North America. Official woodpecker checkers make sure no pine tree with a nest is felled, either for homes or a golf fairway. Off-center placement of some houses reveals the presence of a protected tree! No home builder wants to run into the buzz-saw of the wildlife police.

Behind the croquet and lawn-bowling courts facing the Public Clubhouse, the five golf courses start their first tees at the back exits of the clubhouses and pro shop. The wide, semicircular, covered porch of the Members Club, connected through restricted access to the porch of the Public Clubhouse, offers a clear view of the first tee of the famous Number 2 course, site of many USGA Open and other tournaments, as well as the 18th green of the same course. It is probably the best and most coveted view of the beginning and end of a famous golf course in the United States.

The First Tee does not just designate a place on a golf course. First Tee is the name of a national organization seeking to attract and help talented, eager boys and girls from all walks of life who desire to learn to play golf. It emphasizes character development as well as golf by its focus on nine core values: honesty, integrity, sportsmanship, respect, confidence, responsibility, perseverance, courtesy, and judgment. Regardless of financial circumstances, children seven and above participate in workshops throughout the year, leading to a variety of tournaments in the summer. Much of the support for the organization comes from sponsoring corporations and golf clubs, such as Resorts in Pinehurst, and others around the country. Annual events are often hosted in the Pinehurst area.

Success of the events requires use of multiple courses during the year; lots of pros who can teach the game; chaperones; and an unlimited supply of hamburgers, hotdogs, and fries. Pepsi, the drink invented in New Bern, N.C., is the drink of choice—Coke doesn't have a chance of invading the links at Pinehurst! Pinehurst is one of the few areas in the country that has the accommodations to make large golf outings a celebratory success without disrupting play for regular members and guests.

From 1997, when First Tee was founded, until 2011, ex-President George Herbert Walker Bush served as honorary chair of First Tee. In 2011, the honorary chairmanship was assumed by his son, ex-President George W. Bush.

On one occasion, around 2005-06, I was playing on Pinehurst No. 4 with women in my group of weekly regulars.

"Did you know, Alice, it's rumored that former President 41, George Herbert Walker Bush, is going to be here to kick off a First Tee special event this year?" asked Geraldine Daley, my golfing partner that day.

"When? Where?" I queried. The clubhouses were abuzz with the rumor, and, according to Geraldine, the rumor was correct. President Bush, the honorary chairman, was coming to hit the first ball off the first tee on famous Course No. 2, starting a round of golf with friends.

Both clubhouses filled up early with players and visitors hoping to catch a view of the President. Many local golfers, however, in spite of the electricity in the air about the President's arrival, went about playing their own games instead of standing lookout. Nothing is more important to the regular golfer than his or her own game and score. "Get on with the game, move on through," says the ranger, "because another foursome is coming right behind you in eight minutes. No lingering, no gawking!"

Geraldine and I played No. 4 that morning. Positioned geographically next to Number 2, No. 4 ranks among the toughest courses in the Resort arsenal of nine. Pocket-sand traps are positioned to catch my ball on almost every hole. In spite of that hazard, the expanse of well-manicured fairways and greens made it worthwhile for me to try to play. I say "try" because that was all I could do. Keeping my handicap up-to-date on a regular basis was discouraging and self-defeating to my emotional well-being. The higher my handicap climbed, the lower my interest in golf. I might enjoy the game were it not for the handicap system.

Being classified a novice without a handicap—not beating myself up every time I went out—was more relaxing for me. Even so, no such thing as "relaxing" exists when playing golf. "Equanimity" and "serenity" are not words associated with the game, either. "Determination" and "endurance" characterize it better. But sticking with the novice classification came closest to achieving a level of comfort that enabled me to enjoy the open acreage, the bright skies, and the rolling topography of the land. Green, green everywhere. Birds, too, lots of them!

Like the other courses that make the loop out and back to the clubhouse, No. 4 ends up near the 18th green of No. 2 and not very far from the first tee of that famous course.

When we got to the 18th green, Geraldine suggested, "Drive the cart over to the porch of the Members' Club. We might just see the President and his foursome tee off the first hole of Number 2. Of course, it's after twelve o'clock and we have probably missed him."

As we approached, we noticed four tall men with serious expressions on their faces, their eyes staring forward as if sending daggers out to anyone looking their way or approaching the porch. They wore black suits and we noticed little bugs in their ears with cords running up from their shirt collars.

"Geraldine, see those guys? They won't let us within fifty yards of the porch," I quickly concluded. We figured they were Secret Service and that they would not let anybody on the porch except the President's party.

"Keep going, Alice." Geraldine insisted. She had a gimpy leg, and that day was the first time she had played since surgery on her knee. She held a cane in her right hand as we approached the porch. I drove up but stopped about 50 feet from the porch.

"Drive on, Alice!" she told me.

"We can't go up there. Don't you see the Secret Service guys?" I reminded her. "The President must be nearby. Otherwise the Secret Service would not be crawling all over the porch."

"Keep on going, Alice. Don't be so timid! No one has stopped us yet," she insisted.

We drove up to the steps of the Clubhouse, where I stopped the cart. I figured the President must already be on the course since the men in black did not keep us from reaching the steps. The chairs and tables on the porch were filled with people.

The President's task as honorary chair was to hit the first ball off the tee to start the event and to continue around the course. Because golf carts are not permitted on the fairways of No. 2, there was a cart positioned on the path not too far off the tee box. We assumed it was the President's cart and that we had missed his tee shot. We looked around the fairway but no President, either near or in the cart.

Geraldine stepped out of the cart, leaning on her cane. "Let's go up on the porch, get a chair and wait to see what happens," she suggested, as she started to limp up the stairs. "Maybe he has already teed off, but maybe he hasn't even shown up yet."

Still no one stopped us. No one even looked at us, we thought. Cautiously, I got out of the cart, leaving it at the foot of the steps.

"Geraldine, don't walk up the stairs until I can get you a chair. You need to be careful," I reminded her. I walked up the steps to the porch, looking for a table and chairs from which we could view the people going off the first tee. She hobbled up, holding on to the rail.

Every table was taken. Yet, a few empty chairs were scattered here and there. I spied one to my left at a table with only three people busy eating their lunch. On the right, I saw another chair ajar from a table of four.

"Wait here, Geraldine. I'll get a chair so you can sit down."

The chair on the left was the closest. I walked to the table. Eating sandwiches and fries were a middle-aged woman and man who looked up as I approached. The third man, white-haired, with his head down, was biting into his hamburger.

"May I have this chair, please, if you are not using it?" I asked the man who had looked up at me. The other man turned his head and looked up at me, smiling. I gasped. The electrons in my cerebrum stalled, and I froze! I was tongue-tied. No one said a word. It was President George H. W. Bush!

"*Oh, I know who you are!*" I exclaimed.

With that, he smiled again.

"Not only can you have the chair, I will help you with it," he said, standing.

"No, No, No, Sir. Absolutely not! I can manage. It's very light-weight."

He insisted, saying emphatically, "Dear Lady, my mother would be upset with me if I let a lady take care of her own chair. I won't hear of your carrying the chair."

He picked up the chair and asked where I wanted him to put it. By that time, I had recovered a slight sense of where I was and who I was facing. Still in shock, though, I pointed to a spot about twelve feet away.

As we walked over to Geraldine standing there, I jabbered about how Geraldine had a bad leg and needed a chair. When he put the chair down, I could finally thank him and address him as Mr. President. I apologized for my awkward and improper exclamation a moment before.

He laughed, gave us both a greeting, shook our hands, and made me feel almost human again. "It's good to see you here," he concluded and walked back to his cold hamburger.

I stumbled over to the other empty chair on the other side of the porch, trying to regain my composure. I don't remember who was at that table. People were watching and smiling. I positioned the chair beside Geraldine's and sat down at the front of the porch. We stared straight ahead, not wanting to invade the President's privacy. We did, of course, strain to see out of the corners of our eyes who his companions were.

"Who are those people with him?" I asked Geraldine, who seemed to know everything.

"No one I recognize," she replied, "just golfing friends, most likely. Or, the organizers of the event being rewarded for their work."

The stairs leading to the first tee box were close to our seats. We watched as the President's threesome, along with the security detail, started down to the first tee of No. 2. Thanks to the President, we had the best seats on the porch.

President Bush was playing with the couple at his lunch table and another man who joined them at the tee box. They chatted while each of them took a turn at driving the ball off the first tee. President Bush hit his ball straight down the fairway, a good shot especially for a man his age. We weren't surprised. For a man who could parachute out of a plane at age 80, hitting a golf ball down a fairway was small stuff.

After the other three hit their shots, he walked over to the cart. The driver of the cart, with his passenger in tow, headed down the right side of the fairway. We saw Mr. Bush walk to the center of the fairway and swing at his second shot. We could see the trajectory of his ball but not where it landed. The foursome soon faded from view.

For a few minutes, Geraldine and I watched the other players on the courses, commenting on our luck of the day, musing about our audacious behavior.

"See, Alice," Geraldine bragged, "if I hadn't pushed you, having the courage to ignore the Secret Service fellows and drive straight up to the Members' Club porch, we would have missed out on meeting the President."

I felt a little ashamed, in fact downright impolite, for not calling the President by his proper name and title when I recognized him. My shock had made me blurt out my honest, childlike first thought, and Geraldine was amused. Hmm. She could laugh because she was not the one who had made the *faux pas*.

Despite my lack of manners in addressing the President, we basked in the delight of the happening. Not only had we seen President George Herbert Walker Bush, but we could confirm what people the world over had been saying for years. "He exudes kindness. He is a Gentleman through and through. He exemplifies his Greatest Generation."

Virtue and reason, concepts—principles even—were the bedrock of our Founding Fathers' revolution to create a new nation. It would be one governed by virtuous citizens who reasoned the way forward based on honoring the dignity of all its citizens.

How far we have come to witness now, 230 years later, a dystopian body politic and a crumbling social fabric? Until his death in 2019, George Herbert Walker Bush was a happy warrior. I understand now his Thousand Points of Light: success, prosperity, and social peace come from thousands of individual acts of kindness and compassion. He lived that life, a life of virtue and reason, kindled by kindness every day.

In my memory, he is "A Man for All Seasons." He did not make the earth move that day, but he did move a chair for me.

Winter 2019

Of Pies and Pine Straw

At Christmastime 2016, I was planning dinners and ways to help Andrea. I decided to make pecan pies, one for us and one for Jerry. Pecan was his favorite. Just to make sure I had crust, should I be too rushed to make it myself, I bought a box of ready-made Pillsbury refrigerated crust. The package is still in the refrigerator. Jerry did not return my call. His phone was down. Where can he be? What has happened? We always checked on each other about once a month. No pecan pies for him this year, I supposed.

Jerry McDonald has been my friend for 17 years. Jerry, my yardman or "landscape contractor," farms McDonald land near Foxfire in Moore County, land granted by King George II in the mid-eighteenth century, but he is also a coon-dog hunter, trainer, and breeder. Until he retired at age 80, this honest, dependable father, neighbor, and church deacon employed the Gang: skinny Johnny, who ended up hit on the head in a fight and disabled; Big Johnny, former golf caddie, bright but driven to drink and death; Mitch, who could not keep a nickel in his pocket when liquor was around; and Louis, unpredictable when hung over, always borrowing against his pay, but an excellent worker who had a better eye for cutting hedges and pruning bushes than anyone I ever saw. And he did it with hand shears. The guys were always sober and ready to work when they came to my house.

They called me "Little Bit" behind my back and it's true. I am tiny compared to them. After we got to know each other, they said it to my face. Every week, we joshed and joked a little as they started work. Some weeks I made brownies. One day, I had a birthday cake for Big Johnny. We gathered around the pool and sang "Happy Birthday" as Johnny's eyes filled with tears.

"This is the first time anyone ever had a birthday party for me—and with a cake, too," Johnny spoke haltingly, his head down.

"Well," I said, "It's about time you had a cake. Besides I wanted to make a cake for you today instead of brownies. Now, blow out the candles."

Think about it. No birthday cake until he was a middle-aged man. No wonder he turned to drink, even though he had graduated from high school and had had a good-paying job at the Club as a caddy. At Christmastime, I gave the Gang money and chocolate truffles. I always tried to have a crisp, new $100 bill for Jerry, who divided it equally.

Every week upon his arrival, Jerry and I stood in the driveway, catching up on the latest news. Jerry told me the latest gossip in the neighborhood, and around town for that matter. He loved to talk, and talk he did with all 30 of his customers. He also knew just about everybody mentioned in the newspaper each week—and the background story.

He had lived in the county on his family's land all his life. The happenings on the farms in Foxfire, his hometown nearby, were the spice of our conversation: family feuds; land developers trying to skin the local farm folks; Verizon trying to get Jerry to install a cell tower on the cheap; coon hunting at midnight on private land with his Knight Champion dog.

The gossip concerned funny happenings, because "funny" happened to Jerry all the time. There was the time that his cows got loose and wandered onto the Foxfire golf course. "Come get your cows, Jerry," telephoned the course manager. "They are tearing up the fairways and now they are on a green!"

Jerry dropped everything, ran over to the golf course, and steered the cows off the property toward home. He got them to the road across from his house, but an oncoming car scared the cows and they ran back onto the golf course. Jerry, normally a calm, deliberate man, got agitated and started shouting at the cows, scaring them to fairways farther back on the course.

"These cows got a short life span," Jerry exclaimed, exasperated as he corralled them once more. With a neighbor's help, he got them home.

The next week when Jerry came to my house, I asked about the cows. He confessed, "Those cows are gone. I got shed of 'em the next day. Good thing a guy was willing to buy 'em; I would've killed 'em otherwise."

"Are you going to get some more—maybe a different kind?" I asked.

"No way!" he said. "I am *out* of the cow business. Just dogs, crops, and lawns."

Jerry respected people's privacy. Some of the gossip—and much of what he saw—stayed with him. One serious situation in our neighborhood Jerry kept to himself for a long time, until after the man's death. Even then, Jerry confided in just two of us once some of the information became public.

Jerry and the Gang had seen disturbing activity at that house time and again over several years. Seems one of my neighbors abused his wife for as long as she lived, then subsequently beat his second wife as soon as they returned from their honeymoon.

One day, Ginny, my neighbor across the street, heard screams and ran down the street to see with horror the man knocking his new wife's head against his driveway pavement. She phoned the police, who came and cited the man for domestic violence, resulting later in a restraining order. The fight was all about their cat.

Soon, the new wife got an annulment, though the man stalked her for a while after that. When the man died, in his mid-90s, Jerry; Ginny, the neighbor who rescued the wife; and I attended the funeral. Before the service we three spoke among ourselves—quietly but candidly about the man.

Then, during the service, everyone in the church—save the children and grandchild and others who had suffered the secret—sang his praises. And the eulogies seemed heartfelt and sincere. He was described as generous and kind, a caring husband, a successful businessman. What a double life...and he got away with it! Every now and then, one reads about how maniacal people have the capacity to compartmentalize their lives, projecting two very different personalities at times. It's difficult to comprehend.

The man's children and grandchildren knew, but they were not going to tell. Jerry, Ginny, and I were certainly not going to tell, either. Others who knew the inside story had moved away or died. Safe at last, though in the grave.

I made pies for Jerry. His coming to pick them up was an occasion for a visit. We sat in the kitchen or on the porch, depending upon the season. In the summer I made blueberry or strawberry pies; in winter, pecan pies. Moore County is peach country, but Jerry did not like peaches. Nor tomatoes. How could a good North Carolina soul not like fresh tomatoes or peaches? Maybe his mama overdosed him as a child! Bless his Heart.

Another untold story there.

After he picked up his pie at my house, Jerry typically bought a quart of milk to go with it. By the end of that day, half the pie and all the milk would be gone. The pie lasted only two days, consumed totally by one person. Yet, Jerry never gained a pound. He worked too hard, cleaning yards all day, raking grass and pine straw, and farming in the off-hours of the evening during summer and on the weekends. And every Sunday found him cleaning up the McDonalds Chapel yard before Sunday services.

What did Jerry McDonald have to do with McDonalds Chapel? Everything! His mother owned many acres of land in the Foxfire area. Before she deeded it to her three sons, she gave some of it to build a church, a small Presbyterian chapel. Jerry, the only son remaining on the farm, cared for the property, served on the Board of Deacons, sang in the choir, and opened and closed the doors every Sunday. He supported well the ministers who kindly and diligently served the small congregation; he helped ease out those who didn't. As with many churches, McDonalds Chapel had its clandestine trysts that brightened local gossip from time to time. Jerry's was the calm voice and steady hand that kept matters in focus and moving forward.

That Christmas, I thought, "Maybe one more pie, at least?" What shall it be? Pecan? I'd gotten a shipment of fresh pecan halves for Christmas. Blueberry? Some good blueberries from Chile are in supermarkets now. No refrigerated crust. Just my own homemade one. Wonder if Jerry still has the pie-plate case? When I made baking pies for Jerry a habit, he worried he would mess them up in putting them on the seat of the truck as he drove home, so he bought a nice hard-plastic container to fit the pie plate exactly. Each time I had a pie for him, he took it home in the round case and, when the next pie was ready, brought back the clean pie plate in the container and we switched out. The empty pie plate for me; the full one for him.

The scorecard was never even: I could make pies all day and still not repay Jerry for his kindness. Well before I saw him face to face, I did business with him. During the year I owned the property on Lake Forest Drive but did not live in the house, Jerry maintained the yard. He sent me a bill once a month, always fair and reasonable. No one ever questioned Jerry's honesty—none of the 30 people for whom he managed lawns; none of the people with whom he worked in the plant before turning to yard maintenance; none of the people who dealt with him as a farmer; none of his neighbors or church members.

JERRY TAKING A BREAK

Once I settled into my routine in Pinehurst, Jerry and his Gang were faithful workers every week, mowing, pruning—I had 75 holly bushes in my yard, to say nothing of all the other shrubs—and raking pine straw was an endless task. Pine straw piled up in the vacant lot next door, so we used it to replace the dull, cracked, broken pine straw bleached by summer sun and heat. Not only that, Jerry came by to check on things and to water my annuals while I was away. He came by to help me get out of the driveway during snowstorms. He brought magnolia leaves, pine boughs, and pinecones for me to use in decorating for Christmas. And he came by just to sit and talk, showing me his *American Cooner* magazines and the champion dogs he admired.

Jerry loved coon hunting and coon dogs. From him I learned that coon hunting and breeding is a popular American sport, not just in the South but in the upper Midwest as well. I had heard of coon hunting when growing up in Weldon but that was all—it sounded like a joke then. I had no idea it was a highly developed sport with detailed, precise rules. However, I learned that competitive dogs sell for $20,000 or more, and stud fees are sometimes in the high four figures. Jerry had hunted when young and bred several competitive dogs, one a Knight Champion. His son, Scott, took up the sport, hunting almost every night. And a tough sport it is—men crashing through forests, stomping bushes, running with heavy gear, and following dogs as they race to "tree" the coon. Points are awarded to each night's winner.

Jerry was a thrifty guy. What would you expect of a Scot? But he spent big money on coon dogs. Every year, he and his son went to South Carolina to a regional dog show and sale. Even though he had given up coon hunting—as well as deer hunting—Jerry decided to breed his champion one more time. On this last effort, the bitch failed to be impregnated successfully by the sire, a sire whose owner's dishonesty led him to refuse to honor his guarantee.

One day, Jerry knocked on my door, "Alice, that guy who owns the male coon dog that I used to sire my bitch just won't live up to his promise. It's not fair and I want to do something about it."

"What can I do to help, Jerry?" I asked.

"Can you write a letter for me to send to him? You are a businesswoman; you know how to use words."

"I would be delighted, Jerry. Just come in and give me the facts, the man's name and his address." I helped Jerry write a letter to the disreputable owner. That and a few calls yielded nothing but empty promises. Jerry was mad enough to sue but felt it would be a waste of time and money.

"I know how you feel, Jerry," I said, trying to console him. "You burn inside when someone takes advantage of you."

Disappointment led to sorrow when his prize bitch, one he had bred, raised, and trained, got lost. Jerry looked and looked all over Foxfire and the countryside. Each day after work, he rode around scouring the neighborhood for her. He grieved for her, downcast and brokenhearted, as if a family member had died. Anyone who has loved a pet understands the helplessness that overwhelms from such a loss. About a month later, Jerry's phone rang one evening. A dog like his had been found miles away on the other side of town. Joy! Joy! Joy! She came home much thinner but running straight into the hands of her loving master.

Jerry lived simply. He had a modest red-brick home on his farm, a pond for fishing, an old Jeep and a little red pickup truck he loved to drive. For his business, he drove a flatbed work truck, holding his yard equipment and the Gang, too, one riding shotgun and the others on the back platform. He dressed in simple work clothes and a baseball cap—always a baseball cap. I brought him new caps from cities and countries I visited. He saved some of them for special occasions.

As he aged, he had some of his front teeth pulled, but refused to spend the money to get a bridge made. I prodded him to take the step, if, for no other reason, than to avoid digestive problems. He finally gave in, but he kept the dentures in his pocket unless he came over to converse or he had to appear in public. Reluctantly, he spent money for good glasses after his eyes needed more than Dollar-Store lenses. He needed those for his work. Yet, he didn't think twice about spending money on dogs and tractors. Only after he retired from yard work did he stop acquiring and taking care of coon dogs. Scott had waited a long time to lay claim to those fine animals.

Tractors were another matter. Jerry continued farming, growing corn for feed, wheat for sale, and hay for local farmers. Since the incident with the cows, he shied away from raising farm animals: no cows, no pigs; nothing four-legged except coon dogs. He didn't garden since he did not like tomatoes and peaches. He was a meat-and-potatoes guy—with pie for dessert. For his birthday, I took him to Outback for a steak and gave him a pie to take home.

The farm had grown smaller as a result of his brothers' selling off their shares. Reluctantly, Jerry even sold one piece of land to a man down the road who needed access to the Pinehurst-Foxfire Road. He felt sorry for the man, I guess, not to be able to exit from his property onto the main road. That man didn't know how lucky he was to persuade Jerry to give up even a small strip of his land.

Jerry kept about 150 acres, including the house and pond. How many tractors are needed to till that size tract?

One or two at most. Jerry has seven! Along with the tractors, he owns every imaginable attachment for sowing and harvesting his crops. Even when all the children and grandchildren are gathered around, there are more tractors in his yard than there are cars.

Family holidays were usually celebrated at Jerry's house because he was the patriarch—and he liked to stay at home. Once or twice a year, in addition to Christmas and holidays, Jerry's house was the site of big family gatherings and reunions. His children and neighbors provided the food. Jerry provided everything else, notably the liquor. Year after year, his guests enjoyed their highballs and toddies but seldom, if ever, did they thank Jerry, much less reimburse him for expenses. Jerry got tired of that, concluded it wasn't quite fair; so, after several years, with no announcement to anyone, Jerry quit furnishing the drinks. No loss for Jerry, because he didn't drink.

He told me that as a young man, he was sometimes pretty wild, enjoying people and parties. One day, attending a football game at N.C. State University, he was partying on the second floor of a building and wanted to reach the ground as fast as he could, so he jumped out of the window. Luck, as is said, protects drunks. He broke no bones, incurred no serious injuries. But Jerry figured one crash was enough. He didn't want to chance another, so he quit drinking. Years later, when his kinfolks didn't seem to appreciate his hospitality and he stopped furnishing the drinks, no one stepped up to the plate to take over. After a while, the reunions stopped! He was still a gracious host, however, opening his house for Christmas and special holidays.

But no more.

I have just located Jerry. He is in Hospice in Carthage, N.C., the county seat of Moore County, northwest of Foxfire and Pinehurst, struggling with multiple illnesses. No wonder he could not talk to me when I called. Late in August, after we had spoken weeks before to wish each other "Happy Birthday," and I had apologized for not having a pie for him that year because of medical problems—he developed a debilitating brain abscess. In rehab from surgery, he seemed to improve enough to go home.

Before Scott could get him home, though, he developed a blood clot in his lung, and then one in the right leg and another in the left. He is conscious much of the time but often incoherent. He cannot walk and his weight has dropped to 135 pounds. I am overcome with sadness and worry.

Not only can I not talk with him, I can't see him. As soon as I heard where he was, I prepared to drive down from Raleigh to Carthage. Scott deterred me by telling me Jerry has a very serious infection. Anyone going into his room must wear protective clothing, covering hands and face. Because of an earlier lung problem of my own, my lungs were too fragile to tempt a powerful virus. I had to stay away.

I'm distressed. My only option is to send a card. Jerry may not comprehend it, but I will send it to Scott anyway.

Maybe he can read the card to Jerry in one of his lucid moments. I want him to know how much I treasure his friendship. I want him to know how much I love him. I want him to know how much I miss him.

I wonder if he can eat pie! I will call Scott. Maybe a pecan pie and some milk. Scott can come over and pick it up, as I am the one who has the plastic container this time.

Late winter 2017

My continuing efforts to get news about Jerry from his son had failed. My cards and calls were not answered. When I never heard from Scott, I had written to the church. Mr. Hartsell, Jerry's friend at church, had responded by calling to inform me of Jerry's worsening condition. The circumstances then were still such that I could not visit. Eventually, I got another call from Mr. Hartsell. A kind gentleman, he knew I would want to know: Jerry died several months ago.

I never made pecan pie that Christmas, but Andrea did serve us each a slice of store-bought pecan pie for dessert. It was sweet enough, not too much salt, but neither made with Karo syrup like mine nor stored in a durable plastic container.

September 2017

Spunk—and Grit!

Ever since she squirmed and wriggled to escape the confines of her stroller so she could climb on the wheels and handlebars, my sister's nickname has been Monkey, or some version thereof. Margaret Ray is her given name—fitting, because she is named for our mother, favors her, and is about her size. But Margaret Ray was too big a name for a pint-sized tot who ducked in and out of everything around her and around everybody in her way.

A friend of Mother's said one day, "She looks like a little monkey scampering around the room, bumping into everybody. I am going to call her 'Monkey Ray,' not Margaret Ray." The term stuck. First it was "Monkey Ray," then "Monkey" when she reached high school, then, when older, just "Monk" to the family and close friends. She begged us not to use the nickname in public, but bad habits seldom die.

Yet, in spite of her nickname—or perhaps because of it—her antics paid off and fame touched her early. She had just entered elementary school when she became the cheerleader mascot of the Weldon athletic teams. She dressed like the rest of the cheerleaders, with big blue and yellow W's on our off-white sweaters. Her off-white pleated skirt was like ours, as were her bobby socks and saddle Oxfords. Our lineup positioned her in front of us, and she performed every routine we did. Spectators from visiting teams came to our side of the field to watch her; townspeople came to see her; the coaches and teams spoiled her. Monk was the *Star* and has ever been so: so tiny, yet like a magnet to those around her.

But, there was another side to her spunk. Eight years younger than I, she set out to embarrass me with my male friends. Extortion was her game. For money, she would tell tales on me. If I was still primping when my date came to the door, Monk invited him into the living room and regaled him with imagined stories about my other boyfriends. Mother and Dad thought it all so innocent that she escaped her mischief with impunity.

They simply laughed, "Monk is just playing, Alice. She doesn't mean any harm." Not to me—she wasn't so darling and "just playing." She didn't need an allowance; her piggy bank filled up from her dastardly deeds. She earned enough quarters to pay for her own Cokes and movies, and even those of a few friends. I was furious but helpless.

In spite of my sister's attempted annihilation of my nascent courtships, there were times I was proud of her, quite proud, in fact. When George went to college, Dad needed someone to show his two horses. Monk was tiny, but a strong rider. Dad decided to let her enter horseshows even though she would be competing with men, and sometimes women, much older and more practiced than she. Just imagine a tiny preteen, shorter than five feet tall, sitting atop a thousand-pound animal in an English saddle, controlling dual reins and leading her horse through his paces. She looked like a Little Women doll sitting astride a toy pony.

Of the Little Women dolls, Monk looked like Jo. She was tiny but shapely, with a flawless oval face, big, limpid, hazel eyes, and a broad, welcoming smile like Mother's. She was clearly the beauty of the family. As she aged, she looked even more like Mother and has continued to be the prettiest person in the room wherever she is.

Viewers at the track could not believe that Dad would let his tiny daughter compete against grown men three or four times her size in a ring of high-strung, gaited American Saddle Breeds.

MARGARET RAY ON LADY KALORAMA

"Mr. Joyner, how can you put that child on top of that big animal?" spectators asked in surprise.

"She'll be okay," Dad responded modestly but confidently. He knew her skill.

When people in the stands saw what she could do, they stood agape, cheered for her, shouting and clapping. She won many ribbons and looked most elegant on two of Dad's favorites, in addition to Lady Kalorama. Little Joe, a bay gelding just barely the 14.2 hands minimum height for a horse, had a perfect stride with sure-footed legs and balance. And Sweet Sensation, a chestnut mare with a striking conformation and movements, held her head high with neck curved—and feet prancing high off the ground. Sweet Sensation epitomized her name. She was a sweet-tempered horse and responded immediately and gracefully to every instruction from Monk. I swelled with pride every time I saw my little sister enter the ring.

Monk spent her adult years in North Carolina, first in Weldon, then in Cary, and finally in the Pinehurst area. During those years, I moved from Greensboro to Princeton, N.J., and Washington, D.C., following my own career path. She started her family when young, and even though her husband, Bob Kinker, was a salesman in a local automobile dealership, she needed to enlarge the family coffers. The farm economy of Weldon, however, with its few thousand residents, offered few employment opportunities for young women, even those with college degrees.

Always prim and pretty in appearance, Monk developed her skills in cosmetology, studying and then working in a beauty parlor. Southern women are always mindful of their appearance, so beauty salons did not lack for customers seeking all kinds of cosmetic services. Those were the "beehive" days of the 1960s, styles with hair piled high on top of the head.

She thrived for a while, but standing on her feet all day and taking care of two children when at home took its toll. For reasons of both income and health, she needed a different avenue for applying her talents. Never one to aim low, Monk studied for a teacher's certificate, then switched her career to teaching, following in Mother's footsteps. She taught at a small private school, the Halifax Academy, preparing students for college.

Just as with Mother's former students who sing her praises even now, twenty-five years after her death, Monk is thanked many times over when she meets up with a former student.

One such student operates a Weldon restaurant, Ralph's, famous for its barbecue and located right off the Interstate 95 ramp. Ever since leaving town to settle elsewhere, Monk and I have always gone to Ralph's Barbecue for lunch when back in Weldon.

"Mrs. Kinker, I am so glad to see you in town," Kim, the third-generation owner, called out one time when we walked through the door.

Turning to me, Kim added, "I can't tell you how much Mrs. Kinker taught me in school! I'll never forget her classes. She was tiny but never let those big boys get out of control."

Both Mother and Monk made life-changing contributions to the lives of numerous Halifax County children, many of whom had grown up on farms, remote from cultural and educational opportunities other than school. It never fails that, every time I go to an event in Weldon or Halifax, one or more of Mother's students walk over to me, introduce themselves, then praise her by saying that she gave them hope, opportunity, and confidence to learn and aim high. Some who never thought of leaving Weldon went to college and became doctors, lawyers, and professors because of Mother's and Monk's tutelage and encouragement.

For years, I saw Monk at holiday times in Weldon—Thanksgiving and Christmas—but when she moved to the Raleigh area and subsequently to Pinehurst, our paths seldom crossed. Those were busy years for each of us and we lived hundreds of miles apart. Monk was busy with family, children, and her work in a Pinehurst bank. I was rearing Andrea, working at Educational Testing Service in Princeton, and traveling around the country for my job. Monk and I were in the same family, but I sometimes felt as if we were generations and continents apart.

Then in May 1999, years later, Bohren Moving's eighteen-wheeler moving van pulled up to my new home in Pinehurst. I was not only entering my new home but the next phase of my life: retirement.

Thanks to my sister, who had introduced me to a capable and persistent real-estate agent, I had found a house on Pinehurst Lake in an architectural style I liked and a pool in the backyard. Seemed like Heaven!

Later that first day, Monk and Kay Beran, the real-estate agent, dropped by to welcome me, though I had nothing to offer except box cutters, nothing to drink except water. We found places to sit on the sofa and the fireplace hearth. Joking about the trials of relocating, unpacking, and getting settled into my new life of retirement, I addressed my sister as "Monk."

She screamed, "Oh, no! You promised, Alice!"

Kay laughed and exclaimed, "So, that's your real name? Been hiding it from us all these years! Just wait, now that I know...."

"Oh, Monk—I mean Margaret—I am so sorry." Calling my sister "Monk" was so ingrained in my mind I'd long forgotten her admonition to call her by her given name.

She had started anew in Pinehurst to build her business using the name Margaret, certain that she had left "Monk" behind. My slip of the tongue was the first that anyone in town knew of her secret. Her colleagues and friends thought of her as a dignified, serious-minded professional banker, not the mischievous practical jokester of her early years.

In spite of my betrayal, she treated me royally, introducing me to her friends and business acquaintances, hosting me in her home, gathering the family together on special occasions. Her son and daughter and their families lived in the area. My brother and his family had moved back to Morehead City, North Carolina, from Maryland, and my daughter and grandson, Andrea and James, were in Apex.

Imagine: our small family—all in one state again. That in itself made retirement to North Carolina worthwhile.

"Ties that bind." My hope was realized: to get all of us within striking distance of each other again.

I assured her that this time, I had no boyfriends for her to keep tabs on. The tables were turned; I was on her territory. What would I do? I could cast a keen eye on her social circle of friends and remind them of her childhood specialty: blackmailing her older sister! Soon I saw, though, that rather than hazing and *my* practical jokes, Monk needed my support. She and her husband, Bob, were in the process of getting a divorce.

Despite that and her busy work schedule, Monk made time for me. We had swimming parties and cookouts around my pool. Good thing the first one was just for family. Using the cover on the hot tub as a counter, I placed the food there in family-size containers and opened the bar. By dessert time, we gathered around to cut the cake, only to find that the icing had melted around the lower rim of the layers, having been heated by the water in the spa. Oh, the folly of a first-time hot-tub owner!

"Hey, Alice," called Karen, my niece, "we don't need a knife. Bring spoons!"

The multi-layer chocolate cake broke into clumps of cake with hot-fudge icing.

"Nana," yelled James, "it's good anyway. I just got a glob of chocolate with my finger. Bring bowls; these plates don't work."

No one cared because the kids were back in the pool momentarily, washing the cake down (or off) as they hit the water in cannonballs, splashing all of us on the deck.

About a week later, Monk's granddaughter wanted to have a pool party with some of her friends to celebrate her graduation from high school.

"Great," I said. "That's what homes like this were designed for." The "Little Easy," I called it. Confident that I knew the ropes by then, I entertained ten young girls with Karen, Monk, and me as chaperones. I even rented a paddle boat from the marina so the youngsters could get out on the lake and paddle around the coastline or just swim out in the lake.

It was hot enough on that June day to curl straight hair. Soon thunderheads gathered in the sky while the sand in the beach area was too hot for bare feet: just the right combination of weather conditions to produce an intense electrical storm that knocked out phone lines and closed roads down to the lake area.

"When is this storm going to end?" asked one distressed young girl as we hovered under the roof of the patio. "How long do we have to stay here in wet bathing suits, getting wet?" said another youngster. Still another exclaimed, "I have to go to the bathroom." Why were they worried about getting wet? They had just come out of the pool!

That started the parade. We retreated to the dry garage where there were yard chairs to provide seats for a few. Once I opened the door to the house, the girls trailed water dripping from wet bathing suits along the hallway leading to the bathrooms. Politely, the girls formed a queue, still dripping. But where were their towels?

As I started to look for them, one girl coming back down the hall called, "Mrs. Irby, there's water dripping from the ceiling in the corner of the dining room."

Before I could assess the situation there, another guest cried from a different area of the house, "Mrs. Irby, there is water coming from the high ceiling in the kitchen." And I ran there, then recalled that my buckets were outside in the room housing the pool equipment.

"Pots. Pans. Get some out of the cabinets, quick," I instructed them. But the teens stopped in their tracks, eyes big and staring at the falling water.

How could this happen? The house had been inspected before I purchased it. According to the inspector's report, the roof was sound. I was shocked and in disarray.

Then, another girl leaving the bathroom at the end of the hall started to call out and I interrupted her, "Oh no. Another leak! I can't deal with another."

"Mrs. Irby, No, not a leak; we need toilet paper. Where is it?" How should I know? I had not unpacked all the boxes from the move. Hastily, I peeled some off from a roll in another bathroom and ran it over to her.

That wasn't the end. When the last parent had worked his car through the tree limbs strewn across the roads and picked up his daughter, the paddle boat was still at the end of my dock. It cost $15 per hour and I didn't want to pay for it to rock in the waves while I slept—or tried to sleep—through the night. Marty, Karen's husband, had arrived and agreed to paddle the mile downstream with me to the marina to turn in the boat.

No one was on the lake. Black clouds still hung low in the sky. The waves on the lake lapped whitecaps. Not a bird or duck in sight. The wind was calm but the air was heavy; Marty and I were cautious and alert. Is this the calm before another storm, I wondered? As we neared the marina, the scene was eerie and desolate, with just one duckling looking for rescue bobbing in the waves with his head barely out of the water.

No one was there. The marina and the hot-dog stand were shut tight. After leaving the paddle boat on the beach where boats were stored, we walked to the gate at the chain-link fence. Locked. *And we were on the inside!*

Karen and Monk had driven their van down to pick us up. Good! *But they were on the outside!*

They started laughing. Marty and I were stuck behind the fence with no chairs or tables or boats—nothing to use in climbing over the fence. Luckily, barbed wire was not rolled on top of the fence. If we could get to the top, we could jump over.

Marty scaled the fence. His upper body was strong. Mine was that of a retired, skinny female. With my small toes and feet inserted in the holes of the fence, I managed to climb to the top, but the drop to the ground on the other side was too steep. Finally, with the help of all three— Marty, Karen, and Monk—I was lifted more or less gently to safety, and we made our way back to the leftover uneaten cake and flat Cokes.

What a baptism of immersion—to begin my retirement. I had come home to enjoy the summer sun, the water, and the sandy soil. It had to get better than a trial by water.

Ever loyal and helpful, my sister came to my rescue often during my early years in Pinehurst. When I was recovering from a hysterectomy in 2001, she made sure I was comfortable with enough food to last a week, having helped me find a woman to stay with me day and night until I could manage by myself.

About ten years later, when I developed shingles in the trigeminal nerve in my head, unable to drive because of heavy doses of strong pain medicine, she drove me where I needed to go. She bought my groceries; she took me to church. Monk even tried out a new car for me, enabling me to get a good price on sale at the end of the calendar year. She drove while I dozed. I understand how people can get hooked. Narcotics soothe anxiety and erase pain, enabling one to exist in a world of euphoria.

Simultaneously, Monk was busy with her own responsibilities. And busy she was! She had opened a mortgage-banking office for Wells Fargo in Southern Pines, purchasing the building herself, painting and furnishing it and hiring staff so she could arrange mortgages for many newcomers to the area as well for current residents. Because she developed a reputation for prompt service, accurate calculations, and careful attention, she was able to go out on her own. She didn't advertise because real-estate agents and their customers came to her; they knew she would treat them fairly. Some of them became lasting friends.

She retired in 2006, looking forward to having time for her children and grandchildren, all of whom were in the Pinehurst area. Several years earlier, she coped with her divorce and subsequent death of her former husband. Since then, she had found companionship with an attractive retired executive who had moved to town. Life was looking up for her. Maybe she had cleared her last fence and could go on to green pastures beside the sea.

Suddenly, she was struck by the Big C—breast cancer. She was frightened; I was devastated because I had suffered the same disease fifteen years earlier. I knew the pain, fear, and anxiety she would experience. She had to have chemo, which for breast-cancer patients is among the most toxic of drug combinations doctors can administer. I wept as I sat by her bed in the hospital when I realized what was in front of her: a double mastectomy, reconstruction, followed by months of chemo. How could she keep up with her business?

Her new partner, Charlie Pulley, cared for her when she was flat on her back. Charlie, a retired medical-equipment executive, became her best friend and caregiver, insisting on helping her every day by getting groceries, feeding her water and soup when she could barely lift her head off the pillow, keeping her bed fresh, washing sheets and clothes, and sitting by her as she slept in case she needed something when she woke up. He did everything for her a fine nurse would do.

One night when he and I were eating a simple supper in her kitchen, Charlie said, "Alice, you know...since I met Margaret, I have been happier than at any time in my life."

"That touches my heart, Charlie. I am so glad you have brought love and pleasure into her life, because only her raw courage kept her going at times," I replied. "And, you know, I'm sure, how important you are to her healing. You are her main source of emotional support."

For Halloween, once she was back on her feet but still void of every strand of hair, she and Charlie went trick-or-treating. Charlie drew a face on the back of Monk's bald head, dressed her in a straight-line red-colored gown, and helped her walk backwards up the sidewalks of houses, approaching them with an empty plastic pumpkin in hand. Talk about spunk!

"Trick or treat!" she said as the doors opened to shocked faces.

"Who *are* you?" residents asked, aghast.

"I am *not* a witch. I *am* the Red Devil, and I'll put a hex on you if you don't put something in my pumpkin."

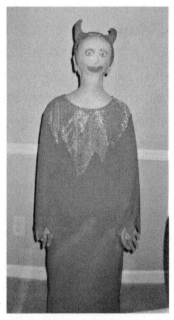

MONK, THE RED DEVIL, IN 2007

Not only did neighbors give her treats, they invited her inside to see who she really was. When they realized it was Monk, they exclaimed, "Oh, how did you do that? You're hilarious."

"It was Charlie," she said. "His idea, his help and humor, and his artwork on the back of my bald head. More fun than a wig—and a lot cooler."

Her spirits, buoyed by Charlie's devotion, humor, and care, brought her back to working and socializing sooner than anyone expected. She wanted to spend time with him and they wanted to take trips abroad as well as here in the U.S., so she told Wells Fargo she was retiring. A group of us, friends and family, had a party for her with all the streamers, balloons, cake, and gifts to send her off to see the world.

They travelled...first to Italy for a month, then to California for a month. But, before their backpacks were broken in, a call came from Wells Fargo asking her to return. She went back to work to help them with the big re-financing craze of 2007 and 2008. Finally, in 2010, she retired for the second time. The sub-prime roller coaster was enough! We had a second party for her, again with balloons, cake, confetti, and gifts.

"Monk," I told her, "happily, I am giving you another gift, but I want to give you fair warning. If you go back to work again, I want the gift back. So don't use it yet."

Judy Worthy seconded my idea, "Alice is right, Margaret. You can't use any of our gifts for six months, not until we are sure you are staying retired."

Kay Beran chimed in, "And stay away from Wells Fargo. We are not going to support a retirement revolving-door!"

MONK IN 2017, FINALLY RETIRED, AND HAPPILY SO

This time retirement stuck. Monk and Charlie resumed their traveling to places she had only read about. Along with their extended trips, she started spending time at Edisto Island in South Carolina. Like me, she thrives on being near a large body of water—and the Atlantic Ocean qualifies! She and Charlie decided to buy a house and move there. Joining a group of Sea Coast volunteers to walk the beach marking nests to protect turtle eggs provided her daily exercise, but more importantly, contributed to the preservation of our environment.

It was her turn to leave me behind. She deserved a new home in a lovely place with a caring companion. Over her full and active life, she has faced many hurdles and cleared many fences, but now, she could start down an open path and anticipate a future with equanimity and calm. I cheered for her.

So we are apart again, though we find ways to join with our brother, George, to travel around North Carolina and Virginia searching for our ancestors' graves, churches, and histories. And occasionally we spend a weekend together, just the three of us—weekends filled with laughter, love, and gratitude for our life together—back home where barbecue is king, church bells still ring, and cicadas sing through the long summer nights.

September 2017

Mary, Mary

Two good friends of mine, Mary Brown and Mary Bowers: One has "gone to another place," and one is cramming for finals, as she might call it. I met one when I retired to Pinehurst. The other I have known since college days. Both are bright and engaging. Both are articulate with a sense of humor. Both are entrepreneurs, and both smoke, with the bad lungs that result.

Mary Brown

Pinehurst is a couples' town, though I did not know that when I retired there. Not by law but by custom, Pinehurst segregates many of its activities: women's golf, women's church groups, and women's book clubs. The friends I came to know through Newcomers and the book club turn into housewives and partners when the clock strikes 5:00 p.m. each day. When the sexes come together for social events, again that means couples. Singles can stay home or go to the symphony, movies, or clubs with friends.

When I moved into my house on Lake Pinehurst in 1999, even my lake association did not permit dates from out of town to attend its Christmas Dance; the social event was for members only. Fortunately, that symbol of discrimination and exclusivity has gone the way of others—to the bottom of the lake.

Mary and Fred Brown ignored these unwritten expectations. They joined other couples for dinners and social events, but they included me in the gatherings they hosted. Often, Mary invited me to dinner with just the two of them, or with other family members or an occasional friend. It never occurred to them to narrow their guest lists to couples only.

Mary and I played golf together, sometimes with Fred and another fellow to make a foursome. Even when it was just the three of us, we had healthy discussions and debates around the dinner table. Mary was an avid, eclectic reader, not limiting herself to just the books of book clubs. A Holyoke grad, she had studied history and was still expanding and deepening her knowledge. We read history together, focusing for a while on numerous books about the Founding Fathers.

I learned much from Mary, who included me in visits of her family. Her daughter, Jenny; son-in-law, Perry; and two grandchildren, Katy and P.J., visited once or twice a year from Detroit. The two families spent part of their summers together at a family cabin in Maine. I witnessed firsthand Mary's unconditional love of P.J., her physically disabled grandson. P.J. could not read well, write, or carry on an easy conversation. In addition to his other disabilities, he evidenced all the attributes of Asperger's, as well as a lack of physical coordination. Even so, P.J. could learn and think clearly and was progressing through school toward graduation.

He had personal tutors for each academic class, then Mary and Fred took up tutoring him in summer, reading history and other subjects to him. They taught him to fish and to enjoy their lake in Maine. They taught him table manners. They remembered to reinforce the care and love P.J. soaked up every day from his mother, father, and sister. In short, he was treated like a regular member of the family, a boy living normally.

"I can hardly wait to get to our cabin in Maine," said Mary, who was ready to leave North Carolina on the first hot day of summer. "Having P.J. with us is such a thrill, especially when we can see that he can handle his studies but also develop marine and camping skills. His being with Fred and me gives his parents in Detroit a month's break as well."

"Don't they join you in August for a family retreat?" I asked.

"Yes," said Mary, "and my brother joins us, too. A happy family time."

One summer, soon after I returned from a trip to Normandy and Bastogne and before they went to Maine, I was having dinner with Mary and Fred and P.J. I was describing some of the sites that had made a lasting impression on me. One American-German encounter in the Battle of the Bulge occurred as the German 1st SS Panzer Division, then running out of gasoline, was trying to break through American lines to reach Antwerp to get fuel. At the Baugnez Crossroads in the Belgian countryside, a monument stands to the 84 American soldiers who were massacred there. Before I could describe fully the site and the massacre, P.J. bellowed, "Malmedy, that was where they were killed. Did you really see the monument?"

"Yes, P.J. I saw the monument with every name on it. You really know your history!" I then went on to finish the story. He knew more World War II history than Mary and I combined!

P.J. went on to graduate from high school, to continue his vocational education, and to hold down a part-time job. Mary and Fred did not live to see all that, but they felt certain that he would achieve his goals. P.J. had all the confidence that powerful love and devotion can give. From the Heavens, I imagine Mary still gives him a lift and a pat on the back when he stumbles.

Mary learned from an oncologist at Duke that she had pulmonary fibrosis, an incurable, hereditary disease of the lungs. Her condition was clearly exacerbated by her smoking well into her retirement. Her brother suffered from the same disease. She lived on oxygen for a while—maybe a year or 18 months. And, she had treatments at Duke. One day upon her return from the hospital, she asked me to drop by. She said, "Alice, I won't be going back there. They have told me my time is limited." She never complained, even when she had to carry an oxygen tank around with her.

In fact, two weeks before she died, Mary entertained all her family, including me, at a series of birthday parties for her daughter, her granddaughter, and herself! Her granddaughter, Berkeley, a talented amateur artist, decorated the house with balloons and streamers. Fred tended bar.

Perry, who grew up in Southwest Louisiana around Abbeville, prepared an authentic Cajun dinner with crab and shrimp—seasoned with Zatarain's spices—and, of course, rice and okra. Like many others from that part of the world, he was an excellent cook.

Katy and Jenny, expert bakers, offered homemade cake and ice cream to accompany birthday wishes sung by all with special effects by the tiny tots. Under the watchful eye of Kylee, Mary's granddaughter, children ran around the house and the yard, playing games with rules known only to them. Mary was celebrating life fully, and I was gladdened by her spirit. For my gifts, I wrote amateurish verse and read a couple of poems at the parties. Along with a gardenia, I penned these lines to take her mind back to an earlier time.

FOR MARY
On her birthday

THE GARDENIA

Its face as arresting as a Madonna,
Its petals as soft as velvet,
Its texture as fragile as fine porcelain,
Its fragrance more intoxicating than
      Chanel.
Remember days of your youth....
      With a blossom in your hair,
      Arm in arm with your beau,
      You were early for the Dance—
      And, ready for
           Romance...Romance...Romance

During her illness when I visited, she always invited me to have a gin, her favorite drink.

"Alice, come have a gin," she said, holding her glass high as if toasting us.

"Mary, it is only 2:00 p.m. If I start drinking this early, I will never make it to dinner." We talked as she sipped.

She thought gin helped with the pain much more than the multiple medicines the doctors had prescribed. When Jenny held Mary's pills in her hand, giving her mother a glass of water to use in swallowing them, Mary chose those she would take and discarded the others, asking all the while for "a gin." I learned later that Jenny and Fred would put just enough gin in a glass of water to make Mary think she was drinking gin. That way, she could have as many as she desired.

Days before she died, she asked me to step into her bedroom. "Alice, I don't have much longer. I know I'm dying."

We talked about friendship, then she said she did not know about eternity. "Some days I believe in an afterlife, some days not. In any event, 'I am going to another place.' We'll see what it's like." She was reconciled and at peace with that image and belief.

I went to see her again on what turned out to be her last day. She was sitting in the living room right after lunch. When I left to pick up the mail at the post office, she told me she was tired and going to take a nap. Before I left, she said, "Let's have a gin." By the time I returned with the mail, we had lost her.

Yet Mary was in charge until her last breath.

Mary Beacom Bowers

Rarely in one's life is there a friendship so deep it does not depend upon frequent communication or visits. Instead, an indescribable common bond and an unspoken shared experience that cannot be erased by time or distance links two friends. My closeness to Mary Bowers is like that although I have no idea what made it that way.

I don't even know exactly how we met. In 1950, the Woman's College (UNCG) had 2,500 students. We think we were both in Miss Alexander's political science course sophomore year, but probably we met first in our freshman year. We were in adjacent dormitories, but we started hanging out with a group from both of our dorms. Mary Lib worked in the dining hall, which took up a lot of her time. I was dating Claud, which took up a lot of my time on the weekends.

Then, during our sophomore year, she and I bonded as we developed our world view and began our political awakening. She was a big-city girl from Winston-Salem and I was a country girl from Weldon. But we both had a lot of country in us: growing up near farmland, close to the land; mothers with similar approaches to child-rearing; and churchgoing parents with high standards. We both liked history and political science. She was better at English than I; I leaned toward the quantitative. We both liked to laugh, though we were known as serious students. We were full of vim, vigor, and an expectation of changing the world!

Together we went to Washington to learn how. In 1954, Warren Ashby, our philosophy professor, took a handful of seniors to D.C. to an institute sponsored by the American Friends Service Committee. Experts spoke about the threats of the Cold War, and domestically, about the threats to free speech by Senator Joseph McCarthy's attacks, among others. Today, I wonder why there are not more defenders standing up for free speech, especially on the campuses.

Current threats to free speech are different than they were in the 1950s and 60s. Then, the threats came from outside the academy. Remember the Speaker Ban Law of the late 1960s? Now, the threat is often from *inside* the academy—unheard of in my time—as well as from without. Then, the university was the bulwark against censorship. Today, in numerous instances, the academy is complicit in quashing free speech, e.g., protesting and cancelling speakers, intimidation of faculty, disinviting commencement speakers. Additionally, serious legislation had been introduced into Congress to restrict the First Amendment. Whether attacks come from the Right or the Left—or from somewhere else—I will always object to actions that threaten to undermine our freedom and liberty.

Three of us, Nancy, Mary, and I, slipped away from the institute seminars and went to the Russian Embassy, asking to speak with someone about Russia's military adventures in Europe and elsewhere. In an elegant, red-carpeted sitting room, a polite attaché gave us the predictable propaganda pitch. Nothing was accomplished, except that we got to see the fancy inside of the Embassy with its long hall of tinted mirrors. Were people watching or filming us from behind what appeared to be typical one-way mirrors? Who knows, photos of us might be deep in Russia's counter-intelligence archives.

The Woman's College stamped us with a sense of purpose—its motto of "Service" permeating all of our career searches to find a way to serve in some small corner of the world. In our own way, each of us became a vagabond, moving from one opportunity to another. In doing so, each of us pursued very different paths.

Nancy, after graduate school at Radcliffe and a stint as governess for a French family in Besançon, France, did end up trying to change the world beyond our borders, spending most of her adult life in Africa working for the American Friends Service Committee.

Twice widowed, Mary turned from teaching English at the college level to become an entrepreneur when she formed, along with two partners, the *Bird Watcher's Digest*, a magazine to educate the general public about birds, their habitats, and behavior.

Newly graduated from WC in 1954, Mary started out with the Red Cross, which was then extremely active in serving U.S. soldiers stationed all over the world. The draft was still in force, and hundreds of new draftees streamed into Fort Jackson every day. Mary was assigned to that army base where she encountered both out-of-school high-school graduates as well as college graduates out in the workplace.

Soon, John Beacom found Mary Elizabeth Alspaugh. At their wedding, I was Mary's Matron of Honor in a simple church service in Jacksonville, South Carolina. The location was determined by John's enrollment in the Army and Mary Lib's job with the Red Cross.

John was a total misfit for the Army. He cataloged its every flaw and shortcoming. All Mary and John could talk about was what they were going to do when he got out of the Army. Once married, the two of them spent most of their time planning graduate study in English—somewhere, anywhere they could pay their way.

They made their way to Kent, Ohio. Once John got his Ph.D., he became a professor in the English Department at Kent State University. Mary supported John during his years of study by working as an editor at an art museum in Akron.

Given her marriage and the arrival of a daughter, she was never able to finish her dissertation for her Ph.D., but completing her coursework enabled her to teach lower-level courses in English at Kent State. They were well established in the community when the shootings at Kent State occurred on May 4, 1970. The killings of four unarmed students shook them to their roots. And the carnage put a lasting, indelible black mark on the community and on local political leaders attempting to protect people and place.

Mary had a daughter, Susanna, the same age as Andrea. We both ended up as single moms: Mary twice from widowhood and I from divorce. While we were far apart geographically and too poor to travel to see each other, we stayed in touch over the years, comparing notes on child-rearing and on good books. Mary always had a good book to recommend, one I had not considered.

Now and then, I visited her in Marietta, Ohio, where she had settled upon the death of her second husband to start a magazine with two of her friends. The husband and wife were to handle the financial side of the business. Mary became the editor of the *The Bird Watcher's Digest*, even though she had no scientific background in ornithology or field-birding experience. But Mary was an excellent editor and fast learner. In time, she not only edited but imagined, wrote, and produced it as well. It was a hit, modeled on *The Reader's Digest*: full of stories about birds and people. Mary became known in birding circles nationally and counted Roger Tory Peterson a friend. He wrote the introduction to her own book about birds, *Stories about Birds and Bird Watchers from Bird Watcher's Digest*, which Athenaeum Books published in 1981.

Bored with small-town Ohio, she thought long and hard about quitting. I remember extended telephone conversations about career, location, and financial possibilities.

"Your partners need you, but they can't keep you in Ohio," I told her repeatedly. "Pick a place you would enjoy, one not so far away you can't get to headquarters several times a year." As with most of us, striking out on your own in middle-age is daunting, and this was in the 1980s when women in business were just finding their way. Mary thought long and hard, and then made her move.

She picked Baltimore; close enough to Washington to visit museums, not too far by train to see her sisters in Philadelphia and New York, yet a real "working" city. Unlike the transitory nature of Washington, Baltimore was a city with roots: a place where she could make her own new friends, discover new game trails, and participate in the artistic and literary life of the community.

Susanna, her daughter, had been out of the nest for years, first in high school at Dana Hall, then at Kenyon College, and then in Washington in an editing job she took temporarily before deciding her own future. In a few years, she wound up in New York City. At that time, I was splitting my time between Princeton and Washington where I headed up the ETS government affairs office. I was able to see Mary much more often than in the past.

To no one's surprise, Mary was a success, not only continuing to edit *The Bird Watcher's Digest* but moving the physical production of the magazine to Baltimore, which added to her already-heavy responsibilities. She even did the physical layout of every page.

In her spare time, which she carved out of her daily routine purposefully, she joined the Walters Art Museum and became a patron of the arts to the extent her modest resources would permit. Living in an historic apartment building in Roland Park not far from Johns Hopkins, she became friends with two other residents, Bill and Frances Muller, former professors at the Woman's College, and served on the building's board of directors.

Her cultural life flourished. I think of Mary as my authentically intellectual friend because she has one of the most fully developed literary minds I have ever observed. She is not only well read, but aware of the social and political forces at work in the world. She thinks critically about societal forces that hamper or encourage individual growth. She also thinks philosophically about the spiritual dimensions of life, and she's attuned to nature, especially to the ways of birds.

Through all of the trials of aging, and she has had many, she has kept her keen sense of humor and her desire to consume as much knowledge as her time on earth will permit.

ALICE AND MARY IN MARY'S BALTIMORE APARTMENT

On occasion, when in her company, her friends and I will hear her break out in song. With her low and sultry, sensual voice, she will laugh and sing a tune from years ago.

"So you met someone who set you back on your heels,
Goody, goody....
Goody goody for her, goody goody for me,
And I hope you're satisfied, you rascal you."

We all join in, and one song leads to another until we are all laughing and reliving our days in college.

Mary Lib is a voracious yet thoughtful consumer of the written word. To this day, she charms anyone who meets her and spends an hour with her. Her broad knowledge, her quick wit, her gracious smile with a twinkle in her clear blue eyes engage even the wariest traveler.

Now, it is eventide for her. She is in extended innings. Until last week, my times with her have been happy times, sometimes with serious overtones, but always pleasant to remember. We took trips together: to Biloxi, Mississippi; to New Orleans with Nancy, our classmate and friend; to Nancy's home in the mountains outside Blowing Rock, N.C.; to the North Carolina shore with Barbara, another classmate at UNCG. That time, we three celebrated our 80th birthdays. Most recently, about two years ago, Barbara, Mary, and I got together in her apartment on Upland Drive, in Baltimore. We lunched together on her sun porch, talking and laughing for hours. What fun, but we also felt a sadness because we sensed it might be our last celebration.

Mary Lib spends her days now in an assisted living facility in Baltimore not far from her apartment. Susanna comes down from New York City about every ten days. Her four sisters visit from time to time. A couple of years ago, when her body continued to fail and she was in the hospital and then in rehab, she talked about not wanting to live, given her inability to remain active. She is bedridden.

"I *hate* 'nursing homes'," she said in every telephone call.

"Me, too," I responded, "but I will most likely end up there as well when I go blind."

I did not plead, but I urged her not to give up. We concluded that as long as the mind is clear and sane, one still has purpose in life. Her body is wracked with illness and disease but Mary's mind is sharp and her sparkle energizes her smile and glance. She treasures her life and closeness with Susanna. An independent woman, Mary acknowledges her growing dependence on Susanna but does not want to be a burden on her.

Andrea and I visited Mary in April 2017. We marveled at her spirit...and her humor. She laughed and said, "This facility is called 'assisted living,' but, really, it ought to be called 'assisted dying.' That's what we're here for."

"You are right, of course, Mary," I replied jokingly.

With a mischievous smile on her face, she told us, "I have exceeded my 'sell-by date' three times." Meaning that Hospice, which expects death within six months of entry, has been caring for her for almost two years!

She jokes with the staff about her surroundings, noting the miniature size of the patient rooms compared with the spacious and empty lobbies. "Turn it all around," she says, "so the patients get bigger rooms and there is less unused space. Nobody sits in that big lobby anyway."

The planners and architects of places like that should listen to Mary. She has a practical sense they lack.

A couple of times while Andrea and I were there, a well-dressed woman walked into the room, using a walker, though she had no idea where she was. That encounter led Mary to comment, "I lament the fact that I have not been able to develop a few friends here. Most occupants have functioning bodies but inactive minds, and I can't converse with them."

While her body is giving way and she is going blind, she is still sharp mentally. "I have a large TV that even with blurred vision I can see, but it can't yet talk back to me," Mary jokes. "You know, my best friends here are, perforce, my caretakers. I like it when they come by to talk, but if they spend too much time here, they can't complete their daily tasks."

She asks about my grandson, James, now in graduate school in Germany studying to be an ornithologist. Mary was instrumental in encouraging him to pursue such a career and actually recommended the university where he did his undergraduate work. Given his interests, I called Mary when he was a high-school junior and asked her advice about college programs.

"There are only two schools I would recommend," she told me, "Cornell and Louisiana State University (LSU)."

"In all my years in higher education, Mary, I have never heard of LSU specializing in ornithology. What's the program?" I asked.

Thanks to Mary, we learned that although LSU has no undergraduate major in ornithology—the major is Biology—its graduate program is outstanding, a leader in the field. And the focus of their research is in the area of James' research interest.

Andrea, James, and I visited LSU during his senior year in high school. He spent the day with the head of the department, several graduate students, and a professor specializing in the DNA of birds. The head of the department showed him their extensive specimen collection in the lab. He had lunch with graduate students. In other words, people there treated him as a serious student—pretty unusual for a prospective freshman. Right there on the spot, James decided to go to LSU.

Andrea told Mary that he found not only birds in Baton Rouge but Samantha, a very able and attractive young woman who turned his head and captured his heart. Now, six years later, he is in Konstanz, Germany, in graduate school.

Samantha is headed to the University of Michigan in an MFA program. That pleased Mary, too, given her background in English composition and literature.

The two young folks are far apart geographically but not so far as to deter James from coming home this summer to help Samantha move from the warm climate of Cajun country in Louisiana to the cold North. Mary was thrilled to think she had set James on his way. She told us of one more young man she had helped. He now has his Ph.D. and is head of a nature conservancy on the coast of Alabama.

Andrea and I stayed for three hours, far too long. We wore her out, and ourselves as well, but Mary said, "I am happy to be worn out. After all, why not? I certainly don't have other plans. Fill up every day!"

We thought about taking a picture of her and of us with her. Then decided "no" because she knows her appearance is not what she would like. We are all vain, no matter what stage of life. Also, a picture of her now would not enhance my recollections and memories of her. I want to remember us both in an earlier times, laughing, even giggling in the street outside the Russian Embassy at having been spied upon, or later having lunch at the harbor in Baltimore after a morning at the Walters.

Either because of her demise, or my own infirmities, I am not likely to see her again. That saddens me. At the same time, I have a very special life to carry around in my memory and in my heart. Mary Lib Bowers has been my best friend.

Just recently, in reading a book by another Woman's College alumna, I read a quote that Emily Herring Wilson, the author of *The Three Graces of Val-Kill* (2017), attributes to Eleanor Roosevelt:

"I think perhaps I would prefer when I am dead to have it said that I had a gift for friendship."

The two Marys had it. I smile, even laugh sometimes, when I think of them, remembering our times together. Images of them restore my soul in my waking hours during the long night. They soothe me in times of stress. They occupy a special corner, deep inside. And they are there to stay.

September 2017

The Heart of an Angel

Having three remarkable women named Mary in my past and present, each of whom has enhanced and changed my life for the better, has been an undeserved blessing. I feel as if I had won the Trifecta at Churchill Downs. The Trifecta—or any horse race—stirs mental images of majestic animals, creatures of beauty, power, strength, courage, endurance, and determination under pressure. This third Mary, petite at 5'1" tall and about the height of a horse's withers, has all those qualities and more. And she is also a *mighty* force for me—and for others, too.

Mary Moseley, with a graduate degree in counseling psychology from N.C. State University, is a specialist in family counseling and the owner of the Lochmere Family Counseling Center. Since 1983, she has served hundreds of people of all ages, occupations, and family circumstances as guide, teacher, coach, and mentor. In her own words, this is what she is about, as stated on her website:

Welcome!

I look forward to our work together as a time of learning and positive growth for you and your family. I have had the pleasure of serving hundreds of adults, children, and families in Wake County since 1983. Being invited to team with those who choose healing or other life changes that promote inner and outer peace is a joy and privilege for me.

Or to put it more simply, as my daughter says, "Mary can help anybody!"

What led this hundred-pound ball of energy, strength, and wisdom to her ministry among us?

At an early age, Mary wanted to heal the distressed. To her caring parents she brought home numerous cats, lame birds, turtles, snakes, and other injured animals to get them well. From the time she was five years old, she wanted to lay hands on the wounded—on anything sick or broken.

Her mother had shown the way by caring for people in her community, including the garbage men or yard men to whom she provided sandwiches or cool drinks of water on a hot day. She was a joyful, loving mother with her own kind of ministry.

Mary's father also led the way with his calm manner and his disciplined reason.

"Now, Mary Agnes," he would say when he got home from work to learn she had been mischievous. "Did your mother give you permission to rummage through her pocketbook?"

"No, Sir," admitted Mary.

"Would you like for someone to go through your things without your permission?" he continued.

"No, Sir," replied Mary.

Never employing physical punishment, always using reason, always grounded in right action, her father let Mary have her say but also held her accountable, often asking, "How are you going to fix this?"

This was also the way her father dealt with his other children, Mary's three sisters and a brother; his colleagues; and his customers. Mary refers to him as an "entertainment entrepreneur," an unusual man in an unusual business. Early in life, he was a professional jockey, and later he was a professional billiards player, at one time the straight man for the famed Willie Mosconi. When he opened his own billiards parlor on Hillsborough Street in Raleigh, his rules were: No Alcohol and No Cussing. In upholding his standards, he was always calm, definitive, but insistent. "You want to leave now, Boys—or change your language and keep playing?"

There was another force at work in molding Mary. It came from inside her—from the very beginning: an open heart with a spiritual core, an ability to release healing and life-sustaining forces within those she served.

Always interested in metaphysics, psychology, and the interface of the mind with behavior and physical well-being, Mary continued her studies, after her degree at N.C. State, with the Family Therapy Institute in Washington, D.C. And she later became Advanced Level Certified in the trauma treatment method developed by Francine Shapiro, called EMDR. This powerful trauma treatment protocol has demonstrated that the mind *can* change its capacity to analyze personal conditions and reach a higher self-knowledge.

Using her training and experience, Mary developed her own model of counseling, one that focuses on non-coercive, non-violent parenting when disciplining their children. She taught parents how to analyze situations so that they did not create conditions of hostility toward their children. She counseled children to think clearly in the context of bonding and connecting with others and how to make smart choices that meet personal needs but don't hurt self or others. For many years she trained others in this model, conducting workshops throughout the state at schools and churches, and in corporate settings. She designed and implemented the first elementary-school guidance program in Wake County.

In one of these workshops Andrea encountered her at the McGregor Creative School where James, about three years old at the time, spent the day while Andrea was working at N.C. State. Parents were invited to a workshop, and Andrea listened to Mary talk about how, with assistance in understanding behavioral patterns and in self-awareness, a single member of a family could bring healing to other family members and change the dynamic of the entire family unit.

As she listened, Andrea thought to herself, "Who is this diminutive lady with the broad smile, dancing eyes, and commanding lyrical voice? Optimism is written all over her face. I can learn from her." That was the beginning of Mary's relationship with our family, now going back twenty-five years.

When we "hurt bad," we turn to Mary. Her insight is penetrating. She goes to the heart of the problem and does not shy away from pointing to destructive or self-defeating behavior. She is no pushover and can make us uncomfortable as she guides us—as her father did her—in a calm, non-threatening way to reason about our negative actions and then turn our thoughts toward positive change. She doesn't waste hours spouting sweet nothings; she is frank about what she sees. Her purpose is not to make us feel good but to *do* good—for ourselves and for those we may harm. And she does not try to predict outcomes but can help us imagine what the results of our changed behavior might be.

Her presence exudes confidence and brings hope. Her caring nature enables her to mobilize her strength, knowledge, and grace to forge safety nets for the distressed, the troubled, and the apparently defeated. She has the skills, methods, and experience to engage the wounded in ways that bring relief, comfort, and inner peace.

Whether it is pain from betrayal, isolation from mistreatment, despair from addiction, smoldering anger from hurt, or a child finding his voice, Mary can enable the children and adults she serves to cope with the dark sides of their existence.

"My heart has always been most open to parenting—whatever the age of the parents and children," she says. "But, in recent years, I have been more focused on adults in marriage difficulty and, for the last four years, engaged in skilled trauma work. We are all eternal, spiritual beings here to serve one another with our unique gifts." Like her mother, Mary serves her community and extends her hand to anyone she can heal or help.

One friend has told me, "Mary saved my life. When I think of Rodin's sculpture of the two vertically placed hands, I see Mary holding up her hand, taking mine, and lifting me up."

From my own perspective, I have found her to be perceptive in understanding circumstances and feelings, analytical in disaggregating problems, extraordinary in solving complex behavioral puzzles, and, unlike anyone I have known, able to help me connect with spiritual forces I have so often neglected in my daily existence.

The word that comes to mind is *grace*. Grace is not earned; it's a gift—bestowed by a friend, a counselor, a parent, the Eternal Spirit. It does for someone what she cannot do for herself and offers kindnesses she does not deserve, hasn't earned, and cannot repay.

Mary is a conduit for God's grace to troubled souls, and her profession is a ministry of service. She creates a deep level of awareness in those she helps and extends a generosity of spirit to embrace those in pain. In the highest sense, she restores torn hearts and mends broken souls.

Again, Andrea has said it best: "Over twenty-five years I have sent many students and friends to Mary and I have *never, ever* seen anyone she could not help. Mary is God's angel on earth."

October 22, 2019

MAGICAL HARMONIES AND CONNECTIONS

Music and Memory: for James

April 21, 2013, wasn't the date of Mother's birthday, but it was close. And though it wasn't a woman's day, in part it turned out that way. As the afternoon in my house unfolded with Chris Watkins at my piano, beautiful sounds recalled from youth took me to a different place. Soon the room was filled with souls both present and past: Andrea, my brother and sister here—and others hovering overhead: my mother; Louise, my piano teacher; my grandmother, a versatile musician; and Genie, my aunt with the lovely contralto voice. These were the important women in my young life.

James, your mom delivered her Christmas present to me that April 21: a piano recital in my home by the organist and choral director of The Village Chapel, Pinehurst—Chris Watkins. I can no longer play; arthritis has taken its toll on my hands. But Andrea gave Chris a list of pieces I had played in my senior high-school recital and a list of hymns, soaring hymns familiar to all who have worshipped at the Weldon Methodist Church. He chose some of those but also other more complicated pieces—above my ability level!—filling the space between those long walls and high ceilings with transcending tones that brought back to me both tears and vivid images stored safely away for years, then forgotten in a sunny corner of my brain: Bach, Haydn, Mozart, and Chopin.

ALICE, CHRIS WATKINS, ANDREA

George and Gwen came from Morehead City. Monk was here. Cecil and Philip accompanied Andrea. Close friends from the church and community numbered about 18 altogether. An engaging master of ceremonies, Chris described the music, and for the lighter pieces, kept us in stitches as he played his own variations on a theme from an exercise he had to perform in a recital as a child himself. No wonder people in the Chapel, both children and adults, enjoy being in his choirs!

Oh, the music, James, as the sounds rang from the Knabe baby grand that my dad had given me for a high-school graduation gift. I imagined Dad sitting in a big chair behind the piano at home in Weldon as I played classical pieces and hymns that he loved. Mother was there reminding me to practice two hours every day and, with pride, enjoying my recitals. Louise Farber, my piano teacher, was pushing down my wrist and curving my fingers to correct my hand position.

"Relax your arm and wrist," she would say over and over. "Feel the pressure in your fingertips, not your elbow."

I saw Granny, seated at the organ, conducting the choir at the Methodist Church. Up in the choir, Bill, Mother's brother, and Genie, her sister, were singing with vigor. I envisioned Josephine Pierce's elaborate Christmas chorales with as many as ninety voices filling the sanctuary of the Methodist Church at Christmas. Music was everywhere in the life of Weldon, and Chris had now brought it all back.

I hummed a few duets that Blanche and I had sung in the choir and at Sunday school. She and I had started our piano lessons with Louise on the same day and wore identical dresses as we performed solos and duets in our recitals. Piano was a main extracurricular activity from the time I started taking lessons at age five until I graduated from high school.

Certainly swimming and hanging out at the community pool were starred on my calendar during the summer, but come September, my hands found the piano keyboard for practice every day. During my high-school years, working on technique and memorizing pieces consumed about two hours each afternoon. I was taken aback when Louise suggested I give a one-person recital for family and friends at the end of my senior year. She had more confidence in me than I did, but I accepted the challenge and poured effort into becoming proficient in a dozen or so classical or semi-classical scores.

The day of the recital—it was held in the spacious music room of Louise's home—I wore a white eyelet full-skirted dress, one that would not cramp my arms and legs. She provided printed programs for the audience and reserved seats for Mother and Daddy.

Once I began to play, the butterflies in my stomach settled down to listen. I announced each piece before I played it, starting with Bach, then Mozart, Chopin, Grieg, Haydn, and on down to Tchaikovsky. Never would Louise consider anything low-brow, or even contemporary, for a recital. That kind of music was left for my leisure time with friends. No point in wasting her time, skill, and Daddy's money on scores that did not advance my proficiency, she thought.

I am sure I made mistakes as I played, but not many. I had worked hard to achieve perfection. And, Louise reassured me, "Nobody will know if you make a mistake; you know the music better than anyone. If you do, just keep playing."

To my surprise and relief, the recital was a success. I thrilled at the compliments and flattery showered on me as the guests enjoyed refreshments. Playing well that day gave me a very real sense of achievement. But, today, many years later, I feel a void—a big zero in my life—because I did not continue to study piano in college and beyond. I know I disappointed both Louise and Mother, though they never let on or pressured me to continue. But now, I realize I have disappointed myself.

Louise, my piano teacher, taught me so much more than the techniques of hand position and loose elbows, and an appreciation of the great classical composers. A Jewish woman of the Reform congregation, she was patient, too, in answering my questions about the anti-Semitism Jews faced in this country and in other parts of the world. She had a sober, unemotional manner of describing the treatment of Jewish families she knew in the Northeast: "Alice, they had to have separate social clubs; were prohibited from visiting ski resorts in the Poconos; and were denied admission to some of the leading colleges and universities."

Until our conversations, I had no idea of the discrimination the Jewish people had suffered throughout the centuries. It did not seem possible because the Jewish community in Weldon was an integral part of our small town and a very important part of our social world. Louise was my mother's best friend and had been my mother's roommate at the Woman's College. All the years Louise taught me to play the piano, she was also preparing me for a world beyond my cocoon. No wonder that I thought of her again this "Music Day."

People listen to music for different reasons: for comfort, for worship, for intellectual stimulation, for dancing and entertainment. Ah, the dancing....

I remember a Friday-night dance as I let the melody of "Some Enchanted Evening" sweep me off my feet in the arms of my date as we glided across the floor of the Community Center in Weldon. I was seventeen. I imagined I was floating across the sky, touching each star lightly as my partner guided me far above the South Pacific. The lyrics and the music transported me into an imaginary and uncertain future, searching for that unforgettable stranger "across a crowded room." In those early days, I was not in love with anyone; I was in love with everyone! And with love itself.

All the boys, just like all the girls, were good dancers. They had to be; they couldn't get dates otherwise. I couldn't pick one dancer over the others except that Jimmy Bridgeman was the smoothest and lightest on his feet. He was tall, thin, not handsome but nice-looking, and ever the gentleman, thanking me at the end of the dance, then continuing to dance with me until someone cut in. Boys knew not to abandon their partners on the dance floor. "Some Enchanted Evening" turned us all into dreamers, certain our futures would be enchanted, too.

Now, like all adults, I admit to innocence lost, but I still thrill at the images of dancing in my bobby socks, loafers, and full skirts at the local Boy Scout hut, or in long gowns with dance cards on my wrist at the Country Club, or in a restaurant with the tables pushed aside and the jukebox blasting. My high-school crowd danced and danced and danced—to Tommy Dorsey's "In The Mood" at the Dunes Club in Virginia Beach; to Artie Shaw's rhythms at the June Germans on the floors of tobacco warehouses in Rocky

Mount; to the Shag—a gentleman's jitterbug—in bare feet on the only dance floor in Nags Head; and jumped into the snake-line to Ray Anthony's beat on the UNC-Chapel Hill campus.

And, ask my few remaining high-school friends. Age has not stopped our toes from tapping to a good beat nor our feet shuffling close to our dance partner's. Not too long ago, several Weldon friends gathered at a local restaurant in Roanoke Rapids. Jimmy Johnson and his daughter, Harriet; Henry, his brother and wife Jenna; and Andrea and I took to the floor in David's. Most customers had left, the owner turned the music up, the tables were pushed aside, and our feet fell into motion doing the Shag—beach music—as we relived our youth for an hour or so.

Now, I listen to music mostly to remember ties that bind us to each other, sounds that transport me into contemplation of my angels, both men and women who have loved and guided me; my God, the Source as some call it; and the majesty of my surroundings. I appreciate my life and the freedom I have enjoyed in making my own way. The revealed beauty, the simplicity, and the complexity of nature's world takes my breath away. Outside on my deck, I have learned to listen to the birds sing every afternoon when the weather is good. Unlike you, James, I cannot identify all of them and don't know their habits. However, I can appreciate fully their struggle to live, their beauty, and the joy they bring to me just by their nature. I have advanced to novice birdwatcher, thanks to your occasional tutoring of me when you are home.

Someday, I will have to leave this comfortable home on Lake Pinehurst, with its Louis Kahn architecture and tall glass windows that give me an expanded view of the lake. My eyes and age won't let me stay here much longer by myself. But today's musical sounds filling the open spaces of my living room and library will raise songs in my psyche for my remaining days. On this special day in April 2013, the music brought it all to the fore. Music filled the air at the touch of Chris's fingers, a day Andrea—your mother, James—made possible, with my siblings gathered around, along with friends who celebrated the day and our lives together.

James, I wish you could have been here. Maybe you were lying on the grass at LSU watching the birds fly overhead, imagining their flight patterns, their habitats, their struggle for survival and, above all, the joy their songs bring to our lives. That's how I picture you.

I am glad you have chosen ornithology for your profession, offering you the chance for an unconventional life. Being half Greek, you may know about Zorba. He has some lessons for us all. If you don't know already, look him up. The man who brought Zorba to life in a novel, Nikos Kazantzakis, was born, lived, and died in Heraklion, on the island of Crete. The book is *Zorba the Greek*, published by Simon & Schuster, in 1952.

I know that your interest is the study of the evolution of birds and its lessons for our species. You are right, James, to focus on scientific inquiry, especially animal behavior, because that research will benefit our living world in the long run. But with your keen sense of hearing and seeing, as well as your appreciation of animals, you are fortunate in your choice of career because the specimens of your inquiry enable you to experience as well the soaring grace of small and large creatures, their extravagant beauty, and the cheerful, grounding music they offer.

Every day, a song sparrow—I call it my *very own* song sparrow—sits on the bush by my pool and serenades me during my swim. When I hear that song, I close out the rest of the world and am peaceful in every way—focused, too, like a scientist, knowing what's at stake in each moment.

I will experience joy vicariously, James, through your discoveries. Your choice of profession will lead to a fruitful, enchanting life. I know you were attracted initially by birds of prey and the miracle of their rapid flight. As you have discovered, though, there is much more than the value of speed. You will have that rare opportunity, experienced by so few, to live your life among a symphony of song in the midst of a rainbow of colors. You will have your dream lab and make a substantial contribution to our understanding of this complex and astounding world—I know you will. Along the way, the symphonies you will hear from the choruses of birds you observe will lead you to heights of awareness yet unknown. Welcome them, my dear grandson!

I love you, James, and am proud of you.

June 2013

Awakened

He's back! That he had been away was my doing, no doubt. But why do we cast aside pleasures, often even forget them? That can be our undoing. Antonín Dvořák and his symphony *From the New World* have been gone from my life for years. Why? Mental laziness on my part? The forgetfulness of age? With a loss of hearing, do I give in to the quiet of silence and listen less to music than in my earlier years?

No—none of the above. I've been too busy trying to be useful. Seduced into a strong sense of obligation to "give back," volunteerism has controlled my schedule, and church or club activities have filled my waking hours with plans and projects. Yet, upon reflection, I am not even sure I've been that useful.

Latent in my musical senses for the past thirty years, Dvořák's second movement, the "Largo," played by the North Carolina Symphony orchestra last night, February 22, 2015, kindled flashbacks to my youth. Scenes from the movie, *The Snake Pit* (1948), crowded my consciousness: Olivia de Havilland distraught, wandering the halls of an insane asylum, not knowing how or why she got there; the awful Nurse Davis who traumatizes her; these scenes are enacted to the soulful music in the "Largo" with Dvořák's original melody of "Going Home."

The score of that film is based on the second movement of his symphony *From the New World*, created after listening to the music of African American composers such as Harry Burleigh, a student at the National Conservatory of Music, in New York City; after reading the poetry of H.W. Longfellow, particularly *The Song of Hiawatha*; and exploring native American music on Dvořák's trip to the Midwest.

In the 1890s, Dvořák had been invited to America to be director of the first conservatory in the United States. Burleigh was a student there, Dvořák having insisted that the student body include minorities. Dvořák believed that Indian folk songs, as well as the spirituals and blues songs of black Americans, made up a unique body of American music. While totally original, the compositions he wrote while here were derived from that music of our people, people whose music he discovered as he explored the dimensions of indigenous cultures of the South and West.

"In the Negro melodies of America I discover all that is needed for a great and noble school of music," Dvořák said. He saw what Americans had not seen, perhaps because they were too close to the material, or because classical concert masters and music critics of that era chose to ignore other-than-European composers. As a result of his discoveries, Dvořák produced orchestral scores demonstrating a variety and blend of songs reflecting the expanse of our continent and the richness of our eclectic heritage.

The Snake Pit is memorable, too, because of the exposure it gave at its première to the dehumanizing treatment of mentally ill patients in traditional asylums. The music turns the subject into much more than a social-political idea, though. It prompts emotions that seep into and haunt one's soul for a lifetime: The idea of being lost and confused yet trying ever to go home. The fear of being entrapped in a labyrinth with no escape, no control over one's will and independence. The feeling of being flooded with a cascade of unraveling emotions of sorrow, yearning, and unremitting despair.

Dvořák's symphony *From the New World* is also far more than a melodic score for a movie classic. It echoes an America at the turn of the twentieth century: a land of robust, boundless energy; frontier cowboys; vigorous expansion; and folk music woven into original melodies, dances, and symphonic displays of the varied traditions of new immigrant groups. Dvořák captured all this in one vital musical melting pot of heart-rending melodies, loud percussive rhythms of Indian (native American) drums and dances, and folk songs embedded in stirring orchestral scores. He forged a controlled explosion of sound that makes one cheer and applaud and shuffle his/her feet as well as experience the longing for home and hearth grounded in spirituals, the longing for comfort and order. Had he known Teddy Roosevelt then, he might have represented TR charging up San Juan Hill in bombastic, kettle-drum 4/4 time for just that high purpose.

Last night's production brought back another memory. Before there was stereo, I had a Fisher record player with very good speakers, housed in a lovely cherry-wood chest on four legs. I had ordered it from New York City—my first mail order—because there was nothing quite like it in Greensboro. I could almost get my head under the front of the chest; so, stretched out on the floor with my head near the speakers, I could imitate the sound effects of stereo. In the dark, lying on my back, I listened to my favorite symphonies, concertos, operas, and big bands of the day. Of these, Dvořák's *New World Symphony* was one of my favorites, capturing images of my country, my people, and what I imagined unfolding in my future, a thoroughly generative state of affairs. As I listened, I contemplated my new life in Greensboro and my own dreams of the years to follow.

Just beginning my career as a college administrator at the Woman's College, I renewed my acquaintance with the Ashbys. Claud and I lived near their home; walking over for a visit and stimulating conversation was appealing and easy. Their doors were always open to friends.

Helen, Warren's wife, was a candidate for a Ph.D. in Child Development but not so busy she couldn't play a constructive role in the community. As Executive Director of the Greensboro YWCA, Helen had been instrumental in merging and integrating the local branch and invited me to join the board. This was in the 1950s, before the civil rights legislation of the 1960s, and being a part of one of the first organizations in Greensboro to integrate fully made it possible for me to try to live my convictions. I marveled at the competence and talent of the women of all races who sat on the board.

Helen was also an artist and musician. She devoted her spacious basement to two large floor looms. She made rugs, wall-hangings, and anything else the looms could produce. Her weavings became well-known locally and regionally and were purchased by individuals and organizations near and far. She was a serious, professional artisan who studied regularly at the Penland School of Craft in N.C.'s Blue Ridge Mountains. Ultimately, with her knees failing from constant motion at the loom, she had to retire from her craft. But she always had an insatiable appetite for art, music, and for reading—even when she became blind and read books-on-tape from the North Carolina Library for the Blind.

Today, one of her weavings hangs majestically on the entry wall of the UNCG library. Two of her small modern pieces—donated by her children—grace the walls of the parlor in Cotten Hall named for my parents, Margaret and William Joyner. She was as lovely as her artwork: flawless skin, silky hair—eventually totally white—and sparkling blue eyes.

HELEN AND ONE OF HER WEAVINGS

An accomplished pianist, she enjoyed playing classical music for her family and friends but was always modest about her talent. She liked Dvořák, too. I am grateful to Mr. Dvořák for bringing her back to me. I won't let him go away again.

On a Saturday in the spring of 2017, Dvořák returned by way of a Carolina Ballet performance. Richard Weiss produced Antonín Dvořák's *Serenade for Strings* ballet with ballerinas in classic, flowing pastel gowns and male dancers in matching leotards. The opening tableau of the dancers, along with the opening chords of the music, focused my eye in wonder as if the stage had replicated a Degas painting. Simply, it was pure artistic beauty in a camera-framed portrait. I was breathless. The subtle mix of stage-set colors, cool and quiet, gave form to the music as did the figures, moving together, then apart, flowing in changing patterns over the stage. At an allegro pace, the music then soared upward as if dancing up a circular staircase into the Heavens, enough to make one light-headed.

Then, the stage, like a pastel Impressionist painting, along with the joy emanating from the fast pace of the strings, brought to mind my friendship with Warren Ashby, professor and dear friend. The Dvořák *Serenade* was one of Warren's favorites. Often it was background music to his reading and studying, and, of course, his writing.

A young Ph.D. graduate of Yale, Warren made his way first to Chapel Hill to teach from 1946-49 and then to the Woman's College, where he chaired the Department of Religion and Philosophy, from 1949-83 except for a year in

Princeton on a Ford Foundation grant and two years in India working with the American Friends Service Committee.

Warren was sensitive but strong in holding to his ideals. He was also compassionate but determined in pursuit of his goals. He was patient but persistent, kind but forceful, warm and wise, and generous with his time and knowledge. He held fast to his convictions, standing firm in the face of opposition. His book on the history of Western Ethics was not just a study in ethics; it was a search for meaning—meaning in community, in the West, and in world cultures.

I remember Warren was always asking questions—a young Socrates—and listening intently to his students and any others with whom he was engaged. I believe he was always searching—not for identity, for he knew who he was; not for his ethical principles, for he had formed those during his boyhood days growing up on the banks of the James River in Newport News, Virginia; but searching for the threads that connect our lives with purpose, in the historical context of ethical foundations.

He was a man engaged in the community of family, classroom, and town, always encouraging conversation and debate. He was a man who anticipated in his writings the national and global disruptions and conflicts we are facing in the twenty-first century. Yet he hoped that out of the spoils of disintegration could come a revitalization of community based on self-knowledge, dignity, courage, and love. He was a powerful force for human rights. Ever the philosopher—but an active and courageous one—his compassionate hand reached far beyond the campus to advocate for truth and fairness. As a friend described him, "He was deep-good."

DR. WARREN ASHBY

When he died, his sister Frances gave me a tape recording of the *Serenade for Strings,* along with a recording of a couple of movements of Beethoven Sonatas that Warren also had liked. I played the tape over and over for years, especially during the long hours of driving up and down the highway from Princeton to Washington and on to Weldon for holidays. The tape is lost to me now—for some unknown reason, it did not make the move to Raleigh.

I remember well when Warren died in October 1985. A few days before, as he was failing, I talked with him briefly by phone. His voice was weak, and I felt then that it might be the last time we would speak. The rare intestinal cancer, having been cut out multiple times, won the battle with Warren's surgeons, and his body could take no more. The cancer grew like spaghetti, wrapping itself around his organs, but Warren was never morose or angry over his condition. He simply went on with life as if he would be around every day.

At his request, I presided at his memorial service, held in the Alumni House at UNCG. Before he became ill for the last time, he had requested that three of his former students, all women, participate in the service: Sally Buckner, a poet at Peace College, and Mary Hill from Winston-Salem served along with me. Warren requested no eulogy; rather, readings of poetry by Sally, readings from his diary by Mary, a George Herbert poem and prayer read by James Allen, piano music by his faculty friend Robert Darnell playing Beethoven and a Brahms "Intermezzo," and brief comments by me, concluding with a poem.

The day before the gathering, at the family home in Greensboro, Helen gave me several of his journals to read, telling me that Warren wanted to share them with me. I spent several hours before the service sitting in his study in UNCG's Jackson Library, looking at pictures of his family, scanning the titles of his books, and reading the pages of his journals. I shed a few tears and said a prayer. As I looked at pictures of him, I could feel his presence there and imagined him quiet with contemplation, anticipating a changed world order, or engaged in a conversation with a student. What a force he was for change and for good on the campus, establishing a residential college that thrives to this day within the university.

What a leavening yet expansive influence Warren had on the lives of so many residents of Greensboro, too, as he worked with McNeill Smith, a well-known lawyer, and others to ensure a smooth transition to integration of schools in Greensboro! I count myself among the multitudes who benefitted time and again from his wisdom. As I sat in his office reading words he had penned by hand, my head spun with a jumble of sensations: of loss and grief, yet equanimity, optimism, and hope, too. His spirit, infused by the harmonies of Dvořák and Beethoven, would continue to enliven campus and city life and be a source of strength for his family.

Such, too, were the last entries in his last journal I read at his service:

"It might be nice to have some refreshments catered so persons present would be encouraged to greet friends and talk as they do at any meaningful and happy time. Do what is right for you. If nothing, fine. If something entirely different, fine. Above all, make it a satisfying happiness. I have been and am."

Along with messages of encouragement and love to his family and friends, Warren's last entry, on September 12, 1985, in the journal he carried with him to the hospital quoted this poem by British poet Ruth Pitter:

FOR SLEEP, OR DEATH
>Cure me with quietness,
>Bless me with peace;
>Comfort my heaviness,
>Stay me with ease.
>Stillness in solitude,
>Send down like dew;
>Mine armor of fortitude
>Piece and make new;
>That when I rise again
>I may shine bright
>As the sky after rain,
>Day after night.

I have memorized this poem-prayer and say it to myself often, day or night. I would like it read at my graveside service.

It was as if Warren's and Helen's souls merged in a mystical dependence, for Helen loved Dvořák's *Serenade*, too. I know from Paul, her son: "...Mother also loved the piece and after Dad died in 1985, she kept a diary of every time she heard [it]. She kept the diary from 1985 until 2005, by which time she had heard it 50 times."

"On each entry," Paul writes, "she would write a brief description of where she was, how she was feeling, or what she was doing. She always felt the occurrences were Dad taking care of, or soothing, her. Ironically, I notice the first three entries, the first in 1985, the other two in 1986, all took place when she was visiting Frances in Washington and

Accokeek. For her first entry, for example, she wrote: 'One night when I was feeling <u>very</u> sad (1985)'."

Paul explains that the entries from 1985-1996 were typed, probably by Allen, Ann, or him, based on notes Helen must have kept about the times she heard the piece.

The remainder, entries 28-50, were handwritten by one of the children. She stopped writing the diary in 2005, because she had gone blind by then. Paul wrote the last three entries for 01/02/05; 06/19/05; and 09/23/05.

"One entry really got to me and spoke to me like Dad and Mother did all my life. Number 26, on the 26th time Mother had heard the music, she wrote: '26. February 5, 1996 10:15 PM on NPR, *Music Through the Night* which I seldom listen to. Everything OK. So set me to thinking: Are these occurrences for my comfort alone? Or is something required of me? Some response? Some effort?'[This was the] quintessential Helen and Warren Ashby way of thinking, of dealing with life, I do believe," Paul concludes.

Frances Wright, Warren's sister, and I stayed in touch after we returned to Washington. She lived on a five-acre plot of land in a conservancy down on the Potomac in Accokeek, Maryland. When the trees were bare in winter, she could walk down to the river and look across to Mount Vernon. Frances was a professional musician with two baby-grand pianos in her living room. She and friends gave concerts for small audiences. Before her husband, Jack, a research scientist with the Naval Research Lab, and her daughter, Marion, were killed in an automobile accident, Frances and Jack held neighborhood dinner parties with square dancing and live music groups in their living room—

which had a tile floor made for dancing and a dominant stone fireplace on the room's left side. The house was designed for music and dancing.

WARREN AND HELEN'S CHILDREN: PAUL (LEFT), ANN (2ND RIGHT), ALLEN (RIGHT) WITH ALICE (2ND LEFT) IN THE JOYNER PARLOR WITH HELEN'S WEAVINGS ON THE WALL—NOT SHOWN.

Frances and I enjoyed going to art galleries—the Phillips being our favorite—and to the Kennedy Center for music concerts. On holidays such as July 4, she came over to my house and we walked to the Mall to hear the National Symphony play as part of the celebration and fireworks display. A young female violinist in the Symphony lived in Frances' guest cottage. We subscribed to performances at Arena Stage, located on the same street as my townhouse. We even chased culture to London as part of a trip to a Dorchester farm to visit her former neighbor.

A couple of times a year, Helen visited Frances; they entertained each other as well as friends by playing two-piano pieces on Frances' two baby-grands. On Saturdays, they joined me in the City for dinner, and off we went down the street to Arena Stage for the play of the month. A favorite daytime spot for us was the café in the East Wing of the National Art Museum—after viewing and discussing current exhibits, of course. Not wasting a minute, Helen saturated her schedule when in town with one art show or music event after another.

Now, Warren, Frances, and Helen are gone far from my earthly life—Warren died in 1985, Frances in 2011, and Helen at the age of 99 in 2014, but I feel their presence around me as I did at the ballet. I have not lost them; I just can't touch them. Their joy in beauty—whatever its form—and their optimism about life still fills halls of music, rooms of students, offices of scholars, and the cozy reading and listening corner of my home. I remember them thus:

> From school days at WC in the '50s
> To museum days in DC in the '80s
> Helen and Warren were present to listen and guide.
>
> From the late '80s to the '90s at Accokeek,
> Arena, and around town
> Frances and Helen made word and song abound.

In perpetuity their legacy fashions the future.
The Ashby Residential College came true
And for generations a door opened to adventure.

First Warren, then Frances, now Helen.
Adieu,
With thanks for more than a half-century
Of profound bonds of friendship, love and joy.

Dvořák connected the melodic strings of memory again on September 15, 2017, in a concert at Raleigh's Meymandi Hall when the UNCG School of Music performed an extraordinary "Collage: Atlantic Crossings" of music and musical adaptations from countries in the Atlantic World. An institute at UNCG, Atlantic World Research Network, directed by Christopher Hodgkins, an English Professor, a George Herbert scholar, and friend of mine, had hosted a conference earlier in September, titled "Collision, Fusion, Revision," that examined and commented upon works of literature, art, and music that reflect peoples, cultures, and ecologies of the Atlantic Rim.

Last night, one of the pieces performed was "Allegro con Fuoco" from Dvořák's Symphony No. 9 in E minor, Op 95. *From the New World.* There it was again—that grand, open, generous work that has meant much to me.

Through his compositions, Dvořák links the strands of my life with friends present as well as those resting in my heart. His symphonic melodies, his cello concertos, his serenades—together they weave, as Helen did with her exquisite artistry, patterns of common experience, longing, and passion that bind people together. His themes insert themselves into my consciousness in unexpected moments with tones that swell my senses with overwhelming wonder and make me aware of the undying bonds of friendship threaded through my history and into my twilight age.

September 2017
revised September 2019

A Big Part of Me

I gave a big part of me away today. I am sad, even grieving, but I know it was the right thing to do. My most prized possession, carrying memories of my dad and his generosity and love of music, has been with me for 67 years—never out of my house. Never stored. Never lent out. Never anywhere but near me in my home. Even when I rented small apartments, my piano went with me. Any place I lived, whether rented or owned, had to be spacious enough to house my Knabe baby grand.

My eyes moisten with tears as I think back. Until the deed was done, I didn't give it much thought. Then, the impact of the loss hit me. I had considered all ramifications, been decisive, and had taken action immediately to give the piano to my niece, Meg, and her family. Now I'm not regretful but simply sobered by the fact that I will no longer have the Little Knabe with me.

It is the right decision, and I know it. It's time for the next generation to enjoy the piano, and this is the right time to make the change. I want to inspire Riley Belle, Meg's oldest daughter, to develop her talent for the piano. Right now, she has only an electronic keyboard, but she needs to learn to command and appreciate a mechanical keyboard with a solid touch. The Knabe has a keyboard on which her small fingers can learn to be strong, and her hands can develop an appropriate position for playing scales, runs, and chords. The pedals are not too hard or too soft—she will be able to manage them. And the strings will fill their house with the sounds of angels. What a perfect treasure, I hope, for Meg and Michael's family.

When the flood of memories passes, I realize that it is better to make the gift now rather than later. Riley Belle needs to start out on a good instrument so that she can come to feel one with the piano. When she learns to use it, she will cherish it for many years. It will become her friend—in good times and bad. My dream is for her to enjoy playing the Little Knabe as much as I have over the many years of my life. If she enjoys this heritage piece even half as much as I, she will bring pleasure to herself and happiness to her siblings, parents, and grandparents. She will fulfill the wish of my dad: to fill the halls of a family home with music and pleasure. She will add to the memories stored in its strings and keys. The Little Knabe, my treasure, will keep on giving.

Of course, that is what pianos do: they are useful, they generate beautiful sounds, they transform the moods of listeners, and they infuse students' minds with dreams. Increasingly, I could not enjoy those benefits because my hands cramped with arthritis every time I tried to play, whether for my own pleasure or to entertain others in my family—especially by playing hymns at Christmastime for a sing-along. The keys have remained silent for a year. Every time I saw the Little Knabe sitting alone in the corner of my apartment, I grew sad. And, my heart skipped a beat when I gazed ahead to a time I was no longer around to protect it. That time has come.

How did it happen that I owned a fine piano, one that has been the source of my passion and my comfort since high-school days? Pedal back to 1938. Blanche and I, each six years old, started piano lessons with Louise Farber, my mother's best friend and college roommate. Even though it was in the middle of the Depression, our mothers decided music must be an important part of our education.

"Margaret," Sue Selden said when she called on the telephone, "I want Blanche to take piano lessons and I understand that Louise Farber is beginning to accept students. Do you know anything about her plans?"

"Sue," replied Mother, "that's correct. I want Alice to take lessons from her as well, even though it will stretch our budget."

"Will you talk to Louise about it?" Sue continued. "You are a friend of hers."

That was how a new world opened up to me. Until my senior year in high school, I played on an old but substantial upright with a moderately-hard keyboard housed in a black-carved wooden cabinet. It was the instrument my mother and my grandmother had used; so, it was good enough for me, too, even though I played on Louise's grand piano when taking lessons. The sound on the upright was adequate, certainly for a young student, but nothing like that of a baby grand. We often played ragtime on it, pretending we were performing in a speakeasy during Prohibition.

I remember everything about the day I got the Knabe: the drive to Richmond, the sunny fall day, the Artur Rubinstein concert we went to hear, and the store where Daddy took Mother and me. After lunch at Miller & Rhoads, Daddy said, "Margaret, I want you and Alice to walk down the street with me to a music store. I have a customer who is interested in a piano, and I told him I would investigate this company up here in Richmond."

"Do we have time before we go to the Mosque Theater for the concert?" I asked, wanting to be sure to be on time. The Mosque—now the Altria—was an elaborate art-deco concert hall about a mile from downtown. It was not unusual for us to drive up to Richmond for concerts. Daddy and Mother had taken me there to see Toscanini conduct the New York Philharmonic on his last tour. Only now do I appreciate fully what sacrifices they made so that I could listen to fine music and observe famous musicians close up.

"It won't take me long. I called the salesman before I left Weldon," Daddy responded.

When we entered the store, the salesman greeted us as if he had been expecting us.

"Well, Young Lady, would you like to try out one or two of the pianos for your father?"

I was reluctant to do so. Actually, I was shy about playing openly in a store.

"Alice, it's okay. I want you to try out several because, you see, this is for you. It is your graduation present," said Dad. "I want you to have the one you like."

I was thunderstruck! I didn't know what to say or do. The salesman showed me two or three in Dad's price range: a Baldwin and a couple of Knabes. I tried them out, choosing to play two Chopin preludes that I knew from memory. That seemed fitting because we were going to hear Rubinstein give an all-Chopin concert.

When I played the piano I later chose, the salesman complimented me—flattery never hurts a sale!

"Miss Joyner, you have strong fingers and good hand position that give the music a balanced sound. I like your interpretation of the prelude. Congratulations," the salesman smiled.

Clearly, it was meant to be. My hands, and the touch of the keys—firm but not really hard—went together. Sound rang through the store—clear and vibrant. My hands were small but my fingers were strong and my thumbs worked in proper position. I couldn't decide whether to cry or faint, but I simply gave my father a huge hug, whispering many thank-you's in his ear. Mother was smiling, satisfied that the surprise worked.

The piano soon appeared at our front door. How exciting for me, standing at the door, watching the men unload it and set it up in our front foyer. It looked *grand*, perfectly suited to that space, and the sound filled the entry hall, the living room, and the stairway into the second floor. I had never heard sound like that in our house. As a result, practicing for my senior recital was easy, even welcomed. Two hours a day seemed like fifteen minutes.

Friends came by to sing and play. Blanche had not continued her lessons, but she was gifted in that she played "by ear." Because of that skill, she was the accompanist when our group, both boys and girls, gathered every Sunday to sing.

Often I played for my own enjoyment. I also played when I was upset because playing calmed me—took me to another place. It was easy for me to memorize music, which meant that I could play without searching for music books all the time. Sometimes, Daddy slipped quietly behind me and sat in a comfortable chair about three feet from the bench and keyboard, listening to me play. Only when I looked around did I realize he was there. I practiced Bach and Mozart a lot; the finger work was intricate. Dad didn't mind my mistakes and repeats.

I played hymns from the Weldon Methodist Church hymnbook that he loved. Methodist hymns are, without doubt, the best hymns in all of Christendom. That's because the Methodists had Charles Wesley. To this day, Dad's favorite, "How Great Thou Art," brings to mind memories of the fullness of his life and serenity of his death. I played that hymn whenever he requested it. The last time the hymn was played for him was at his funeral when a church full of mourners, with strong voices, sang every stanza.

The Knabe got me through rough times. When dealing with my separation and divorce in Greensboro, I spent hours playing the piano in the evenings. Most of the time, I played from memory. Sometimes I used sheet music of contemporary songs, occasionally jazz. I liked Errol Garner, as well as Dave Brubeck.

Burdened by my first big failure—one I admitted at least—and anxious about my rudderless future, I found refuge each day among my associates at the Woman's College where I served as Director of Admissions. They provided intellectual stimulation when I needed to focus on something other than my personal sorrow and mistakes. But, what sustained me through months of sadness and defeat were touching and hugging a happy daughter when I got home each day, and the transcendent sounds of the Little Knabe's keys every night as I played until I was spent. Andrea and the piano revived my spirit. I determined to endure.

Doubt about my future, and my ability to provide for Andrea, persisted. A couplet from Thomas Gray's *Elegy Written in a Country Churchyard* that I learned in college kept inserting itself into my consciousness and clouded my confidence.

"Full many a gem of purest ray serene.
The dark unfathomed depths of ocean bear:
Full many a flow'r is born to blush unseen,
And waste its sweetness on the desert air."

Was that my future?

My hopes rose when I was offered the job at ETS. Andrea and I packed up, left Greensboro in 1962, and settled in Princeton, New Jersey, with piano in tow. Housed in a spacious rental duplex for a couple of years, we had a living room big enough for the piano, and ample space for Andrea to run and dance. I started piano lessons again and even participated in a recital.

But work at ETS, caring for Andrea, and maintaining a home did not allow two hours a day for practice. I could not keep up. That did not stop the music, however. Between dinner and Andrea's bedtime, I accompanied her on the piano as she ran around the living room playing and dancing. Dancing turned out to be her love. She started ballet lessons shortly after starting school and continued through high school. Without doubt, her early-age choreography was central to her success in the dance company!

When she was five, I was able to build a house near the center of town on one of the last quarter-acre lots in Princeton, and Andrea could walk to the neighborhood school. Loretta DeWitt, a colleague at ETS who knew my situation, suggested that I contact her husband, Bob, the foreman of a housing development, about building a house I could afford on a tract of small, centrally located lots.

"Bob, I would really like to have a home on one of your lots. They are small enough for me to maintain and located close to schools so that Andrea can walk each way every day. But I am a single mom and can't afford to build a home as large as the others," I explained when I met him.

"The lots are too valuable to put small houses on them. Let me talk to the developer and see if there is something we can do," he replied.

"How nice," I thought. "He didn't reject the idea out of hand, and I know he could sell the property to an affluent prospect."

"Alice, I talked to the builder and he thinks we can build the shell of a three-story home—which the others are—finish the main floor, put electrical and plumbing in the second floor and basement living areas, and put fireplaces on the main and basement floors. Then you can have heat, lights, and plumbing so your daughter can have a playroom in the basement until you can afford to finish it. We can add a laundry and build the garage so you enter into the basement level."

"That sounds ideal, Bob. I can't thank you enough for your consideration and help," I said. "What's next?"

"The lot we suggest is the one on the hill at the end of the cul-de-sac where traffic will be minimal. You will need a set of plans and a mortgage. We have an architect who has worked with us, if you would like to use him."

The architect was perfect for me—he adapted some plans of a Cape Cod to accommodate three floors, including a garage and my needs for Andrea. The Nassau Savings and Loan mortgage broker, after checking with ETS and my bank, was willing to take a chance on me.

Those acts of kindness and consideration I can never repay; they provided critical support for my well-being and security. Those three people—all men—did not have to extend a helping hand to a young, unknown single mom with little credit history when mores and laws didn't require it. Their confidence in me gave me assurance that I could provide a good home for Andrea and that I could hold my own as a woman of independent means.

Number 42 Turner Court became my home for 35 years, and Andrea's until she settled in Washington, D.C. The piano was front and center in the living room. For several years, graduate students lived with us to provide care for Andrea after school until I got home. Some of them enjoyed playing the piano—one young man, Ed Beasley, in particular. He was getting a Master of Arts in teaching and was preparing to teach middle-school kids. Andrea gave him practice; she was a seventh grader then. They got along well, and Sally, the breadwinner of the couple, was kind and helpful.

Andrea took piano lessons for a while but soon turned to the violin, the piano being too lonely a pursuit. She preferred being among friends, playing in an orchestra. In our early years in Princeton, we continued our evening performances: I played the piano while Andrea danced around the living and dining room. Sometimes we ended up lying together on the floor in front of the fire, just the two of us—quiet times of affection and love.

Next stop: Washington, D.C. In 1978, my piano traveled with me to a small apartment I rented until I could find a place to buy. Andrea spent her senior year in a converted upstairs apartment in our house in Princeton and then went to the University of Virginia as a freshman in 1979. By that time, I had found a townhouse down the street at 701 Sixth Street, S.W. It needed lots of renovation, but the living room was in good enough shape to house the piano, a necessary attribute of any purchase I would consider.

The piano was the center of family gatherings in our townhouse. The house was large enough to accommodate my mother, father, and Genie, my aunt, when they visited from North Carolina. George, my brother, and Gwen, his wife, lived forty-five minutes away in Bowie, Maryland, with their two girls, Jennifer and Meg. Frank and Pauline lived in Foggy Bottom, near The Kennedy Center. Andrea came home from the University of Virginia for holidays. Birthdays, Christmas, graduations, even wedding parties, were celebrated in our townhouse or sometimes at George's. Always, the piano was the center of family singing. Genie's beautiful contralto voice rang out, as did the young girls'.

Each year, the entire family were Frank's guests at the Christmas concert of the Washington Performing Arts Society at The Kennedy Center. The organ, the piano, the singers, and the orchestra combined to soar in a *frisson* of delight celebrating the spirit of the season. What could be better than having my family together, the townhouse filled with decorations, and the Little Knabe's keys dancing with all of us singing Christmas carols after dinner? We were all together, except for Margaret Ray who always had to stay in North Carolina with her family.

In the years on either side of 1990, my world started spinning like a top. Maybe "implode" is a better word, for lives crumbled. In Weldon, Genie had a second or third stroke and lost her memory. Ellen, her daughter, took her to Alabama to live her last days with her grandchildren. I developed breast cancer, which altered forever my attitude about life and mortality. My father entered a nursing home at age 89, after he was hospitalized several times because of falls. He was diagnosed with Parkinson's disease. Mother was devastated, so much so that she could not sign the admissions papers to the home without my steadying her hand. He died about two years later. A few months after Dad died, Andrea gave birth to James, which was the one bright event amid successive sorrows. Then, blow of all blows, Mother died unexpectedly in December 1991 from pneumonia contracted in the hospital following carotid-artery surgery.

The piano went silent. My hands froze. Turmoil filled my days, as if I was ricocheting off one wall and then another.

I drove up and down the East Coast from Princeton to Weldon to meet George and Monk to handle family matters, all the while trying to perform adequately in a job that required traveling around the country. Some days, I didn't know where I was when I woke up—"What city today?" I do remember waking up sad, weak in the pit of my stomach, or heartbroken almost every day.

The cohesion, the glue that held the family together, Mother and Dad and the home place in Weldon, no longer cemented our lives. Our center caved. George and Gwen began plans to retire from Maryland to the North Carolina coast. Frank lost Pauline and became seriously depressed. Andrea, by then a single mom, worked at American University in Washington, D.C., while trying to be a good mother to James, her baby son. I commuted from D.C. to Princeton and back every week.

Family were scattered. Gatherings ceased. The piano remained in my Washington living room—silent, its keys still. In time, I began to stretch my fingers over the keys. I played a hymn or two that Mother and Dad had liked. It brought their spirits close to me. I opened the music books containing scores of my high-school recital pieces. My fingers were not flexible enough to play Bach, so I tried something else, with more chords than runs. Even playing badly brought calm and solace. Through my fingers, the Knabe was bringing my life back.

When I retired, the Knabe made the trip to Pinehurst with me and remained the featured item in my living room for 16 years until I moved to Raleigh. It was the center again, this time of the concert Andrea planned with Chris

Watkins when she invited friends to join with family and to gather in my living room for an afternoon of music. It was Andrea's Christmas present to me. What a present! Andrea presided, introducing Chris and giving background about her gift and how she'd arranged it. Chris made the Little Knabe burst once more with song and heavenly sounds, as I recounted in my letter to James, who could not be with us.

The Knabe is not just a big part of me. It strums the strings of my heart. It stores in its keys and cabinet many secrets, events, and emotions—entire parts of my life over my 83 years. It activates the fountainhead of my feelings, the spirit of the Eternal as I experience it, and things unremembered but felt.

I am losing my mind's filing cabinet. It contains my thinking—in this case, my finger memory and scores of music, my schedule of days and practices, my plans for my recital, the Christmas songs for family sing-a-longs, the pieces I played for Andrea when she danced, and much more. After the Knabe leaves my apartment, I must rely on sensory memory: sounds from the stereo; fingers tapping on a table; feet striking a beat on the floor. I can no longer turn to the boxes of sheet music or the piano bench full of exercises to spark my pleasure. Bravely, I tell myself that nothing is really lost. I will visit Riley Belle and her family to touch and hear the Little Knabe again. And from afar, I will imagine Riley Belle creating her own stories and memories. The Little Knabe is ready to shape another life, to preserve the dreams and ambitions of another child and family.

RILEY BELLE AT THE KNABE WHEN IT ARRIVED AT HER HOME

Grieving a loss is natural if one has loved. My grief over the loss of my Little Knabe reflects my love for my father and mother and the life we children had in my grandmother's big, rambling house in Weldon. There could have been no better place to grow up, no more beautiful church to attend—the neo-Gothic Weldon Methodist Church with its lovely stained-glass windows, and no better community of families to support young children. There could have been no better siblings than my brother, George, and my sister, Margaret Ray. And, later, no better daughter, Andrea, and grandson, James, who loved running around the home's big halls. In a real sense, my tears of grief are tears of joy for the strong bond I still feel with my family and the spirits of my parents, Margaret and William Joyner, and my grandmother, Alice Hudson. I love them all and the Little Knabe too.

July 15, 2019

The Sound of Music

Sequel to "A Big Part of Me"

Laissez les bons temps rouler!
 August 3, 2016, will be a day of transition and celebration. Meg and Michael will bring their children to my house: Riley Belle, Zoe, Henry, and Ruby. Jennifer will bring Jack and Drew. Karen may bring her grandchildren. Children will outnumber adults—by design. Isn't that the way it should be? Andrea, George, and Gwen will watch! But the Little Knabe will be the center of attention at our party.
 My sadness over the loss of the Knabe has grown into excitement and joy at the thought of Riley Belle, and perhaps others, learning to play the piano that has meant so much to me. The Knabe has been the storehouse of my joy, comfort, and strength. And now, it is fitting that it pass from one generation to another—from my dad to me, from me to the next generation, and on.
 Yesterday, a Polish man, Christopher Lech, tuned the piano. He told me he escaped Communist Poland to come to America. He now has his own business: tuning pianos; performing; and teaching piano to young people.
 His story makes me cheer. I asked him about his experience here in the United States.

"I am very happy here, and I can't understand why others don't appreciate America," he said. "But, there is one thing that puzzles me."

"What is that?" I asked.

"I am totally confused by the health-care system. I can't make sense out of the bills I get, and I never know what anything costs."

"Well, join the club! I can't help you there," I said. "We all feel the same way."

After tuning the piano, Mr. Lech reported that the Knabe should stay in tune for a couple of years. I hadn't told him that it had to travel to another home.

"Given that," he said, "it should be tuned in six months to a year and before too many years, some of the cushions will need to be replaced so that the touch on the keyboard is consistent throughout."

Keeping the piano in good shape will be important if Riley Belle, or other family members, become serious students and invite guests to the house for recitals. Maybe one or more of the children will dream such a dream, which would make my dad and me very happy...and make the Little Knabe sing!

Chris Watkins and I went to dinner the other night when he came to Raleigh to plan the music for the party. He will be helping me. We both got excited about growing up playing the piano, remembering the way we learned to play: practicing scales, scales, scales until our fingers were numb. Drumming on the table top in the restaurant we played trills, chords and arpeggios with our fingers, pretending we were doing our daily practices.

"Chris, I'd like you to perform for a few minutes at the beginning, playing pieces that demonstrate the capability and power of the Knabe," I said. "The children, I'm sure, will be charmed."

He also agreed to coach Riley Belle about ways to position her hands, practice her scales, and perform for her family. He is a musician who inspires and loves children, but he is also a performer who will enjoy having an audience. I remember well the concert Chris gave in 2013 in my living room in Pinehurst on the same Little Knabe.

We will listen. We will sing. We will eat. The walls of my small apartment will reverberate with sound, maybe even some noise. Fifteen vivacious people in an 1,800-square-foot apartment! I have warned the neighbors: either come and join in, or have appointments elsewhere.

Andrea will bring the lunch, along with decorations. She is practiced at putting on parties for children. When she lived in Apex, she was the Pied Piper of the neighborhood, with every child following her everywhere to be sure they joined in the next surprise.

"Mom, I will spread out Roly-Poly sandwiches, sodas, and cookies on the balcony. Do you suppose the children can wait until the recital is over? Maybe I should hold back on the cookies...," she wondered.

"We'll see," I said. "Don't fret. Chris will adjust as necessary."

They held out until the recital was over but couldn't resist digging into the sandwiches before the sing-a-long. Henry got his sandwich with smooth-creamy peanut butter. Ruby got her apple juice. The others grabbed Roly-Poly sandwiches and all the drinks Meg had identified as their favorites. Cookies topped off the lunch, which meant they were wired with sugar and would stay awake.

The day of the celebration, clear skies brightened the walls of my apartment, sun shining benevolently on the Little Knabe in the den as Andrea and I hosted the Quinn and Joyner families. Who could better welcome a special piano into a family than four cherubs and two teenagers—Drew, 15; Jack, 13; Riley Belle, 11; Zoe, 9; Henry, 7; and Ruby, 4? The piano was older than all six together: 68 years compared with their total of 59 years. Who cares about the age of the piano when the sounds from the strings are still pure? Who cares about age when the notes of hymns are closeted in the keys, waiting to be discovered by young fingers? Who cares about age when the ivories are waiting for small hands to touch, gain courage, and press them? Who cares that the children's feet cannot yet reach the pedals?

Touching and pressing those keys is exactly what Chris did as he demonstrated to Riley Belle the workings of the Knabe, showing her how to position her fingers and depress the keys.

"No banging allowed!" Chris announced so the all the children could hear. "Doing that is like spanking the piano, hurting it. Instead, the touch should be more like tickling its ribs, making it sound with bell-like laughter!" He tickled himself to demonstrate the touch. The children laughed.

With the big top of the piano propped up so that the Knabe's sounds soared to the garden outside, Chris led us all—adults included—in songs of *celebration and commencement…*

Celebration because many of our family were together.

Celebration because the piano is a special treasure, spanning generations.

Celebration because Meg and Michael and their children and grandchildren can enjoy it and learn from it over their own lifetimes.

And...

Commencement because it is a new life for the Little Knabe.

Commencement because it is a new adventure for Riley Belle.

Commencement because it is a new center of family life for the Quinns.

Just a few weeks earlier, Riley Belle had started piano camp. She had learned enough so that she and Chris could play a duet. She also learned from him how to care for the Knabe and when to give it a tune-up—about a year hence. She sat in awe on a small stool facing the keyboard as he played compositions she would hope to play one day. She wanted to observe how his hands moved over the keys. The other children gathered around to watch the keys make the cushions bounce up and down on the strings and to watch Chris's hands strike the white and black keys in rapid-fire fashion.

On this day, family pleasure—the spark of life—included the joy of the "sounds of music."

A day or so after the celebration, I said good-bye to the piano when the men from the music company picked it up for its journey to Arapahoe, N.C.

RILEY BELLE AND CHRIS IN ALICE'S APARTMENT, AUGUST 2, 2016.
LEARNING ABOUT THE PIANO.

I knew the sadness would creep back into my heart after my piano no longer graced my home. A big something would be lost. Yet I realized that this was another chapter in my end-of-life time. I had asked Meg to take pictures of the Quinn children receiving the Little Knabe. That would bring cheer back to my heart.

The Little Knabe was loaded and taken away that day, August 4, 2016.

"Mrs. Irby, the Little Knabe is going to be all right. We'll take good care of her," the movers called out to me as they drove out of the parking lot.

"Thanks, Fellows," I replied. "I know it is in good hands. I watched you wrap and load. I have confidence in you."

They transported the piano to Arapahoe as if it were their child: tenderly but with strong hands embracing and lifting each piece with care. They were so attentive and efficient that the piano reached its destination—four hours away—still in perfect tune. Those guys knew the Little Knabe was a special item, with a special history, for a special family. They were not about to disappoint the children!

One picture shows me smiling, but I was "smiling on the outside, crying on the inside," as the old song goes. Everything did turn to smiles and joy when I saw pictures of Riley Belle seated at the piano in her living room. My father and mother would be smiling, too, if they could only be with her now and follow along as she makes musical harmony with the Little Knabe.

All year, the Little Knabe's keys stroked its strings under the delicate finger-touch of Riley Belle during her practices and performances. It never tired but sounded with joy each time she made its notes ring out. Riley Belle is now an able student. In just one year, she has learned to play numerous songs of many genres. She has talent, and the Knabe yields willingly to her touch, making magical sounds for her siblings. Zoe and Ruby dance to its music. They like ballet and design elaborate choreography which they display in dances performed on their living-room floor. In their tutus and other costumes, they sparkle as they move gracefully in step with Riley Belle's piano renditions.

Henry is not a dancer but has a musician's ear and sensitivity. I thought he would play the drums. But, no. Henry has picked the piano for next year! The Little Knabe has cast its magic again.

RILEY BELLE AT HER FIRST RECITAL AT THE BAPTIST CHURCH IN ARAPAHOE WITH ALICE ON JUNE 5, 2017. SHE WAS THE STAR.

But I am getting ahead of myself. On June 5, Riley Belle's year with the Knabe culminated in her recital at the local Baptist Church in Arapahoe. Would that she could have shown off the Knabe, but recitals have to be in a facility large enough to accommodate the fans. Many parents and other relatives were there to cheer for eight pupils. Even though Riley Belle had completed only one year, she was one of the two most advanced students at the event. The other was a young boy who had been taking lessons for four or five years. What does that tell you? That Riley Belle loves her music and instrument; that the Little Knabe responds well to Riley Belle's affection and attention; and that the two of them together have a bright future.

Perhaps Riley Belle will give her very own recital about the time she is ready to graduate from high school, and maybe she can give it in her home so that she can show off the Little Knabe and its melodious tones. Am I getting ahead of myself again? I keep dreaming about its future.

Summertime is a time for play—and for playing the piano! Meg invited Chris to the recital, and he came all the way to Arapahoe from Wilson, N.C.

"Chris, I am glad you could come," I said as I welcomed him. "I would appreciate your sharing with me your observations of Riley Belle's performance. She has learned to read music and play a few pieces, but I am not sure she is getting sufficient instruction in technique and theory."

"Riley Belle clearly has talent, and she loves to play," Chris told me at the end of the recital. "You can tell she is dedicated by observing her concentration and manner. And, she *is* old enough to be able to handle more than what seems to have been demanded of her."

"Do you think there is a way you could manage to give Riley Belle a few lessons this summer, both to give her an opportunity to continue learning and to give her a more comprehensive approach to studying music?" He paused, frowned as if thinking hard, and then, immediately, said *yes*—probably not realizing what it would mean in commuting time.

Meg arranged to drive Riley Belle to Little Washington once a week or every other week when Chris is there on church business so that Riley Belle can have an hour's lesson.

The summer lessons extended into the academic year. Meg and Chris worked out a transportation system that each could manage. The lessons continued, and now—a serendipity! Henry has started taking lessons as well. Another pair of small hands will learn to read notes and play scales and arpeggios up and down the keyboard. The Little Knabe is happy; it would dance along with Zoe and Ruby if it could!

What's in its future? Who knows, but I anticipate that it may become the center of a music/dance group with Riley Belle and Henry as the musicians and Zoe and Ruby as the dance group. Mother Meg, also a good musician, will conduct. Michael will be the manager and booking agent. Wouldn't it be great if right there in Eastern North Carolina, we could have a newly-minted Trapp family entertaining friends and neighbors—all because the Little Knabe passed the *Sound of Music* along to the Quinn family?

Fall 2017

Amazing Grace

Israel, that ancient place. History has catalogued millennia of war, mayhem, savagery, familial assassinations, and terror in the small strip of land bordering the Mediterranean Sea and called, at times, Canaan, Judea, Israel, and Palestine. A cemetery of civilizations, though today it is a cauldron of conflict as well.

For 70 years, Jews have laid claim to the land, have established borders through waging wars, have sought legitimacy among their neighbors, have turned the desert into green farmland, and have defied enemies trying to wipe them off the face of the earth. Established in 1948 by a vote of the United Nations, Israel has populated and controlled most of the land west of the Jordan River from the Sea of Galilee to south of the Dead Sea.

Despite this turbulence and perhaps because of it, too, the descendants of Abraham have brought forth in this tiny landmass three religions dominant in the world and lasting for thousands of years.

I was anxious to see that land, with its layered remnants of earlier civilizations, and to trace Biblical history, especially from the time of the first unified Israel under David around 1000 B.C. through the time of Christ. Early in 2017 I traveled to Israel with friends and a group from a Methodist church in Raleigh. I wanted to enhance my understanding of the history that has shaped much of the world for centuries and to explore dimensions of my own faith.

Before we entered Israel from Jordan, we had the thrill of seeing the famous pink archeological ruins of Petra, the third-century B.C. home of the Nabateans. Located at an opening at the end of a long canyon, the community included finely developed commercial buildings with homes and burial places in rock caves. Their tall commercial buildings carved out of pink hillside rock, such as the Treasury building, were incredibly impressive—I had no idea that such architectural masterpieces were possible then! But more amazing were their skills in developing water-management systems of aqueducts comparable to what the Romans achieved.

"Can you imagine the ingenuity of these people!" exclaimed Janet Lowry, a fellow tourist. "If alive today, they would be ahead of us in technology and in everything else."

Once in Israel, our journey was fast-paced. There was much rushing, no free time, no time for meditation—except once or twice. The lectures were long—too much for me to absorb each day. Given that I had fallen and injured my left pelvic bone on the second day of the trip, I hobbled about the land and sites of interest, often finding the daily tour requirements exhausting and the terrain too rugged to manage. Without my friend Sally, I would have had to abandon the trip. The extensive territory we raced to cover in a few days almost sapped my spirit for adventure. Though I know our guide tried to expose us to as much history as possible and to give us a broad understanding of the history of the area, it took grit and fortitude to persist. At the end of every day—when Sally was getting a bucket of ice for her cocktail and another bucket for the swelling in my painful

TREASURY, PETRA

hip—I lay on the bed trying to associate facts we heard with places we visited. It was impossible; my mind blurred with images and facts. Even photographs I took helped only for a short while—until the next lecture when I added more facts and images to confuse with the previous ones. Yet, even with those drawbacks, I appreciated this opportunity to see Biblical places that had been of interest to me for many years.

Sandwiched into the many miles of walking among and studying historic sites, such as Qumran and the Garden of Gethsemane, were heartfelt moments of inspiration and learning. Those moments easily exceeded my hours of discomfort.

Even now, the veil of memory lifts and moments of awareness flash into my consciousness, prompting a smile or a word of thanks. Such an image appeared to me—an image of my family—when I was seated in a place of quiet meditation: a majestic stone Catholic Church near the Via Dolorosa in Jerusalem. Its middle-aged priest, dressed in a white robe, welcomed visitors at the open, arched doorway as we approached.

The church is significant in multiple ways, but three stand out. It stands in the area where Jesus's maternal grandparents, Anne and Joachim, lived—and where his mother Mary was born. Behind the church are the remains of ancient pools and a Roman temple, but also fresh gardens. The pools have been identified as the Pool of Bethesda mentioned in the New Testament, where Jesus healed a crippled man by speaking to him. Last, the church was not destroyed after Saladin's 1187 conquest of Jerusalem, but in 1192 it was converted into a madrasa.

When I walked into the church, parishioners were singing "How Great Thou Art," my father's favorite hymn and one our congregation sang at his funeral. When they finished, we proceeded to move into the pews for our meditation. The acoustics were extraordinary, making the singers' voices rise to the Heavens. I sat facing the altar, and George Deaton, a member of our group with a concert-tenor voice, led us in singing "Amazing Grace," one of my mother's favorite songs and the one I sang to her over and

MADONNA AND CHILD

over as she lay dying in a Rocky Mount hospital bed. An indelible image of her taking her last breaths on a Sunday morning in December 1991, disturbed my composure then and for the rest of that morning.

With plain, even austere, gray/white stone arches, wooden pews, and a simple altar adorned only with a Cross, the atmosphere encouraged contemplation and prayer. An all-white, life-size sculpture of Mary and Child beautified the plain side wall of the church, offering a place of worship for parishioners and visitors alike. I gravitated toward the sculpture and paused in reverence.

Suddenly I was startled. "Ladies!" our guide called out. "We don't want to leave without you." Sally and I pulled ourselves away, but it was another solemn moment interrupted by the need to move on.

Even before I discovered the Jerusalem stone church, I experienced moments of inspiration in unexpected places. During the first eventide in Israel, my friends—Sally, Betty, Janet, and Tolu—and I watched the sun set from a boat gliding gently on the Sea of Galilee. Stillness and quiet, peace and calm, surrounded us. But the cliffs above the sea told a different story, one of past conflict and current danger.

The Golan Heights towered above us from the opposite side of the water. "Look at those cliffs and mountains rising out of the sea. You can understand how critical they are to the defense of Israel," said Janet. "The terrain below is exposed to easy attack."

In the time of Jesus, the shore below the giant cliffs was called The Other Side. He took his ministry there as well as to towns in Galilee. We saw the towns, the ruins, and the rocky terrain of the land beside the Sea: Tiberias and Capernaum and, between them, Tabgha, the site of the first feeding of the multitudes. The memory of the Sermon on the Mount is preserved in a church at The Mount of Beatitudes—names known to me since childhood but also kept in my mental history book as if they were exotic places in an ancient fantasy land.

THE GOLAN HEIGHTS VIEWED FROM THE SEA OF GALILEE

Setting foot on the land of Jesus' ministry evoked a breathless awareness of place and significance: a land that, in many ways, is as much the cradle of our civilization as is the Tigris and Euphrates basin, a land of ancient emperors and kings. Israel is a land of *so* many religions, *so* many invaders, *so* many empires, and *so* many believers over the centuries that I could feel Yahweh's firm presence there.

New to me was Caesarea, an important port and fortress built by Herod between 20 and 10 B.C. Originally a small port used by seafaring Phoenicians, it became a thriving capital city by the time of Jesus. Herod named the city, with its aqueduct, a Roman theater, an amphitheater, palace, residences, hippodrome, and deep-sea harbor, for Augustus Caesar, his patron. It was the capital of Judea, and, likely, Pontius Pilate's home was here as well as Herod's palace.

Tolu was our dedicated photographer and scribe. "I got a picture of the harbor and Herod's palace, and I think I got a clear shot of the aqueduct and the water," she said.

I chimed in, "I want to take one of the four of you standing in front of the aqueduct. No one will believe we were actually here if I don't have evidence."

Think of the many peoples who lived and traveled here over the centuries. From here Pontius Pilate set out for the Passover festival in Jerusalem, and while there he sentenced Jesus to death. In 58 A.D., Paul was arrested for presumably causing a riot, then sent to Caesarea for trial by the governor. He was imprisoned for two years. During that time, he preached to the last of the Herods, King Agrippa II, who was tempted to convert to Christianity.

Here also Paul exercised his right as a Roman citizen to be tried by the Emperor, then was sent from Caesarea to Rome, imprisoned and, after several years, executed.

There are so many stories here. The history of these ancient civilizations speaks to us today: imagine how many tribes, armies, and kings have traveled across these hills or sailed into the port. How hard it is to build a civilization; how easy it is to destroy it by war and occupation. Yet that occurred here time and again. In this land of austere beauty and barren, rolling mountains, sophisticated and courageous leaders brought prosperity to their people, but they also brought conflict and destruction often resulting in a ruthless disregard for life. Paul taught salvation by faith—and grace, but grace seemed in scarce supply there.

Tolu, Sally, Betty, Janet at the Aqueduct

A day or so later, our bus made its way at dusk into the City of Jerusalem—no better time to enter the City. Lights across the area shone brightly among the rolling hills covered with monochromatic stone landmarks profiling the ancient center of religions and empires. George stood on the moving bus and sang "Jerusalem" as we entered the city. Familiar to most Christians, the song has a particular significance for me. My grandmother sang it in her home and in the Methodist Church back in Weldon. Daily, during her lifetime, she surrounded herself with music while working around the house or crocheting vanity covers as she sat on the front porch chatting with friends. A picture of Granny occupies a place of distinction by my bed today.

She sang, too, as she lay dying in her bedroom at home, covered by an oxygen tent. I wonder if she was singing "Jerusalem," perhaps auditioning for her part in the chorus of angels she was joining. During her illnesses, I spent my afternoons with her, nestled by her side, propped up in her bed. I told her stories about Mrs. Shirley's kindergarten. Proudly, I showed her what I was learning to read.

All the way from Galilee to Jerusalem, the sounds of music called me to say a prayer in appreciation of my heritage and my family. I even heard familiar compositions in our hotel, The Olive Tree, in Jerusalem. The first morning, I stopped abruptly when I entered the public Ladies' restroom and heard the first movement of a familiar march. For a moment, past and present joined as one.

The restroom's walls were a soft green, accented with blue and black colors, and a waterfall spilled over crystal rocks—soothing and comforting. When I entered the Ladies' room, the music playing over the loudspeaker was Mozart's Turkish March. I stopped, stood still in the lavatory area, and permitted myself to be absorbed by the music. Unintentionally, I blocked traffic coming in the door.

I moved aside and listened to the movement until the end. I knew the piece well, having played it in my senior recital in high school. Instinctively, my fingers started moving along the counter in time with the notes and chords. I imagined myself sitting in Louise Farber's living room at her grand piano with her seated at my right, evaluating my hand position, making sure that every finger touched the keys with precision and equal pressure. She frequently tested my touch by pulling up one of my fingers as I played a chord or run, then letting it drop to measure its resistance.

My piano teacher and my mother's best friend, Louise, was active in the Jewish community in my hometown. Her life had not been easy, given her heart's weakness from atrial fibrillation. There in the middle of Jerusalem, I thought of her and all she had taught me about piano as well as about Jewish life and history. I wished she could have seen Jerusalem, too, but she never got there. But I was there, in the middle of the City of David, thinking about her and grateful for her gifts to me. Listening, I froze in place, going back in time, and failed to hear the call to the bus.

"Come on, Alice!" Sally called, rushing into the room. She grabbed my arm and pulled me toward the front door, admonishing me, "Don't you know Hal will get after us if we are late?"

The day turned into one of real adventure: to Jericho, the world's oldest city; to the River Jordan to witness baptisms; to Qumran to see the caves where the Dead Sea Scrolls were discovered; and to the Dead Sea for a dip in the water for those brave enough to get salt and mud all over their bodies.

"I'm going swimming in the Dead Sea," Sally announced confidently. And she did! The rest of us demurred. Boldly she waded in as we watched from a safe distance on the beach. About all she could do was float, though, because of the high percentage of salt in the water. Others capped off their swim by packing mud all over their bodies: a local myth promising a healthier body! I settled for a bar of soap with Dead Sea salt and other curative features purchased in the gift shop. That was as close as I wanted to get to the salt and mud.

The Jordan River is narrow, and the water is muddy. Yet, like the ancient land, it draws people from afar to be baptized there. Solemnly, ministers immersed white-robed supplicants in the water one by one and guided them safely to the steps on shore. I watched in soulful silence and wonder, repeating to myself as each one entered the water, "He leadeth me beside the still waters. He restoreth my soul." It was as if each of the participants in baptism had experienced a metanoia—a kind of spiritual conversion.

Breaking my reverie, I looked across the River. As the service was underway, I saw evidence of the other feature of life that defines both sides of the Jordan: an armed guard whose bowed head almost seemed to reflect embarrassment or sadness at having to be present for such sacred acts.

In Jerusalem and elsewhere we saw the same contrasts: people going about their lives while armed guards were stationed at key points—and sometimes racing to a city gate to quell an action. Faith and firepower side by side! Where was God's grace? It was found, no doubt, in the persistence of those who struggled daily and unfailingly to work together across the boundaries of religion and ethnic differences.

Perhaps it had been found also in Qumran with the discovery of the Dead Sea Scrolls in the arid desert south of

Jerusalem and west of the Dead Sea—the rocky, hot land where David went to escape Saul, and where a Jewish sect, the Essenes, lived during the Hellenistic period—third century B.C. to first century A.D.

WALKING INTO THE JORDAN RIVER TO BE BAPTIZED

How likely was it that in 1947 a shepherd of the Ta'amireh tribe would discover the Scrolls when he left his flock and went to search for a stray sheep? Amid the limestone cliffs, he found a cave, cast a stone into the dark interior, and heard breaking pots.

AN ARMED GUARD IN DESERT CAMOUFLAGE ON THE OTHER SIDE OF THE JORDAN RIVER, NOT 100 FEET AWAY.

Strange! On entering the cave, the young Bedouin also found intact clay pots, some of which were empty, others containing blackened scrolls wrapped in linen. Hundreds of scrolls! Their content revolutionized our understanding of life among Jewish sects at the time of the beginnings of Christianity, and the scrolls revealed the oldest existing text of the Old Testament.

We saw the scrolls in the Israel museum in Jerusalem in the Shrine of the Book. The entire book of *Isaiah* is displayed there. One stands in awe in the darkened room, the scrolls illuminated by glowing lambent light surrounding the circular display.

QUMRAN CAVES

Betty and Janet said to me in whispered tones, "Are we really seeing what we are seeing? It's almost unbelievable." We marveled at the discoveries and extolled their significance, trying to absorb the enormity of what was in front of us.

Also in that museum is the Tel Dan Stele, the first historical evidence of the existence of David. I had read about it and was eager to see it. Until this archeological find in 1993, several biblical scholars doubted the existence of David, claiming that the Biblical texts in Samuel I and II were mythical representations of tribes and kings of the era. The stele (stone slab) was dated to the ninth century B.C.

But David is very real, historically and religiously, in Jerusalem. Nowhere is that more evident than at his tomb.

Like many sites claiming probable historical authenticity, there is doubt that the tomb in the Hagia Zion, a former

Byzantine church or Roman-era synagogue, is the real burial place of David. It doesn't matter. His presence and that of Jesus and other historical religious figures permeate the narrow streets and shrines across the city. Views of icons of three world religions, sites like the Al-Aqsa Mosque, the Dome of the Rock on the Temple Mount, the Western Wall, the Mount of Olives, and the sarcophagi spreading over the hilly landscape of the city opened my mind to the past and the lessons of Sunday school when I was young. The roots of our civilization grow deep in the soil here.

Our last day in Jerusalem, music set the mood once more for meditation and inspiration. Early in the morning we went to the Garden Tomb.

The site is not likely the location of Calvary, or Golgotha, but it looks much more like what one expects than the Church of the Holy Sepulcher, the commonly recognized location of Jesus's death and burial. Discovered by a British archeologist around the turn of the twentieth century, the Garden Tomb possesses the features enumerated in the Bible about Jesus's tomb: a rock quarry with a skull in the side wall, near the Temple Mount, and adjacent to two roads—one to Jericho with a garden centered by a tomb that looks very much like one that Joseph of Arimathea could afford.

Our group also had a communion service that last day in the outdoor pavilion under a canopy bordered by fragrant shrubs. Rev. Hal Salmon, our tour director, led an appropriately solemn service, distributing memento communion cups made of wood to each of us. But what made my heart turn to the Heavens was a solo by George, who sang "In the Garden": *"I walk in the Garden alone, while the dew is still on the roses...."* His strong, melodious voice filled the fresh morning air and the dew-laden garden.

Again an image of my grandmother flashed before my eyes. I felt tears trickle down my cheeks. That was her favorite hymn, and she sang it many times over the years. I remember her singing it in Sunday School Assembly—and after her death, Genie, my aunt, sang it from the choir loft. George had no idea how much his choice of song meant to me, but I thanked him at the end of the service, describing my talented grandmother and aunt and their love of the hymn.

The garden surroundings were fragrant and still; the visitors were quiet and pensive. I left the group and sat on a stone wall, staring at the door of the tomb and at nature's floral artistry in the garden. To my right, water gurgled from another stone edifice into a rock basin. Right behind me, olive trees provided shade, their swaying leaves dappling the walkways with sunshine.

"Cure me with quietness. Bless me with peace," I whispered, reciting the first two lines of Ruth Pitter's poem as I sat there in silence.

THE TOMB AND ITS ENTRY

At last, on the final day of the trip, I felt my spiritual pilgrimage was complete. I felt close to my family, close to the Holy Spirit, and close to the man known as the Son of God who may have walked or been carried to this place. For all the nattering voices and confusion of the previous week, this time and place was a fitting ending for me. I could start home with equanimity and gratitude, and above all with hope. And *grace*—not deserved but bestowed.

But there's more. Fast forward to today. I realize now what brought me to the interludes of inspiration, comfort, and faith. It was music, music associated with my family and my music teacher. There is good reason why any church that I attend regularly must have a music program that touches my heart as well as having ministers who feed my mind. I know how much I depend on the lives and memories of my family, and I know how much music heals my soul and helps me look forward to the future, whatever that will be. After all, given my age of 85 years, I often contemplate the future, whether on Earth or in the beyond.

Sitting now in my den recalling the emotions and inspiration of my trip, I am listening to a CD of Vladimir Horowitz playing Rachmaninoff's "Concerto No. 3 in D Minor." When I hear that music, I feel suspended in space by the soaring harmonies of the full orchestra accompanying a solo piano. Specific themes in the score draw me close to Louise, to Genie, to Mother, and to Granny. I don't know or understand why.

Maybe it is because those four women—courageous, independent, and spiritual, each in her own way—have bestowed upon me Amazing Grace. They have been models for my life, models to which I aspire but do not yet equal, and that distance and difference leaves a hollowness at my core, though it is one that exists side by side with the fullness of my life.

February 2017

PAST AND PRESENT

My Christmas Angel

She was with me all along on my journey.

Yet there was no sound, no voice or music, not even a slight, momentary breeze.

But she was there. My Christmas Angel. How do I know? Follow me.

For the first time in twenty-four years, since the year of my mother's death in 1991, I decided to spend Christmas in Weldon. The idea hit me in the middle of the night when I was trying to decide whether to go to Florida with Andrea and Cecil to see his parents. I concluded that I needed to do something else.

"Andrea, I really appreciate the opportunity to accompany you and Cecil to Florida. I appreciate his folks' invitation, and I certainly think the two of you should spend Christmas there," I said to her. "But somehow I feel I should stay in North Carolina. Maybe I'll go to Weldon or to see George and his family in Morehead City."

"Do whatever makes you comfortable, Mom," Andrea assured me. "Cecil and his folks will understand. I know that being in Florida at Christmastime wouldn't feel like Christmas to you."

SOUTH TOWARD HOME

Putting wreaths on the graves of my mother and father has been a December ritual since their deaths. I could not forego the gesture for even one year. Each year, Ruth Proctor, a family friend living in Halifax, has the wreaths made and we take them to the Weldon cemetery. When placing the order with her this year, I learned that she had been alone Thanksgiving, an unusual circumstance given her large family of three children and numerous grandchildren. Yet, no one could arrange to be with her, and she can no longer drive. Ruth had no plans for Christmas and was satisfied being alone, but at 87, it was not fitting that she spend Christmas in such a manner. I decided to buy Christmas dinner, take it to Halifax, pick up the wreaths and, with her, visit the cemetery on Christmas Day. From there I could visit my brother and his family in Morehead City, only three hours away.

Soon I had second thoughts. This Christmas would be the first Christmas in Andrea's 53 years that I had not spent it with her. In going home to Weldon, not to Florida, was I letting her down? More likely, I was pitying myself. How would it be, driving alone on Christmas Day, traversing the state from Pinehurst to Weldon, then to Morehead City, and not seeing my immediate family until New Year's Eve?

When I first considered the Weldon trip, my good friend Veda said, "Go ahead, Alice. You will be glad you did. It will bring you close to your roots, unlike being in Florida." She was right. I stuck with my original plan.

Where does all the traffic come from on Christmas Day? Years ago, the highways were empty except for people taking short trips from home to Grandma's. This Christmas, the entire nation appeared to be on wheels. How sad. It seemed like a marker for our society's rootlessness. Where was Santa Claus? Where were the nativity programs in parks? Where were the carolers? Left behind in the malls?

When Ruth opened the door, I knew immediately that an angel had guided me there. I saw trouble. Her face winced with pain. She held her left arm close to her body. She was in distress.

"Ruth, what's wrong?"

"I fell in the garage this morning," she responded weakly while almost sagging to the floor.

"Let me help you to bed."

"No, no. I don't think I can lie down. I can stay on the sofa once seated, as long as I don't move."

Ruth was in a bad way, having fallen in the garage on left-over roof shingles. She could hardly walk, probably a result of broken ribs. A strong-willed, determined woman, she refused to go to the emergency room at the hospital in Roanoke Rapids.

"I know I can't reach a doctor on Christmas Day, and I am not going to any emergency room because I might catch a flu bug," she insisted.

A good point because her coughing would exacerbate the pain in her mid-section. Still, I worried that she had punctured an organ and felt she needed x-rays.

She was breathing normally, and pain medicine and staying immobile kept her as comfortable as possible. She cried out in pain whenever she had to stand or shift her weight. With my help, she got to the bathroom. A tall woman, she has a large-boned, heavyset frame which made walking difficult.

What would she have done without help?

"Do your children know about your fall?" I inquired.

"No. And, I am not about to tell them. I am not going to spoil their Christmas," she shot back.

"One is in Charlotte and another in Asheville. They can come and would want to come if they knew your condition," I argued.

Finally, she phoned her children and grandchildren, wishing them a Merry Christmas and telling them, at my insistence, about the fall, though making light of it. When each one offered to come to her aid, she reported minimal damage to her body and insisted they not come.

"They can't do anything if they come. And, even though you brought enough food for an army, I don't want them to have to prepare meals. Here it is Christmas Day. Their families need to be together and not tending to an old woman with broken ribs. I have suffered broken ribs before. No big deal," she declared emphatically, as if to forestall further argument.

But she kept on, saying, "And I know doctors no longer wrap your arm to your body, nor use a cast. You are just supposed to stay still, and I plan to do that. I have enough willpower to do that."

"How well I know," I thought.

I had brought enough food for a family of six. Leftovers would tide her over for several days. She insisted on getting up and moving to the kitchen table to have dinner. "It's not right to have Christmas dinner sitting on a sofa," she said.

It was a struggle to get Ruth to the table, but we made it. I cut up the turkey on her plate—she could not use a knife—spooned out dressing and gravy on her plate, and put vegetables in small bowls to make handling the food with a soup spoon as easy as possible. She ate like a bird, as Mother would say. It must have hurt to swallow, certainly to breathe deeply. Every now and then, she gasped. But I knew not to say anything about it.

"I'm going to stay tonight, Ruth. Don't try to shush me out," I told her.

Though she wouldn't admit it, she couldn't have reached the bed without help, and I was not about to let her stay immobile on the sofa. How would she have gotten breakfast, or even water?

There was a guest room upstairs already prepared for me, but with twin beds in her bedroom downstairs, I could stay with her overnight and observe her breathing and general condition. She slept fitfully but seldom cried out in pain. She seemed almost comfortable as long as she didn't move. Morning came and she was still breathing normally. With pain medication, Ruth had slept fairly well—better than I had. I woke up frequently to check on her.

She wanted to bathe herself and put on a gown, an unlikely prospect. I helped with a cloth and basin of water, but there was no way to get a gown on her. A change of underclothes and socks freshened her somewhat.

"Ruth, before I go the cemetery and on to Morehead City, I am going to call a friend and have her look in on you. And, I insist that you get in touch with a doctor tomorrow. I can also stay tonight."

"I don't need all that, Alice. I told you there is nothing anyone can do and I can manage right here by myself."

Stubborn? Yes. And older than I am, which made convincing her difficult.

Before I left to go to the cemetery the next day, I called Glenn Dickens, a friend of hers and someone I had known since high school. Glenn was surprised at the news but eagerly volunteered to watch over Ruth.

"I'll make sure she gets her meals and get her to the doctor on Monday," Glenn assured me. Her doctor was not available that day, Friday, and no one was on call. That's rural North Carolina, I guess. No help for miles in any direction except the flu-ridden emergency room.

The day after Christmas brought a clear-blue sky following a couple of days of rain and gloomy, gray surroundings. The grass in the family cemetery lot glistened in the light of the morning sun shining through the trees. The magnolia tree presided majestically over the graves of my parents and grandparents. It was a lovely, serene view. All was calm, all was bright. I felt at peace. Bordering the plot that holds the graves of the Andersons, Whitfields, Hudsons, and Joyners—fourteen altogether—is an iron fence separating our family's resting place from other graves nearby. An obelisk monument at the head of the plot, marking the grave of my great-grandfather Anderson, distinguishes the plot from all others in the cemetery. An oversize headstone of two Whitfield graves anchors the other end of the plot. Angled across the lot from the magnolia tree is a red maple, planted by George, that catches the eastern sunlight as it casts its warming rays on the graves. Such symbolic evidence of life there—glistening green grass, trees dripping with dew, the wreaths of holly and juniper with red ribbon shining bright under morning's early sun—made me feel I could sing Christmas hymns in concert with the all the souls lingering in place. The family plot became a make-believe sanctuary without walls.

FAMILY PLOT, WELDON CEMETERY

As the wreaths, with their fresh green branches and full, deep-red bows, rested comfortably on the headstones, I strained for words to express in full measure my gratitude for the lives of my parents, and my grandmother. How loving. How strong. How stable. How nourishing. Their caring hearts embraced all who needed them. They had all the good "G's": grace, generosity, gratitude, glorification of their God and the good. And, they had given me a strong, capable brother and sister, whom I love very much. My ghosts that day were happy ghosts of a child's Christmas Past, all alive for me again in that old resting place.

Drawn to the earth, I was entranced by the moment of solitude and contemplation. I said my prayer of thanks. I sang a hymn, "Joy to the World," and I felt compelled to stay but, of course, also wanted to get to Morehead City by suppertime. But as I left, my heart affirmed once more that here was an appropriate resting place, one yielding a storehouse of lives loved that will always guide me. My Angel was there, too, joining my chorus and saying a prayer.

GEORGE AND GWEN

And she was not through with me, leading me to a happy place full of Christmas spirit and joy. George and Gwen, my brother and sister-in-law, welcomed me with smiles and hugs to their festive home with lights aglow, warm hospitality spilling out the windows. The pleasure of Christmases past permeated the present, evidenced by children having been there playing and opening gifts.

Meg's four children—George's and Gwen's grandchildren—had gone home the day before with full stomachs but came down with stomach viruses soon thereafter. A virus in that family, when it hits, spreads quickly down the stair-steps of ages: 11, 9, 7 and 3, not dodging a single one. I missed seeing them, because they always like to dress up in Gwen's old clothes and put on a show.

"Aunt Alice, I am so sorry we missed you," said Meg when she called. "The children were looking forward to sharing some cookies they made with you."

"Clearly, I'm disappointed, Meg, because I know they are growing fast and I probably won't see them for another six-to-eight months. I was also looking forward to playing 'dress-up.' Your mother's costume closet is so extensive, there is glamour for everyone. Tell the children I am enjoying the cookies."

Jennifer, my other niece, and Drew, her daughter, came down from New Bern, where they live in an upscale two-story red-brick home overlooking the Trent River. They had escaped the virus of Christmas Day and were enjoying the next day together. She has always been studious, somewhat of a perfectionist, so I am sure her clients appreciate her expertise and wisdom. Drew, at 14, is a dark-haired, fair-skinned, sophisticated beauty and excellent conversationalist, poised, with perfect manners. Soon, young men will be banging on her door.

RUBY, RILEY BELLE, AND ZOE IN COSTUME

"Drew, what's life like now that you are in high school?" I inquired.

"I like some of my classes, especially English and journalism, but I also spend a lot of time with Young Life. It's an interdenominational Christian organization that provides activities and outreach for young people to enhance and enrich their spiritual lives. There are also branches for younger children and for adults," she replied enthusiastically.

"Being dedicated to Christ and to service at your age is admirable, but isn't there time for a boyfriend somewhere? You would be a good catch."

"Well, in fact, there is. Actually, I met him through Young Life. He does not go to my school, but we see each other at Young Life meetings."

It was obvious that Jennifer was moving into an entirely new stage of parenting, with Drew branching out in school and beyond. And Jack, her 11-year old son, was also branching out, trying out for various sports and participating in Rubik's Cube regional competitions. Jennifer has found herself driving all over Craven County and even to Raleigh for Jack's competitions. Not a soccer mom, but close.

Seeing Jennifer, talking with Meg, learning about their children, and observing Drew spreading her wings made this Christmas seem like a real Christmas again: siblings, children, and grandchildren.

Likewise, the food. Two kinds of pound cake, one by Gwen and one by George: my very favorite. Jennifer's son, Jack, can eat one all by himself. Lucky for me, George put aside a half of one cake for me to take home. Weighing down the table were all the things we used to have at home in Weldon: turkey and dressing, cranberry sauce, gravy, country ham, candied sweet potatoes—one of Mother's specialties—and collards plus condiments, and ambrosia with pound cake for dessert. Gwen even made frozen-fruit salad with Mother's recipe, of which I ate gallons as a child. And the children had made us decorated cookies.

We ate and talked and talked and ate. We also walked a bit; the skies were still clear blue, the air fresh. George took us to see the elaborate Christmas decorations on homes facing Spooners Creek and Bogue Sound. Reflections on the water magnified a grand spectacle of connecting yards sparkling with lights that seemed to envelop us as we drove by each one, block after block, and down at the water's edge. It's obvious there's no longer an energy shortage; bright lights gleamed everywhere in all shapes and colors.

"George, what a contrast with Weldon when we were growing up! Do you remember?" I asked. "There were no lights outdoors during the Depression, and few homes could afford electrically-lighted Christmas trees, though most people could afford to place a few real candles in windows."

"I remember going with Daddy into the woods outside of town to fell a tall cedar or fir tree that would reach toward our ten-foot living-room ceiling," George recounted. "Mother always wanted a tall tree, nothing skimpy for that big room.

"It was the woods or nothing," he continued. "There were no tree farms or commercial lots for selling trees and wreaths. I was cold to the bone trudging into those thick-wet woods in December, and helping Dad pull the tree out to put on the truck. I always came home with scratches somewhere—on my face, hands or both."

"Mother and Nanny Kate made wreaths by hand out of holly, juniper, and magnolia leaves from our yards—or from the cemetery! Remember?" I added.

"They also made many of our tree decorations, except for the string of lights that we worried would go out with no warning. One bulb out and the whole string failed. We looked for replacements, sometimes having to go the dime store at the last minute with hope of finding some to fit." I continued.

"Remember that pesky silver tinsel that we hung, a piece at a time, on every branch and twig of the tree? Mother wouldn't let us just throw a handful up on the branches. We had to place each one so that it hung down without touching anything. We decorated the top of the tree with a 'store-bought' lighted star, because Mother wouldn't tolerate an amateur one," George laughed.

George and I always wanted Mother to leave her stockings, rather than Daddy's socks, for Santa to fill because they would stretch out to hold more fruit and nuts; but, nylons were scarce so we made do with the socks. They were hung on mantels covered with evergreen garlands and vases filled with Nandina leaves and berries harvested from our side-yard bushes. Our home back then was as lovely as any of ours today, and much more creatively decorated. What mattered, then as now, were children's voices of joy and excitement that bounced off every wall, and the sharing of food and blessings among families.

Going to church on Sunday with George and Gwen was not to be, though. Storms were predicted, and my eyes are not strong or clear enough to drive home alone in rain. I left George and Gwen so I would reach Pinehurst before the storm. In a way, I welcomed time to myself to absorb the sadness I felt over our family being spread out over the state and no longer able to gather in our Weldon family home at Christmastime. I tell myself that life moves on, that we move through it in stages, and while I look forward to the next stage, mourning the past at special times sweetens our memories and draws us closer together.

This Christmas, I missed going to church for the first time in my life. When I passed back through Weldon after laying wreaths on the graves, I drove by the Weldon Methodist Church, the church of my childhood. As I slowed the car to trace the outlines of the church in my consciousness, a feeling of loss tightened my throat, and tears came to my eyes. The church, so vibrant and full of strong voices fifty years ago performing an elaborate, glorious Christmas concert, was empty and dark. Only a dozen or so members remain, all of them elderly. The organ, with its many pipes echoing blocks away at holiday time, was silent. The majestic, red-brick Gothic structure was crumbling, in need of a new roof and internal repair. The vividly beautiful stained-glass windows—large and arched, filling two sides of the building—needed reinforcement and protection. Maybe some caring congregation will take it over and fill it with voices of worshipful life again!

I may not have been in a church on Christmas Day or on Sunday, but I experienced the living Spirit of the Christmas season in my life all this week. Every day in surprising ways. Around every corner. Above all, I was graced with health good enough to travel and felt my own Christmas Angel guiding me on my journey of memory and mercy, of love and gratitude.

Christmas 2014

To Market, To Market

An email popped up on my laptop: Louis Horne, a Bassett Furniture Company executive, inviting me to the High Point Furniture Market in October.

"I know that Bobby would be bringing you if he was alive, and I thought you might like to come and bring some friends. I will be there Saturday through Monday," he wrote.

"Thank you very much, Louis," I wrote back right away. "You know how much I enjoyed tagging along with Bobby and seeing you in the Bassett showrooms." I jumped at the invitation. With furniture a part of my life since my dad entered the business in the 1930s, how could I refuse?

Twice a year, in spring and fall, High Point, North Carolina, explodes in a vortex of activity. Furniture vendors ply their wares; designers come from afar; displays glitter; company suites host customers; bars fill with excited voices; and guards monitor entry at the door to safeguard 75,000 attendees. Floor after floor of two tall buildings, plus buildings lining the streets throughout the town—11.5 million square feet—are filled with classic, Early American, modern, Art Deco, and funky samples of all kinds of furniture imaginable—for a home, an office, a commercial facility.

The normally quiet university town is transformed into a giant bazaar with 2,000-plus exhibitors. It's as if vendors from all corners of the earth come to town at Furniture Market time. Decorators, retailers, manufacturers, suppliers, and salesmen rush through the halls, bumping into each other and spilling onto the streets as they dash to showrooms.

Bobby George and I had grown up together in Halifax County where he had been a groomsman in my wedding. Just a month before Louis's message in 2017, Andrea and I had joined Bobby George's daughter, Tori, in Macon, Georgia, to say farewell to Bobby, who had died suddenly of a heart attack. Louis Horne was there, too, with his wife and son. It was good to see Bobby's friends and meet family he had talked about through the years.

This time Andrea and I decided to go alone to the market because we needed time and privacy to reminisce about Bobby as we walked through the familiar corridors of the display halls and showrooms.

On the well-traveled Interstate 85, we turned off at the High Point exit, then into the familiar parking lot. We had driven that route many times, but this was the first time without Bobby. Our Bassett passes gained entry for us, and we met Louis in the Bassett suite on the thirteenth floor of the International Home Furnishings Center.

"Are you hungry?" Louis asked. "The buffet is waiting for you."

"Anytime you say, Louis, but we want to be sure to spend some time with you when you are free," replied Andrea.

Going down the cafeteria line, we pointed out to each other the dishes that Bobby would surely have chosen. "He could not have resisted the banana pudding, even if it meant an extra insulin shot," I reminded Andrea and Louis.

We bumped into Bassett salesman Jeff Philpott, a vivacious, articulate go-getter who was standing in the showroom with Jeb Bassett, now Chief Operations Officer of the company. They greeted us graciously, made us feel at home, and joined in telling anecdotes about Bobby.

Louis, a protégé of Bobby and friend for several years, showed us the product lines for which he is responsible. He is one of the young executives who have contributed to Bassett's becoming the industry leader in making furniture once more in the U.S. Louis guided us through the labyrinth of showrooms until he turned us loose so he could meet international colleagues who had come to town.

"Louis is a very creative and energetic entrepreneur," I remarked to Andrea when he left. "Bassett is fortunate to have him."

Andrea and I set out on our own, walking the halls and streets, trying out chair after chair, eyeing lamps and chandeliers, and picking up brochures. Andrea is furnishing a large upstairs suite in her home so it will accommodate the two 6'4" giants in her family: Cecil, her husband, and Philip, her stepson. At the same time, she needs to make the space inviting for overnight guests.

"Andrea, these chairs are so big you can fit two of me in one."

"Ditto. If a chair can accommodate both of us, it will likely fit one of them," she agreed.

To my surprise, the Market offered floor-upon-floor of huge chairs and sofas of all shapes and kinds. If this was what it took to accommodate the American population's girth, that was clear evidence of the market's response to our changing body sizes. I hadn't thought of what human giants need for sitting and sleeping, though in my many trips to doctors' offices in recent years, I have observed very wide chairs and settees.

Clearly, furniture manufacturers know how to accommodate change. They now offer ottomans the size of tables, sectional sofa pieces larger than normal, and beds the size of flatbed trucks. Even occasional chairs offered by specialty companies come in two sizes: regular and roomy. I could sleep in most of the roomy chairs, but I couldn't sit in any of them—they swallowed me.

"Where is all this new furniture going?" I asked a salesman.

"To fill modern mansions that are springing up in cities and towns all across the country," he replied. "Look at these home-theater leather recliners and sofas with drink-cup holders. Everything and more than a theater provides."

The home-theater display area was the size of a small warehouse. The salesman told me developers are razing the small 1950s-1980s ranch houses—those that fit me—to reclaim the land and make room for multi-floor dwellings with cupolas, balconies, and antebellum columns.

While Andrea examined chair samples, I recalled an earlier age when I was first aware of furniture markets. Daddy started going to High Point in 1940, when he went to buy inventory for his new store, the third furniture company in Weldon. He took a substantial personal risk in going up against two well-established furniture companies that had served our small community of 2,500 for decades. George and I looked forward to his trips to the market because he always brought us gifts he had purchased there.

DADDY, IN EARLY 1930S

Mother and Daddy decided to name the business *Joyner Furniture Company*, using our family name. Who were these two bold young entrepreneurs?

Dad was a small, short man, about 5'7" in height, but he was big in every other way. He was slender in frame, had fine features with wavy brown hair and dark eyes.

Mother was about 5' tall, prim and dainty with blue-green eyes and an hourglass figure. Though my parents were small in stature, they were giants in other ways—they had to be for the new venture to succeed. The four of us, Mother and Daddy, George at age six, and I at eight, looked like the Tittlemouse Family walking along together—and we were every bit as industrious.

MOTHER IN THE EARLY 1930S

Mother, orphaned at age eight by the loss of her father, made her way, with Granny's help, to college, earning a bachelor's degree in French and history. At age twelve, Dad, the second oldest of seven children, was put in charge of his siblings working on the farm. Then as a young man, he made his way in the retail business in Weldon.

Hard knocks at an early age taught both to control their circumstances insofar as possible and to shape their destiny by means of their own talents and determination. They grew self-reliant, independent, dedicated to family, faithful in personal dealings, and devoted to the Weldon Methodist Church on Washington Avenue where my mother's people had been founding members.

For a man with a grammar-school education, a wife, and two small children, my father, William Bridgeman Joyner, was remarkably confident, maybe even daring. Some thought him foolish; others called him fearless because he was starting a new company when the country still had not recovered fully from the Depression.

During the 1930s, a quarter of the national work force had been out of work. Our family had come through the Depression without debt, but with little disposable income. George and I each had one pair of shoes for Sunday and one pair for weekdays. We wished for our first bicycles for Christmas but did not really expect them. Santa surprised us with a blue one for me and a red one for George.

Daddy knew something not obvious to others. He and his silent partner knew he would succeed. He had learned the business by doing. Having helped Mr. Garlick manage Weldon Furniture Company for several years, he knew furniture well: the varieties of woods, styles, upholstery, and the difference between well-made and cheap brands.

Inventories in his new company included the best of each line he chose, whether case goods, upholstered sofas and chairs, mattresses, kitchen appliances, or radios and record players. Dad felt many of his customers at Weldon Furniture would follow him to his new business, knowing his intention to offer high quality at reasonable prices, with reliable service. Having grown up in the country, he knew what country folks expected. He focused on conservative or Early-American styles constructed of solid woods such as mahogany, maple, and oak.

Dad knew something else. Country folks, like townspeople, appreciated fine furniture if they could afford it. From personal experience, he knew his farmer neighbors liked comfortable, well-built, durable chairs that would hold up under the wear and weight of heavy men. They took a quiet pride in their possessions, whether their barns, their machinery, or their houses. His targeted customers were like his family in Hertford County: thrifty, unpretentious, proud, serious, and appreciative of nice things.

Dad treated his customers, black or white, landowners big or small, as he would treat his relatives. Some were tenant farmers or families with about 200 acres of farmland, living from harvest to harvest. For those, and other reliable buyers, he granted credit from growing season to the next year's harvest. His customers trusted him and knew they would get a fair deal. And he trusted them in return. He knew they would pay their debts after their crops went to market.

The building had been a former automobile dealership with open space and the front had floor-to-ceiling windows across the width of the building. There was a loading dock in the back and a mezzanine for storage. Easily converted to a furniture showroom with partitions, the giant swinging doors at the back also accommodated out-going furniture ready for loading onto one of the two delivery trucks.

"Joyner, look!" my mother exclaimed, using her nickname for him. "Here come the first shipments. The two Eds are unloading beds, dressers, chests for the bedroom displays." They could hardly wait to set up the window displays.

Last, they placed a modest but precisely printed sign on the building façade at a right angle over the front door: *Joyner Furniture Company*. When they saw that go up, Dad hugged Mother, gave her a kiss on the cheek, and said, "Margaret, we've done it. Now we have to find some customers."

The company was centrally located in town, adjacent to a clothing store on one side and a gas station on the other. Directly across the street from the ABC (Alcoholic Beverage Control), Dad's building was within easy viewing of steadily heavy traffic in and out of the liquor store. Dad—a teetotaler himself—had not anticipated having such a bird's-eye view of the parade of customers frequenting the ABC store. He could have told many stories about the purchases of spirits by the town's finest, but being discreet, he never gossiped.

Dad's youngest brother, Ed Joyner, became his salesman and doubled as one of the delivery men. Frank, his nephew, was his bookkeeper. Another Ed was his delivery man. All four were excited as they opened the doors for the first time. The business grew, month upon month.

No sooner had they settled into their new routine, than the Roanoke River began to rise, developing into a flood of epic proportions—something area residents had never seen. Homes in low-lying areas had to be abandoned, roads into town were impassable, even the automobile and train bridges were compromised. Residents on higher ground took in families from down the street near the creeks.

Daddy moved furniture into his balcony storage, into our house, and into Nanny Kate's attic. Leaving it in the store spelled ruin. Every business owner moved inventory as quickly as possible and stacked sandbags against store doors and windows. Daddy placed sandbags all along the front and back of his store. When done, he could only stand and watch the water rise, inch by inch—and pray. Dad was a man of strong faith.

George and I floated our toy boats in the flooded street until the water got too high. Lapping the sandbags at the door of Joyner Furniture Company for hours, the river then seemed to pause, and slowly started receding. The store was saved; the doors could open again after the clean-up.

Dad, Frank, the two Eds and all our family helped get the furniture back in place. Business picked up again as the towns and farms resumed normal life. Daddy and Mother celebrated the birth of Margaret Ray in December 1940.

The national economy was growing. Prosperity seemed to be right around the corner.

Then another disaster struck and set Dad back. Overnight their world, and the world of every other American, was shaken to its core. SIRENS SOUNDED, AND EVERYTHING STOPPED.

A single day, December 7, 1941, that "Day of Infamy," turned lives in Weldon and everywhere else upside down. Just imagine Joyner Furniture's nascent business, beginning to take root, sales growing, and interest increasing. And then... the U.S. Government had to divert resources to a massive nationwide war effort, reducing raw materials like timber, cloth, rubber, metal, food crops, and cotton to a short supply for the public. Farmers were given 4-F deferments from the draft and told to expand their crop planting where possible. Textile mills in adjacent Roanoke Rapids operated around the clock to produce twill for uniforms and cloth for the military's towels, sheets, and blankets.

The local paper mill poured out particle board made with cuttings from acres of pine trees on local farms. Trains, filled with men and materials, raced over the Atlantic Coast Line high track every eight minutes, and the Seaboard Railway shipped freight daily to ports on the East Coast. Soldiers were stationed to guard the indispensable rail tracks and bridges over the Roanoke River. These routes were major north-south rail and highway lifelines connecting military bases and supply depots all along the East Coast.

Money was no longer the problem; scarcity was. People had jobs, but many goods, including food and gas, were rationed or out of stock entirely. Rubber tires were simply not available. There was little wood to make beds, tables, or chests. Merchants like my father could not get inventory; business shrank.

I have a vision of Dad's face now, preoccupied with figuring out how to survive. A lesser man would have been defeated, yet he accelerated his activity, rushing to buy what he could from existing inventories in the factories in High Point, in western North Carolina, and in Virginia. True to his standards, he still refused to buy cheaply made pieces. He searched every source for solid mahogany, maple, or cherry furniture, calling his manufacturers' reps and saving his ration stamps to buy gas to travel to High Point for whatever the market could offer.

Even so, the High Point market offered slim pickings, and even skipped or scaled back its schedule significantly. Any experienced businessman would have worried, but Dad, a new proprietor, must have worried constantly and even been frightened. George and I never knew it. Dad was always the calm, responsible, steady comfort in our lives. Somehow, he managed to keep the store open, obtaining and selling enough pieces to pay his bills. Mother was called back into teaching when the seventh-grade teacher left to join her Army husband. Unfortunately for her, I was in the seventh grade! No doubt, she qualified for hazardous duty pay, dealing with her own child, but at least her income helped tide us over.

One year during wartime, Dad chose to go to Chicago to the Merchandise Mart and furniture market instead of going to High Point. Traveling by train in a sleeper, he spent two days there. George and I looked on the map to see where he was going; it seemed so far away. We imagined Chicago glittering with lights and sparkling with tinsel. We knew he would bring home special gifts, gifts out of our usual orbit.

He brought George a shirt of fine cotton, me a vest of worsted wool, and Mother a gown of silk. He must have found his way to Marshall Field's.

Dad never displayed much emotion, and his return to Weldon was no exception. Jumping up and down, we begged him to tell us about the market and the city. He assured us it was a big city, full of tall buildings and with a river running through it. The Merchandise Mart was one of those tall buildings. The furniture, he said, was much the same—certainly no better than what he saw in High Point when the market there was in full gear. He had had enough of Chicago, he said, and he never went back. High Point had everything he wanted. We learned then that Dad was not a big-city man. He liked staying home.

With victory declared on September 2, 1945, good times returned. Factories turned to producing consumer goods. Cars rolled off the assembly line. Nylon stockings and lingerie filled the cases in department stores. Shelves in grocery stores offered choices at reasonable prices. And the furniture factories kicked into gear once more. Weldon merchants prospered too! Joyner Furniture Company did so well that Dad planned to open a second store in Roanoke Rapids with Uncle Ed as manager.

But then, Daddy and Mother faced another setback, this the worst yet. Uncle Ed developed an aggressive form of colon cancer that required immediate surgery. This time was different for Dad. Worry spread across his face. Multiple times, Mother, George, and I kept vigil with Dad in the waiting room of the Duke hospital. I remember clearly those waiting rooms: cold, Spartan, painted institutional cream, furnished with uncomfortable plastic-upholstered chairs. Visitors and medical staff spoke in muted tones. Hollow halls of cement walls and floors echoed every footstep.

There was nowhere to go for hot food. George and I walked from one end of the long hall and back again, through what seemed like several connected buildings. Eventually the hall emptied out onto the lawn facing the other buildings in the heart of the campus. We could at least get some fresh air there, for the days were long.

Our father was known to be a steady man with measured movements. In the hospital, he remained quiet, speaking only occasionally to Mother.

"Margaret, it is very serious. Dr. Hart himself is troubled," whispered Dad.

"We can only pray, Joyner, and comfort Eva as much as possible," replied Mother. Eva, Uncle Ed's wife, was sitting quietly, her head bowed, in a chair across the room.

Dad's faith was tested every time Uncle Ed went into the hospital. Unlike the war years, when he could control, adjust, or influence his circumstances, this situation was different; he could not cure Uncle Ed. He could not fix things and make them right. This time his anxiety was palpable. His brow wrinkled, his posture slumped, and his countenance sagged. When Dad felt helpless and unable to make things right for Ed, Eva, and Molly Jean, their daughter, we were all soon immobilized by fear and sadness.

Dr. Deryl Hart, who later became president of Duke University, performed the surgery—and another surgery and several more over a period of ten years. Each time Dad seemed more troubled than before. He knew what we did not. Each operation was riskier than the previous one. Each one could signal the end. The operations lasted six to eight—and then ten hours. It was touch and go each time.

When Uncle Ed returned from the recovery room, Dad, Mother, George, and I were permitted to go in to see him. "Come with me, Alice and George," said Daddy softly, preparing us for what was on the other side of the closed door.

"I know you want to see Uncle Ed but understand—he is not awake and is hooked up to lots of tubes." Daddy was right. Tubes and bottles and monitors were everywhere all over Uncle Ed and near his bed, though he was unconscious.

I have often wondered why my folks took George and me with them into the room. I concluded it was for the same reason I was let into my grandmother's room when she was dying. Pain, trouble, misfortune, then death are part of life. My parents wanted us to understand that truth; they did not try to shield us.

In those days—the early 1940s—chemotherapy drugs, familiar to us now, were not available. The only option for Uncle Ed was multiple surgeries. Dr. Hart, whom we thought a miracle man, kept Uncle Ed alive for ten years, though my uncle was never the energetic young man he had been before his illness, when he would bounce up our back steps every day for lunch.

He died a young man at 39, Dad's baby brother, the youngest of five males and two females, four of whom had died previously. Now Dad and Uncle George, who lived two doors down from us, were the only remaining siblings. It was hard for me to absorb the fact that most of a family's progeny could be wiped out well before middle age. Years later we learned that some members of Dad's family carried a defective gene causing colon cancer that was one hundred percent fatal if not treated early.

Rocked by Ed's death, after some time Dad regrouped and forged ahead with the business in Weldon, but he never again had a desire to expand. He cast around for a replacement for Uncle Ed and found a reliable man, Jennings Kilpatrick, who worked with him for many years. Jennings was a good customer-relations man and excellent second-in-command, but not the outgoing, vivacious salesman that Ed had been. The business stayed small, with four full-time employees, but it was profitable.

It yielded enough income to support us and to enable Dad to pay Uncle Ed's medical bills. A magnanimous man, Dad never mentioned the cost of the medical care.

"Eva, I know that, along with grieving, you are worried about paying Ed's bills and taking care of Molly," Dad said to Eva at home after the funeral. "Don't worry. I'll see that Ed's medical bills are paid."

Eva could not tap into a government safety net to see her through, but her family gave her housing and food while she got her life back together. Eva eventually remarried and had a good life on a farm near Roanoke Rapids. Her new husband was a good father to her only child, Molly, a young girl my age. I loved Molly and grieved with her; I couldn't imagine being left without my father when I was but a teenager.

More than a decade later, Dad stood outside the door of the furniture market's main building, the International Home Furnishings Center, when I approached and gave him a hug.

"Hi, Dad. It's so good to see you and to be here!" I said. "Thank you for helping me pick out furnishings for our new home."

Claud, my husband, and I had just purchased a starter house in Greensboro. It was the late 1950s and I had finished graduate school at Duke. I was now shopping in the mecca of furniture wonderland! With my pass, I felt important, as if I had earned a merit badge.

Dad instructed me, "I need to do some of my own buying. We will start that way, so you can see how purchases are made. Then, we will set out to find the showrooms you want to see."

Dad let me do the choosing; he did the purchasing. Isn't that the normal father-daughter arrangement? But, imagine being in the middle of furniture displays from all over the world. It felt to me as if the Silk Road had offered up all its wares and dumped them in the middle of High Point. Were it not for Dad's discerning guidance, I would have made several gorgeous but regrettable choices.

If Dad had concerns about a piece I was about to select, he would whisper in my ear: "The springs in the seat of that sofa are not substantial." Or, "The drawers are not mitered," or, "That fabric will fade."

In a salesroom that Dad usually visited, I was surprised to see that one of the bedroom suites had been designed by a young man from Weldon, Luther Draper.

"Dad, I didn't know Luther designed furniture!"

"Yes," Dad replied. "Actually, he is very good and has a bright future. He's just starting out."

It was a most unusual design, somewhat contemporary but also bordering on traditional. It would go well with other styles. Made with pine wood, it had dark knots in the light-grained wood that had been varnished a medium-colored tan. Cane doors on the headboard opened to provide storage for pillows. Side tables with open storage extended the headboard height and width. I chose that one.

I still have the suite in my Washington, D.C., apartment as one of those special possessions that carries deep meaning for me, with secret stories buried in its headboards and drawers. Every time I crawl into that bed, I recount all the places that bedroom furniture and I have traveled together—eight places I have lived!

Another piece of my lifelong furniture also has deep personal associations for me. Mr. Foscue, a gracious, kind gentleman, had a factory that made strikingly elegant upholstered furniture. He and Dad were friends. At the market that day, I eyed a barrel chair with soft-gold damask upholstery. That same chair, structurally sound and upholstered several times over by now, occupies a favored spot in my living room today. Today's customers don't have the opportunity to enjoy Mr. Foscue's chairs because his plant closed years ago—and neither can they benefit from his gentlemanly nature. To me, he seemed to be much like my father, a model of honesty and propriety for his time.

What impressed me most about Dad's navigating the market was the way he circulated among the salesrooms, talking with reps who serviced his accounts.

"Mr. Joyner," the rep would begin, "don't you need to buy a little extra to anticipate new customers? And, look at this new design. Folks will love it when they see it."

"I appreciate your wanting to take care of me. I'll let you know if I can find a customer for it. I've done all I can do today." Dad would hold his ground, telling them he would stick with his original order. He was never dismissive but always friendly, courteous, firm, and efficient with the salesmen. Soon, I began to see why he was successful—he bought what his customers valued, not what he thought was attractive or stylish.

Every now and then, I'd ask him, "Why not buy that piece?"

"It won't sell," he'd tell me. "Not in Weldon. My customers like traditional furniture, either sturdy-boxy chairs for comfort or early-American for their parlors." So much for my furniture-business savvy!

Despite his tireless dedication to his customers, Dad was not all work and no play. He took us on vacations to the mountains, to the beach, and to Washington, D.C. At Myrtle Beach, he rode Margaret Ray on his shoulders out into the ocean waves. He liked to go New York when he visited me in Princeton, but only to see the Yankees play.

When business flourished after the War, Dad bought two show horses. All three of us learned as children to ride, but George and my sister, Margaret, went on to participate in horse shows, bringing home many ribbons. Dad was also an active trustee of the Weldon Methodist Church and taught Sunday school classes as well. Truly, to us, he was a man for all seasons.

Like Job, Dad was tested time and time again. In the 1970s, fire broke out downtown in Weldon in the block where his store was located. The clothing store next door was ablaze, as were the two businesses next door to that one. Flames flashed toward and over the roof of Dad's store. Fire engines from Weldon, Roanoke Rapids, and Garysburg tried to contain and control the blaze, but it roared through the other buildings, destroying inventory, furnishings, and walls. To save Dad's store, multiple fire hoses sprayed the sides and roof, hoping to keep the flames at bay. Standing silently across the street, Dad, quiet and stoic as usual, watched for hours as the firemen struggled.

"It's in the hands of the Lord, Margaret. I can't do anything but pray for those firefighters," he said quietly to Mother but mostly to himself.

The store was saved. Some of the furniture was water-damaged but, having been covered, most was intact. Dad's was the lone store standing on the street after the fire. The picture shows the vacant lots where the other three stores had been.

Dad knew Weldon and was happy there. He enjoyed his business colleagues, his customers, and his buddies who came over to the store each day to sit in several comfortable chairs they had used so much he couldn't offer them for sale! When I stopped by, they'd be drinking Cokes and talking about the crops, the weather, or baseball. ("Shooting the bull," we called it.) The men sat directly under a portrait of FDR hanging from a tall column in the middle of the store. Dad put that portrait up the day he opened the store, when FDR was president, and it remained there until the store closed in 1976.

DAD'S STORE AFTER THE FIRE

Joyner Furniture Company stayed in business until Dad was 79 years old. He watched over it six days a week, from 8 o'clock in the morning until 6 o'clock at night, taking only one week's vacation a year. In all those years, he missed only one week of work because of illness.

Early one morning in 1976, before I went to work, my phone in Princeton rang. "Alice, I don't know what to do. I want to sell the business." Dad declared. "I'm tired. Two or three times I've told Margaret I want to retire. I've worked in the store every day for over 35 years. Each time I bring it up, she agrees it is time to step down so we can travel and visit you, George, and Margaret Ray. And, I'd like to start a garden and carve some small wood products

I have in mind for the grandchildren. Yet, when time comes to act, your mother changes her mind!"

Though she wouldn't admit it, Mother did not like change. To her, change meant another chapter in her life was ending.

"Dad, I think you ought to sell. Mother will adjust. She always does. Once the deal is done and the papers are signed, she will be fine. She is resilient and has always faced the future with optimism. When she begins to think of all the advantages, she will be fine."

A week later, he signed the contract to sell the business to the single remaining furniture store in town. Immediately, she got her suitcases out of the closet and started planning for their visits to see their children and grandchildren. She was determined not to miss out on their golden years!

Dad's retirement gave them fourteen more good years together—twelve active years for Dad, with the remaining two in a critical-care facility. When he developed Parkinson's disease, Mother could no longer care for him or find reliable 24-hour-a-day help. She grieved his departure from home so much. Despite that setback, they both made the best of the situation.

She visited him every day, even organizing a social group composed of patients and caregivers that met every afternoon in the sunroom for drinks and cookies. They called it "Afternoon Tea" and invited all newcomers to join the group. Because poor eyesight prevented her from driving, friends picked her up, taking her to and from Guardian Care every day. Sometimes it was a former student, sometimes a patrolman, sometimes other visitors who dropped by.

In addition to Mother, Dad had another guardian angel. Arlene was a nurses' aide employed by the nursing home. She cared for Dad every day she was on duty, requesting that she be assigned his wing. On her days off, she called every day to check on him. We marveled at her attentiveness.

One day, she asked to speak with Mother and me.

"Ms. Joyner, I will always watch over Mr. Joyner. He has been so very good to my family over the years."

"How's that, Arlene?" Mother asked.

"He not only sold us sturdy furniture that has lasted, he gave us a helping hand when we needed to extend our credit. He gave us a rug or lamp for Christmas. He didn't forget us," she said. "And I'm not going to forget him."

"I appreciate that very much, Arlene," Mother replied. "I am grateful for your friendship."

No doubt, Dad helped them in other ways we never knew, but Arlene knew. She was with him until he died, and she joined our family at his funeral.

How many others he helped, I do not know. I do know he got men out of jail after Saturday-night fights. I do know he gave customers substantial gifts at Christmastime, and I do know he gave needy country people money or loans to tide them over in tough times. He never talked about it. I just saw it happen from time to time or heard about it from others.

He was a magnanimous man of honor. When he died, the church overflowed with people from all over the county. He was Weldon's oldest citizen, but he had lived his life in such a way that there were only good things to say about him.

Fifty years after Dad took me to the market in High Point, Bobby George came up from Georgia to take me to the market again. Bobby had recently retired as Vice President of Bassett Furniture Company, which was by 2000 the largest furniture manufacturer in the world. Bobby's factory was in Macon, Georgia, a Southern mini-city that attracts tourists to its tree-lined streets filled with historic three-story buildings decorated with fancy-carved woodwork across the façades of their roof lines. Two city blocks on hills overlooking the downtown are lined with antebellum homes that compete for elegance and expansive views. Macon is a serene, seemingly lazy paradise for those who can tolerate the summer heat and humidity.

In his twenties, fresh out of N.C. State with a degree in furniture manufacturing, Bobby went to work for Art Furniture in Macon. Soon, Art was bought out by Bassett, and Bobby succeeded the previous owner, managing the factory and turning out thousands of tables a month. His factory became one more star in Bassett's crown. With Clara, his wife, and Victoria (Tori), his daughter, he stayed in Macon throughout his career, becoming what outsiders called an *ex-officio* member of the Bassett clan, and caring for Clara through the eight years of her struggle with Alzheimer's.

Bobby found me through a mutual friend, Sonny Hines, and learned that Pinehurst, then my hometown, would be a convenient stop on the way to Bassett, Virginia, to see his cousins and the Bassetts—and the Philpotts and the Spilmans and everybody else in Bassett, all of whom seem related to each other in some way.

At our reunions, we traded tales of growing up in Weldon and Roanoke Rapids. Unknown to me, Bobby had worked for Daddy during his teen years, not in the furniture business but by taking care of one of his horses. In truth, Bobby had hated Tony, a handsome, white-stockinged, black Tennessee walker, because every time Bobby tried to get him to come in from the pasture, the horse bit him.

"But it was a job, Alice, and I needed spending money. I couldn't afford to quit," Bobby chuckled and shook his head.

"All of us needed jobs," I reminded him. "I worked at the swimming pool. It was the only way I had any discretionary income for clothes and fun." Little did Bobby realize then that he, like my father, would be a furniture man.

On his visit to Pinehurst in 2006, Bobby compared Daddy's visits to the market with his own years later. "Not much had changed—during the day, that is!" Bobby said. "I spent the entire market week there, meeting customers and suppliers in the Bassett building and suite. But, evenings off were pretty lively, for the buttoned-down Southern town of High Point."

"I don't imagine Dad wanted any part of the night life," I said. "He came home to Weldon as soon as he had transacted his business. He didn't drink and didn't like nighttime entertainment. He liked to watch baseball on TV."

Talking about the market whetted the appetite of my friends, and Bobby offered to take some of them to market, too. Bassett provided passes for us all, and that was the beginning of our semi-annual adventures. His car, a Jeep Cherokee, accommodated five of us heading to High Point twice a year for several years—not the same friends each time, except for me.

ALICE AND BOBBY IN HIGHLANDS, N.C.

Bobby and I spread the wealth of our tickets and travel among many folks in Pinehurst. One of my friends, Sarah Hargrove, went more than once. She was a fast walker, covering as many salesrooms as possible in the time we had—and also spaces in both the main buildings and salesrooms that lined the streets. After the second trip with Sarah, Bobby said, out of breath, "I just can't keep up with you ladies. You exhaust me. I'll wait for you in the Bassett suite." Truth be known, he wanted to gossip with Ann Holland, Jeff Philpott, Louis Horne, and any other Bassett employee who was around.

LADIES AT THE FRONT DESK
LEFT, DALE BELLE; CENTER, ANN HOLLAND; RIGHT, LAURIE LAPIER

Behind our backs, the women working the desk in the reception area referred to us as Bobby's harem because he brought a carful of female guests each time—and helped us carry small purchases home. They teased him about being a ladies' man. He grinned with pleasure, turned a bright shade of pink, and nodded appreciatively. Bobby's full name was Robert George, so they called him Mr. G. for short. Giving him big hugs, they said, "Mr. G. talks a tall tale but, in real life, he was a kind, steady, humorous, and patient boss when he ran the factory."

And, that's the way it was...for years. Two good men, men I loved very much, made their way in the same industry, Dad in retail, Bobby in manufacturing. A good furniture man needs to be part businessman and part artist. The numbers must work for the bottom line, but without a good eye for wood grains, for proportion in design, and for styles that are popular, one cannot run a furniture business successfully. Both Daddy and Bobby had those skills. The trait that topped it all off for both was their concern for their customers. They wanted the pieces they made and sold to *fit*: to fit the room, the occasion, and the owner.

Dad left our world in 1990. Bobby left in August 2017. Things change; things stay the same. For me, the High Point Furniture Market will always be abundant with stunning furniture and elaborate showrooms, but also with the ever-present ghosts of two of the kindest and most honorable men in the world.

January 2018

Of Fortitude and Courage

It's that time in my life: fourscore and four. Friends don't just fade away. They die.

This year, first it was Jerry, my farmer friend; then Harvey, my book-discussion buddy; then Tom, Teddy Murphy's husband and my friend from days in Princeton; then Lou, husband of my book-club friend Jane Galan; then James' grandmother, Fredericki Klarevas; Bobby, my high-school friend; and now Ruth.

Ruth Proctor, who loved my mother as if she were her own, became my good friend after Mother died in 1991. Ruth and her husband Con retired to their family home in Halifax and became pillars of the close-knit historic community.

Ruth was a Gregory and, when I was young and living in Weldon, there seemed to be more Gregorys in Halifax than all the other residents put together. Gregory houses were everywhere, in town and on the edge. Some family members have lived in Halifax all their lives; some moved to Weldon or Scotland Neck; some, like Ruth and Con, moved away. Along with the Dickens families, the Gregorys kept the economy going and worked to preserve the village's historic character. Historic Halifax, a town of no more than a few thousand inhabitants at its peak, was the location of the first formal resolution for independence in the colonies.

Ruth restored her family home, renewed her membership in St. Mark's Episcopal Church, participated in the preservation efforts to refurbish and open historic houses to the public, and hosted a tea every Christmas as part of Christmas in Halifax.

Ruth Gregory was a Colonial Dame, but she was not "uppity." Until her death, I did not know what pre-Revolutionary roots she had. She was a sharp-featured, large-boned woman who could do anything she set her mind to do. She loved the land. Her gardens were models of horticulture, thriving in the loamy, black delta soil of the Roanoke River. From her tomato crop each year, she harvested her own tomato seeds for next year's crop.

On one visit, she gave me six cherry tomatoes, "Alice, take these six tomatoes, collect the seeds, put them on foil to dry and, when dry, put them in a small glass jar until spring. Then, plant them in the ground or in big pots. When they start growing, stake them because they will grow to four or four-and-a-half feet."

I did as she told me and became the "Tomato Lady" of the neighborhood; I had so many tomatoes I had to give many away. In the sandy, beach-like soil of Pinehurst, North Carolina, my tomato plants increased in number so that I ran out of space to plant them.

One year I had so many green tomatoes at frost time that I gathered them in a bushel basket and taught myself how to make chutney. I had never canned anything in my life—that was the specialty of my mother and sister. Thanks to Ruth's faith in me—as well as a tip or two—and *The Joy of Cooking,* I succeeded. The chutney was good enough to share as homemade Christmas presents.

Just this past week, I bought a cherry tomato plant, thinking of Ruth and her garden. I have a spot for a planter on my 9' x 13' porch. I chose a Sweet Baby Girl variety and a big container that wouldn't blow over with the strong breezes that sweep through my third-floor balcony. Daily, I watch my plant grow.

I miss my plot of land in Pinehurst. Living in Raleigh in a condo deprives me of the habit of going out in the yard, digging a small hole, and putting a plant in it. It is the first place I have ever lived where I could not lay hands on a fistful of dirt or trim a bush with my hand clippers.

Lacking such access intensifies my desire for the sensation of feeling dirt sift through my fingers. I hear birds in the trees nearby, but I can't see them flying around the yard, poking in the grass for food, and then taking off into the sky. Walking on the track in the gym is not the same as walking around the lake, listening to the chorus of bird songs or cicadas interrupting the twilight hours. I am where I am for necessary and good reasons, but I also mark big zeroes in the lifestyle column of the ledger.

Ruth died just when I thought she was improving from another stroke. She had spoken with me a few days earlier and her death was not expected. She died of pneumonia after being rushed to the hospital but not in time. What a twist of fate! My mother died in similar fashion: unexpectedly from contracting pneumonia while in the hospital in Rocky Mount recovering from successful carotid artery surgery.

Ruth and I became close friends as we shared each other's grief when Mother died. Had Mother lived to go home, she was going to live with Ruth for a couple of months until she could return to our family home in Weldon, seven miles away. The unexpected turn of events knocked us back on our heels. Mother had been released from the hospital to go to Ruth's when she collapsed on the hospital floor.

To this day, I fear the doctors were negligent. Had I lived in North Carolina at the time, I would have asked for a Board of Inquiry review. It couldn't have brought her back, but it might have led to an examination of hospital procedures. We learn to live with loss when the misery of causation remains unsolved, but it never leaves us entirely. Even today, on my way to Weldon from Raleigh, I travel Route 64 East to Interstate 95 North, coming within a mile of that Rocky Mount hospital. Were it directly in my path, I would devise an alternate route because I cannot bear to drive by it, the source of my deepest loss. Nor have I been to the town of Rocky Mount since Mother's death. I pass through on the train to Washington, but I don't get out and touch the ground.

Mother developed a hacking cough, but I don't think the doctors x-rayed her lungs until she collapsed. Then it was too late, though they did everything they could to save her during the three weeks that she lingered. Ruth was at the hospital almost every day. George, Margaret, and I took turns staying with her every day and night. Near the end, I lived in the ICU waiting room, sleeping on chairs, or in a sleeping bag on the floor, anywhere to be near. Mother died December 8, 1991, having addressed her Christmas cards, wrapped her gifts, and left everything in order for us. It was a Sunday morning and she died around 11 a.m., just when church bells were ringing.

We drove back to Weldon, needing breakfast or something to eat, and went to the local Cracker Barrel. That spot is now marked forever with a memory of our sadness and grief.

As I walked in the back door at home, I remembered Mother's behavior when she faced the loss of a loved one: She scrubbed the kitchen floor. Physical activity spent her nervousness and restored her composure. In my case, I released my nervous energy by going to the grocery store to fill our pantry with food for the next several days. My siblings and I "picked up" the house, readying it for visitors. *Keep busy*, Mother whispered from afar.

Later, Louis Reinoso, her minister, told us that she had predicted her death. How did she know? How strange, we thought, given that she was in good health. In fact, just three weeks earlier, at age 87, she had given the keynote address at a town Thanksgiving celebration.

Sadness at Christmas for the last 28 years has not disappeared. The family no longer gathers in Weldon at "Home." The home, built in 1916 by my grandmother, was sold as soon as we cleaned it out. I think back to Christmases there as a small child: wreath on the door; candles in the large-paned windows; the full fir tree in the high-ceiling living room; and chairs for meals at every possible spot in the dining room. Two wood-burning stoves dominated the kitchen, each stovetop covered by pots and each oven filled with roasters. Tables loaded with cakes and pies filled the back porch. What Joy!

I need to recognize there is joy now, too, of course. I am settled near Andrea and her family, for whom I am grateful. She is imaginative in suggesting Christmas activities and stretches herself to make me comfortable and happy. She takes me places, making sure I don't shrivel up at home alone in my comfortable, attractive apartment.

For many years Ruth and I took wreaths to the cemetery; stopping to say a prayer of gratitude for my parents. Not since 2013 have we done that. I was ill in 2015 and could not get to Halifax and Weldon. Last year, 2016, Ruth had been moved to an assisted-living facility in Asheville, near her son Bill. Her cognitive powers were intact, but her speech and balance had been affected by several ministrokes. Now, there will be no more trips for the two of us to the Weldon cemetery. But Ruth will not be far away in Halifax—7 miles. I will visit both cemeteries from time to time.

Funerals are reunions, not simply memorial services. That was the case for me at Ruth's gathering. At St. Mark's Episcopal Church in Halifax last Saturday, every pew was filled with Ruth's large family, her friends from Halifax, and those from several other states. Reverend Duffy conducted the service. Ruth's son, Greg, an Episcopal minister, read scripture from *John* and *Romans*. Two psalms were read: the 23rd and the 120th. We all sang "Oh God My Help in Ages Past," without need of a hymnal.

Ruth, strong-willed and insistent, did not want a eulogy. Reverend Duffy abided by her instructions but did tell a story quite typical of Ruth. Because of her strokes, she had lost her ability to drive her car. She was unable to walk long distances unassisted, and golf carts were not permitted on the streets of Halifax. She lived several blocks from the church but was determined not to miss church services.

Without consulting anyone, she got a scooter and proceeded to go from her yard, out onto Hwy 301—a very busy road—and around the corner, down the street to the church. Imagine an octogenarian outfitted in Sunday dress, pedaling down the side street on a scooter. That took guts—and a strong faith! When Rev. Duffy found out about it, he insisted he pick her up every Sunday. Reluctantly, she consented; her sons had given the scooter away.

The celebratory aspect of the gathering was seeing people with whom I had grown up 65-70 years ago. Some I had not been around since high school graduation. A few I had encountered about a decade ago. In the pews were Letha Page, my classmate Clyde's sister; Undine Caudle Garner, my sister's friend; Fred Gregory, my brother's classmate; Sandra Garner, Jimmy Garner's wife; Tommie Bass Cubine, now living in Virginia Beach, and Patterson Wilson, Glenn Dickens' daughter. Glenn took me under her wing, driving me to the cemetery and reception.

St. Mark's has not changed in 60-70 years, except that it has air conditioning, a good heating system, and new paint. And I discovered an artifact in the pew that went back 70 years: a cardboard hand-held fan provided by Branch Funeral Home. The fan has endured whereas the funeral home is in its own grave! Sixty years ago, fans like that saved many a woman's dress when hot flashes suddenly rushed over their faces.

I knew that Ruth had attended the Woman's College and that she became a medical technician. I knew that she was a devoted member of St. Mark's and also a member of The Halifax Historical Restoration Association. She and her home were featured in the Halifax Christmas open house each year. She was so modest that I did not know she had a string of memberships after her name that included the local garden club, the Daughters of the American Revolution, the Colonial Dames, and the First Families of North Carolina. She never spoke of those organizations, but they knew about her. The DAR was represented in force at the funeral: four regional directors decorated with elaborate badges and medals sat right behind the family.

The reception was as elegant as any wedding I have attended. For the first time, I met Tina Gregory, the talented, gracious woman who has made the wreaths for my parents' graves since their deaths. She and her husband, Tommy Gregory, restored the family home of Mr. Quentin, one of the well-known Gregory brothers. The mansion, a large red-brick home on the outskirts of Halifax, had fallen into disrepair. Tina and Tommy rescued it. Her artistic abilities enhanced a home with "good bones," filling it with furniture, appointments, and artworks of historical and current interest. A visit gave the sure sense that Mr. Quentin and his family were still residents. Tommy, in his nineties now, still makes small pieces of furniture. He says that when God knocks a tree down on his property, he picks it up and makes a bench or table out of it. Even crepe myrtle branches serve as legs of a stool.

Tina and Tommy don't live in the home. I couldn't believe it; it is so lovely and comfortable, I'd want to live there always. They say it's too big for two people and requires too much regular care. They live in nearby Roanoke Rapids, so Mr. Quentin's historic home, "The Pines," is used chiefly for special occasions, including weddings and receptions. Tina invited me to visit when next in Halifax. I enjoyed meeting her and would like to see her again.

Ruth's death led me to relive the events surrounding my grandmother's death. I was five years old that year of 1937. Though I was not yet in school, that loss resides deep in my psyche. I store it in my soul's cupboard, far back in the corner of the pantry. But now and then an event opens the pantry door to my memory, all is as it was then.

Granny, Alice Anderson Hudson, died of pneumonia at age 62. Penicillin didn't exist then and thus infections were not easily cured. She had been sick off and on for a while. I remember that she also had gall-bladder trouble, but primarily her lungs were weak. She had had to use an oxygen tent during this illness and the last one, too.

When healthy, she led the choir and sang in the Weldon Methodist Church. As a young child, I loved to watch her. I don't remember her singing a solo in church, but I remember Mother speaking of it. Genie, my aunt, inherited Granny's voice, a deep ruby-colored contralto. What I remember most is that Granny was singing as she was dying. Propped up in the bed, with the oxygen tent over her head and upper part of her body, Granny was leaning back and singing with her eyes closed. Soon after that, she died at home in Weldon.

Alice Belle Anderson was born in Weldon, where she lived all her life except for a few years in Emporia, Virginia. My grandfather, William Henry Hudson, had been transferred there to manage the railroad freight office. Mother never got over the embarrassment of having been born in Virginia rather than in North Carolina.

Granny's bed was in the first-floor bedroom, the same spot as Mother and Dad's in subsequent years. The door was closed all the time, except when Mother and others tending Granny went in. They knew she was dying. Even Dr. Suiter had given up hope. Mother let me in to see her and say goodbye, though I did not know I was saying goodbye. I think Granny wanted to tell me goodbye, but I could not understand her words through the oxygen tent.

Before she got so very ill, but was bedridden, I went home from kindergarten every day and crawled in bed with her to spend the afternoon close by. She was my idol, and I had been named Alice in her honor. Mother said it took a year for me to transfer fully my love back to her. As with Mother's unexpected death in 1991, I never recovered fully from Granny's loss. I moved on, but deep down, even today the losses of both Granny and Mother are still sharp and poignant.

I remember that a friend of the family on Woodlawn Avenue took George and me to her house. I can't remember her name, but she may have been the wife of the chief of police. The husband kept George downstairs to tell him that Granny had died, although, at three years of age, he was too young to realize the significance of it.

The wife took me upstairs into her bedroom and told me Granny had died and would be going to a place where I could not see her. "Alice," she said, "you won't be able to sit on the bed with Granny again. She has gone to another place."

"What do you mean not see her?" I insisted. "She's at home right now. Where is she going? If she's leaving, I am going with her."

The woman tried to comfort me, but I wasn't listening. "I will take you back home so your mother can explain things to you," said the woman, not knowing how to deal with my hostility.

I tried to keep from crying because I was with a stranger, but I was agitated and frightened. I wanted to go with Granny wherever she was going, and I felt a deep sinking in me each time the lady told me I would never see Granny again.

Before the funeral, Mother took me into the room where Granny's casket was positioned. "Why is she in that box with all that cloth around her?" I asked Mother.

"She's ready to take a trip to another place, Alice, and she won't be coming back," Mother said flat out. Immediately, I tried to crawl into the casket, crying out "Don't leave me, Granny!" She couldn't leave me; I had made up my mind!

Mother hugged me tight and cried along with me. "The Lord has taken her home to him," she said. "And it is not time for us to go yet."

I remember trying to wake Granny up, calling her by name. "She's just asleep," I kept insisting as Mother hugged me tighter. Finally, I realized she was not going to wake up. I fell on Mother's shoulder, sobbing frantically because I loved Granny with all my being.

I don't remember the funeral; it was at home. Maybe a family member stayed with George and me in Mother's bedroom. I do remember the graveside service and the flowers. The wreaths spread out beyond the fenced-in family plot.

Mother and Daddy, Uncle Bill and his wife Doots, and Aunt Genie and Tommy, her husband, were devastated—lost. Granny had been the matriarch of her extended family, the centripetal force that kept everything together. Mother and Bill, along with their spouses and my brother and I, lived in Granny's boarding and rooming house. Genie, the younger daughter, lived down the street in a bungalow.

The three siblings received guests at the Hudson home at 401 Elm Street. People came from everywhere. They sat in the living room, stood in the hall, rocked on the porch, convened in the dining room and the kitchen. The boarders came wearing their hats and gloves, the roomers in their Sunday dress. Church members and elders came to pay respects to my granny. Alice Anderson Hudson had been a pillar of the community, a woman devoted to family, church, and community.

Her ancestors, the early Andersons, were Methodist ministers and farmers, but Granny's father became a railroad man. The Hudsons came to North Carolina from Alabama and took jobs on the railroad. Her husband and brother took railroad jobs. Such jobs were highly prized,

Weldon becoming a busy terminus during the Civil War, and, for decades beyond, Weldon had shifting yards and multiple tracks requiring more workers. And after the war, additional track was laid and well-paying jobs were added. The railroads brought prosperity to the town, and, along with the river, provided modern means of transporting farm crops to market. The standard of living was good, drawing newcomers from all around.

Railroads brought heartbreak as well. Granny's father, T. F. Anderson, was killed by an oncoming train as he moved to switch a line on the track. Her husband Henry's brother was killed in a train accident too. And Henry, also a railroad man, was sent to Johns Hopkins for what turned out to be an appendectomy and died suddenly in 1913 at age 41 from blood poisoning.

Granny was widowed with three children but no means of support because a fluke in Henry's insurance policy left the proceeds to his family, who chose not to share them with Granny. Granny was literate, well-educated for the time, a good musician but not trained professionally for any vocation. Her losses, coming in quick succession, would have defeated a lesser woman. But her will, self-discipline and determination, along with her faith, gave her strength to cope with the present and future.

Kate, her sister, was also married to a railroad man, Captain George Hawks, a kind, generous man of regal bearing, attired daily in a long-tailed coat for work. He was a conductor on the Seaboard branch from Weldon to Kinston and back.

CAPTAIN GEORGE AND NANNY KATE HAWKS

Regulars who rode the train every day, to and from work, held him in such high regard that when he began walking with a cane, they took their tickets to him rather than waiting for him to collect them by walking unsteadily down the aisle. He had provided well for Kate and offered to help Granny build a home next door to them that would be large enough for her to establish a board-and-room business. She struggled for many years with that work until her children were old enough to lend a hand. Gradually, she was able to employ adequate household help to cook, clean, chop wood, and do yard work.

THE HOME PLACE, 401 ELM STREET, WELDON, N. C.

Her business was not a tourist home that served the itinerant traveling public in towns with no hotels. There were two such homes in Weldon. Granny housed individuals or couples who stayed for several months or a year, so-called permanent or repeating guests. She also welcomed spinster teachers who came to town for the academic year. One resident was a patrolman. In addition to a few boarders, she served meals to 15-20 people daily at lunch and at dinner. To those she housed, she gave free breakfasts. Each day, boarders arrived early to get the first seating. Otherwise, they would have to wait the better part of an hour because Granny's reputation for fine food had spread far beyond the town's borders.

Her offerings were not what we would now call *gourmet*, but they typified bountiful, tasty Southern cooking.

George and I liked most of the dishes: apple float with homemade custard, collards with ham hock, fresh butter beans and corn, lemon chess pie with meringue, huckleberry fool, pot roast, and, of course, Southern fried chicken with mashed potatoes. Whether we liked all those dishes or not, we had to clean our plates. No one could waste food, especially during the Depression when people all around us were hungry.

Granny's business provided the safety net for our large family's welfare during the 1930s, but especially a cushion in case Dad and Bill suffered reduced wages from their retail jobs. Mother and Doots continued the business for several years after Granny died until they paid off the debts for Granny's repeated illnesses. Rainy-day funds to dip into for paying the expense of medical care were rare then, nor was there medical insurance, or Social Security of any kind. Except for a few wealthy landowners with deep pockets, residents often exhausted their savings in times of trouble, and then endured dispiriting poverty for years to come.

Every woman on my family tree going back several generations was a strong, self-sufficient woman with independent ways. They were models of courage and hope, giving me the confidence to strike out on my own when the time came. Sometimes, as I look down upon their graves, I imagine their daily lives and some of the hurdles they overcame.

Granny in her black taffeta gown with full skirt, tight bodice and high-neck collar with cameo pinned in the middle, pictured below, was as strong and courageous as any pioneer woman.

GRANNY WITH FRIEND, EARLY TWENTIETH CENTURY

Her hair is swept up in a bun on top of her head with the fullness of soft brown hair shaping her face. I imagine she has been to church, served the midday meal, and is sitting on the porch conversing with one of her boarders. The boarder compliments her on her Sunday dinner, especially the pound cake she had made from scratch using the long, curved wooden platter to mix the ingredients by hand: sugar, shortening, milk, eggs, flour, and lemon and vanilla flavoring. She claimed that you had to feel the batter to know whether it was light enough. You also had to feel the heat in the oven to gauge the temperature because there were no thermometers then to measure it.

I can see Mother in her gingham dress overlaid with a homemade apron—always with pockets to hold her small hand towels—standing in the 100-degree, humid kitchen, laboring over two wood- and coal-burning stoves to prepare lunch for the boarders.

"How much longer before we have fed all of the boarders? It is so hot in here—like Hades itself!" she exclaims, wiping her brow, "Lord help me."

"Miss Margaret," Geneva, the cook, says, "it's summertime in the South! Not enough fans in all creation to keep us cool. We *all* drippin'."

Doots, in charge of the dining room, is setting the table and making sure the tablecloths and linens are fresh. A good-humored woman, she always brought cheer to the busy kitchen, cracking harmless jokes about the boarders and their behavior in the dining room.

"You won't believe what the Sisters are talking about now," she reports, "telling everybody why they can't come to lunch if anyone here complains about a cold. They're sure they will get pneumonia. So, count them out for tomorrow. They probably just want to save a dollar, so let 'em eat canned soup at home."

The portable fans are whirling, the windows are open, and the doors to the rest of the house are closed to lessen the temperature in the dining room. Mother is looking forward to a cool shower and an afternoon nap, but there may not be time since she has to be sure George and I are not in trouble. We like to hide and spy on the boarders, hoping to hear gossip we can pass on to our friends.

I see Genie sitting at the sewing machine or in a straight-back chair with folds of cloth around her, turning a hem, patching a hole, crocheting a monogram on the linens used in the bedrooms of the roomers. She is perched inside where it is cooler, but she, too, is wiping her brow, trying to manage all that heavy cloth on her lap.

Genie is the seamstress with the golden thumb; she can do anything with a needle and thread! When not overworked with household linens, she creates her own designs and patterns, then transforms them into dresses and even wedding gowns for young brides. She makes clothes for all of us. Years later, Mother sent me off to spend a week with Genie with instructions to learn to sew. From that time on, I was able to make many of my clothes and fashion outfits for my family for Christmas.

On wash day, all our able-bodied women gather on the back porch, turning it into a laundry with big black pots on the floor and a round-tubbed washer and wringer. Before transferring the linens from the pots where they are soaking to the washer, Doots scrubs each piece with Octagon soap, moving her knuckles and strong fingers fast as lightning in rubbing the cloth against the washboard. Mother wrings the clothes out, three times through the wringer, frowning down on the endless quantity of soiled linens.

"There are so many sheets here, the wringers are going to break before we can finish," Mother sighs with fatigue.

"Not many more—just think one at a time," Bessie, always the calm one, says as she grabs them up next and hangs them on the three outside lines to dry.

They all pray for wash days to be sunny days.

Better than a fortune teller, the hands of the women tell of hard work and little leisure. Yet, I know they are happy women who enjoy visiting with family, friends, members of their church circles, and the many people who cross the threshold of their home.

THE FAMILY, *CIRCA* 1942.

ALICE; BILL WITH ALAN GRAY, HIS AND DOOTS' SON; TOMMY, GENIE'S HUSBAND; GENIE; DOOTS; MOTHER HOLDING ELLEN, GENIE'S DAUGHTER; DADDY HOLDING MARGARET RAY. NOT PRESENT: GEORGE.

They laugh at their mistakes and celebrate their achievements. They love with open energy and are loved by the men in our family. I have good reason still to mourn their loss, but I also feel the fullness of their lives and the daily joy that sustained them until they found their resting place in the family cemetery.

Now that I have reached my four-score decade and more, perception of loss has become a big part of my life. I am trying to cope, though, concluding that loss makes living more precious. That became apparent recently when I was notified about Bobby George's death. One little illness after another had gotten in his way, though each time, he had bounced back. On Sunday, August 20, 2017, I talked with him by phone. A blood clot in his leg had put him in the hospital, full of frustrations about having to be in rehab again and learning to walk without a walker. At that moment, he was watching the Atlanta Braves—and griping about them because they were losing!

We made plans for our next meeting, deciding to go to Weldon and Roanoke Rapids to put flowers on the graves of family members. We had done that a couple of years earlier.

Tori, his daughter, told me when she called a day or so later that I was probably the last person to speak to him. Bobby's death was sudden, a heart attack in the middle of the night. Another shock, another unexpected loss.

We are told that memory is selective. By grace, our minds sift out the ugly and painful, leaving a past dominated by the bright scenes of warm friendships, sustaining loves, and professional successes. That's what we are told, but I am not so sure. I believe grief can rekindle memories that come gushing into consciousness like a runaway garden hose. In those times, I experience discomfort and pain again for a while, but in the end, there is reconciliation, acceptance, and peace.

Every day I'm aware that I can breech the unknown anytime. And, every day, I thank the Lord and my parents for my life and mental capacity to enjoy that day. I am grateful for my brother and sister. I am more in love than ever with my daughter and my grandson. On any given day, I list the friends with whom I have been in touch that day: business associates, childhood buddies, college classmates, new residents of my apartment building. An elderly friend in Pinehurst, Ellen Woodard, who has suffered much loss in her life, always answers my salutation of "How are you today, Ellen?" with "Nothing but Blessings, Alice, Nothing but Blessings." No matter how dire the circumstances, she finds a way to see the good in life every day. I want to face every day with her cheerfulness.

I try. I am no longer driven—to achieve, to succeed, and to fix a thing or a person. I'm no longer that intrepid upstart daredevil who climbed the sheer walls of success in a man's world. A dose of equanimity and contentment has finally buoyed my being. "Retiring from retirement," as Jimmy, my dear friend from Weldon, says, has made a big difference for me. In July 2016, I ceased all commitments to organizations, whether as a leader or a follower or in any role that involved time and sustained mental commitment over months or years.

I now concentrate on nurturing friendships and my familial relationships. I try to see my siblings more often. I enjoy being with my daughter, Andrea, and taking trips with her. I see her frequently now that I have moved to

Raleigh. She saved my life—literally—and my sanity a year ago. I look forward to traveling with her before the holidays to see my grandson in Konstanz, Germany.

City life in Raleigh provides the stimulation of the symphony and the enjoyment of the ballet. There are many places to shop, but at my age, who wants to buy more stuff? I do enjoy good restaurants in town, such as Caffé Luna, the Midtown Grille, and Saint Jacques. I still get to Washington, D.C., to check out my apartment and see friends. I don't nap but I require eight hours of sleep. I used to think anything more than six hours of sleep was wasting my life away! I take more trips to doctors than I ever imagined, but I also take Tai Chi for arthritis and get gel shots in my knees. I go to the gym several times a week so that I can keep moving every day. It's not a bad life.

Yet I sense I am winding down. I am winding down the exhilarating, exuberant life of seventy years of involvement, trying to be useful, and enjoying new adventures. Now I am assuming the quieter, contemplative life of reading books with my book-club friends and recording the search for ancestors with my brother and sister. Since I will be one of those ancestors soon enough, I'd better make their good, lively acquaintance now.

August 2017

South Toward Home

I got halfway toward home in 1978, when I moved to Washington from Princeton.

Twenty years later, I made it all the way home.

But how did I finally decide where in North Carolina to settle?

I mean "settle," not visit, not immigrate, but settle. I am a North Carolinian by birth, a Southerner by genealogy, and a Country Girl by geography.

Remember, George, my brother, had retired to Morehead City near the Atlantic Ocean. Having grown up on the shores of the Roanoke River, summered at Nags Head in my teens, and lived not far from the Potomac River in Washington, I wanted to live on or near a body of water now, too. It would be idyllic to be near both the water and George. As we grew up, he and I were very close, loving and fighting along the way—mostly loving.

First, I looked for a home on the water in Beaufort, near Morehead City. I liked it, but there were too many log trucks rolling along the highways, and it was too far from Andrea and James, my daughter and young grandson, who lived in Cary, slightly west of Raleigh. I needed to be close enough to them to relieve Andrea of household duties and childcare from time to time, but not too close. At this point, James was about to enter the third grade.

Or, being near Cary and Raleigh, a growing metropolis, would give me some of the social and cultural opportunities of a city. And I knew two or three classmates from the Woman's College who lived in Raleigh and could show me around.

Margaret (Monk), of course, lobbied for Pinehurst, since it was just about an hour's drive south of Cary. I *had* grown up in a small town, and I liked the idea of becoming part of a close-knit community. But where was the water? I was reluctant.

"I see no point in retiring to a rinky-dink village with one hotel, several golf courses, and a few cottages for jocks and seasonal residents. It's not even a town, just a place governed by Mr. Tufts from his front porch with Donald Ross, his golf guru, sitting by his side. Golf? Who cares? I am not a golfer."

"Just come, take a look, stay several days, and get to know the place," Monk said, smiling as if she had inside information.

I had concluded that after life in Washington, Princeton, New York, and Philadelphia—in other words, along the Eastern corridor from DC to NYC—I would smother in tiny Pinehurst. I remembered it as a "ghost town" when I was a teenager. No one went there except rich golfers and hunters.

Monk arranged for me to stay in the Pine Crest Inn during the height of the golf season. She knew the hotel's lobby—the most popular spot in town—would be full of golfers hitting whiffle balls across the lobby into the fireplace. Guests would be eating and drinking everywhere—in the bar, the restaurant, the lobby, and on the porch. Monk, knowing the manager, turned on her persuasive charm to reserve a room, telling her why I was reluctant to live in Pinehurst.

"Marty, Alice thinks life will be too slow and pokey for her here," observed Monk. "I want her to stay in the heart of the village at the Inn, with its bustling bar and lively crowd. I know it's the peak of the golf season and you are jammed, but at the Pine Crest she will see there really is life in the old town and will fall in love with it."

The only vacant room was one used for staff in emergencies. When I saw it, I could understand why it wasn't usually rented: it was a small space with an antique bed, a mattress, and a single lightbulb hanging from a ceiling cord. But this tiny room at the top of the stairs, within earshot of the jolly mayhem going on below, was all I needed to get an introduction to the real Pinehurst.

The bar rocked, the front door never stopped swinging open, whiffle balls barely missed the waitresses' full trays of drinks. There *was* life in Pinehurst after all, lots of it, noisy and spirited!

Mr. Tufts gave up the reins around 1970, I learned, and Pinehurst had become a municipality in 1980, growing to over five thousand residents. The neighboring towns of Southern Pines and Aberdeen, each with about ten thousand residents, shopping plazas, and grocery stores, made Pinehurst livable and attractive, even to non-golfers.

When I left North Carolina in 1962, I already had my sights set on Chapel Hill for retirement. The university town appealed to me with its small population; retail establishments stretched along one side of Main Street and the university along the other—much like Princeton which had so entranced me. On the same scouting trip to Pinehurst, I also drove around Chapel Hill. When I saw the congestion, the over-populated neighborhoods, and street signs reading "speed table" and "traffic-calming area," I knew the local suburban academic elite did not need another newcomer, especially a country girl from peanut country in Halifax County.

Turning back to the Sandhills, I decided to look there for a house. The small towns, the soft, fertile, sandy soil, and the closeness to my sister would sustain and rejuvenate me. When my sister's good friend, Kay, showed me houses in established neighborhoods, not one had a swimming pool or even a pond within view. A few available lots were large enough to accommodate a pool but were farther from the center of town than I wanted to be. And no body of water was in sight. I told Kay I could live in a tent if the property had a pool or was overlooking a lake. With nothing that qualified, I went back to Princeton.

Months later, I returned to Pinehurst to see Monk when visiting Andrea in Cary. Kay was still on the lookout for something for me. Walking through the lobby of the Carolina Hotel, I picked up a real estate brochure. Whoa! Right there on the cover was a brown ranch house, fitted with an appealing irregular cedar-shake roof, and it was located on Lake Pinehurst. And it had a swimming pool! I couldn't believe it.

PINEHURST HOME, PINEHURST LAKE

Kay said it had just come onto the market but the price was higher than I had set. It was easy to change that, given that it seemed to have everything I wanted. I looked it over, liked it, and made a good offer. Instead of signing the contract, though, the owner took it off the market. No one could understand why because even he thought the price was fair. Again I returned to Princeton.

Almost a year later I attended a business meeting in Pinehurst. While I was still interested in settling there, I had about given up.

"You won't believe this, Alice," Kay phoned me. "The house on the lake you liked so much came back on the market this week."

"Put an offer down, Kay, right away. Before the owner changes his mind again." Providence favored me that day. It was mine. I still had several months of employment with ETS before I could move permanently, but I had laid claim to my spot and started moving furniture in.

All this time, Kay could not understand why I kept up my interest in Pinehurst.

"Why did you want to come here, Alice, if you don't play golf or tennis or bridge?" she asked. "Everybody does at least one of those things. What else is there?"

I thought for a minute. "I guess it boils down to three main reasons. I always knew I would end up in North Carolina. The more I thought about living in a small town again, the more Pinehurst became appealing.

"And you know how important water is to me. Now that I have found the house on Lake Forest Drive, I have both water and a small town."

"But what are you going to do when everyone else is playing golf, tennis, or bridge?" she pointed out.

"Get to know my sister. I left home when Monk was in grammar school. Since then, we have never lived in the same town."

Kay knew nothing of our past, so I told her. Monk was a spunky eight-year-old when I was a senior in high school. After George and I went to college, she grew up as an only child, the apple of Daddy's eye and the princess of the castle. But she was no princess to me. If you had asked me then, I would have said that she was more menace than princess. Between extorting money from my dates and gossiping about my social life, she made a bundle of quarters, and I lost a few boyfriends. Of course, she was being a typical eight-year old seizing any and every opportunity for mischief, and, I admit, I was an easy target. I loved her anyway.

She's different now—so am I—and we have much in common. She has a son and daughter just several years younger than my daughter. Her daughter, Karen, lives in Southern Pines. With Andrea in Cary, it is easy for us all to get together for a day. Among other things we have in common is our love for our brother, George. For the first time in about forty years, we are all living in the same state, able to get together now and then.

Here I was, back on North Carolina soil, living in Pinehurst, "going barefoot" as I did in my youth.

It was not Halifax County but a good place nevertheless. The soil was sandy, mixed with dirt, not the rich alluvial bottomland of the Roanoke River, but soft. This was a land of pine trees, with low, rolling hills, not the open, flat fields of Weldon's Coastal Plain. There was a lake, not a river, but one big enough for swimming, for sailing, and for coasting along the shore in electric pontoon boats. Instead of fields of peanuts, there were golf courses at every turn, green and spacious. The sand of my small beach and the mud of the lake felt good to my bare feet. I was finally home in the Old North State.

Folks in Pinehurst knew little about peanuts except that they come in a can. Most of the residents were Yankees or imports from the Midwest. Not only that, no one noticed peanuts except at cocktail time. It was all about golf, or tennis, or bridge, as Kay had warned. How would I survive? I didn't do any of those things.

ALICE, GEORGE, MARGARET (MONK), AND GWEN (GEORGE'S WIFE)
RALEIGH, N.C., SUMMER 2017

I was too excited by my new home to care. I had my own mini-resort with pool, spa, and lake. New friends enjoyed coming by for a dip in the pool, a cup of tea, or a glass of wine. One day, Matthew Mills, a friend who was an architect, and his wife Cynthia, came over for dinner along with Monk and her friend, Charlie.

"No wonder you like this home, Alice; Louis Kahn could have done it," remarked Matthew, who had been a student of Louis Kahn and knew I liked buildings he had designed. He said, "Kahn always asked, 'What does a space want to be?' Without a doubt, this space on the lake wants to be an invitation to the water, high enough off the ground to see the creatures and activities of Nature and open enough to permit the out-of-doors to come in."

The high cathedral ceiling in the living room opened the house to the sky through tall, irregular windows and lines leading the eye upward. A library with a louvered wood ceiling and surrounding windows led the eye to the water and to the garden sculpture. Every room across the lake side created a different feeling. The parlor, as Kahn might say, invited one to tea and offered a view of the camellia and azalea garden and the lake beyond. The enclosed porch created the feeling of a boat deck with a panoramic view of the lake through expansive glass windows, then back through double glass doors into the master bedroom and kitchen.

With its eastern exposure and high, irregular ceiling and windows, the master bedroom awakened one to spectacular sunrises of reds and pinks through the pine boughs. In response, I began each day with a spiritual moment of offering thanks.

This home was as smooth and as pleasurable as any bourbon—and every Southerner knows bourbon. Its spaces welcomed people, giving pleasure to groups of from twenty to eighty.

Its curious halls were inviting to children for running and hiding. Its grounds harbored animals of all sorts that fascinated guests young and old. Its shrubbery and trees housed so many different kinds of birds and fowl that I needed Sibley's guidebook to identify them.

And, for those who love water as I do, there was the pool and spa delicately situated with a patio shading the area in the afternoon so that the water in the pool never got too hot. As Kahn might say here, "That space wanted to be fun without sunburn!"

SUNRISE FROM MASTER BEDROOM DOOR

The small beach and dock were ready for kayaks, canoes, and fishing/pleasure boats. They have both felt many little boys' small feet jumping in surprise at the first fish they ever caught. And the pool has splashed high from a sudden cannonball and many a jump for a Frisbee. You have heard of The Big Easy? Mine was *The Little Easy*, a different kind of resort, perfect for children and grandchildren.

One weekend, I took James, my grandson, and three of his friends from Cary down to Pinehurst to go fishing. Only two of the four had ever been fishing, so the boys were happy to visit *The Little Easy*.

"The best fishing in the South is early in the morning, especially in summer before the day gets hot," I told them. "When the sun is high in the sky, fish go to the bottom of the lake to stay cool. So we'll need to get going early in the morning."

ANDREA AND HER FAMILY: JAMES, CECIL, PHILIP

A quick dinner of hamburgers, Cokes, and cookies prepared them for an evening closeted in the parlor in front of the TV. James was not permitted to watch TV very much at home, and Andrea had chosen not to have cable.

"Nana, we would like to watch *Animal Planet*," James said, careful to check with me so he wouldn't get in trouble with his mom. Already, he was exhibiting a fascination with animals and birds.

"Sure, but don't stay up too late. Remember, fishing is for early birds."

The parlor had a sleep sofa and big chairs, and with their sleeping bags on the floor, the boys had plenty of space. The benefit for them was that the room and its adjoining bath could be closed off from the rest of the house. James and his friends thought of it as their hide-out, away from parental oversight. Who knows what went on in that bedroom-parlor that night?

I had told the boys that our best chance of success was to launch the boat about 6:30 a.m. I doubted that they could wake up that early, but thought I would set a target anyway, planning to wake them up about that time.

Early the next morning, around 6:15, I tiptoed into the kitchen to get a cup of coffee before I woke them up.

"Nana, when do we start?" James asked. "We don't want to miss the fish, even if it means we miss breakfast."

All four of them were sitting at the kitchen table fully dressed, waiting for something to eat so they could get to the boat. We had a quick breakfast of milk, juice, and toast, gathered the fishing rods and live bait, and headed out.

Randy caught his first fish ever as soon as he threw his line out. He was so shocked and surprised that he dropped his rod and reel.

"Oh, what do I do?" he yelled as he fell back against the boat rail. "I'll help you," James called, "and show you how to get the fish off the line."

With several good-size bass in the cooler—they have to be 14 inches long to keep—the boys were ready to get wet themselves. They swam ashore and dived in the pool with the Frisbee. By noon, they were ready for pizza and a trip to the horse track to watch the trotters and pacers practice. They had to be home in Apex for dinner, and as soon as the car reached the outskirts of Pinehurst, heads were nodding, and all was quiet. What's the saying, "All work and no play...?" What about "All play and no work?" I was giving that a try, too, in Pinehurst.

"Alice, you really need to play golf. You will meet interesting people and make new friends. You don't have many friends here," Monk said one afternoon.

"OK, but how and where?"

"The best program around here for women is at Pine Needles," she replied.

I signed up for a Golfari for beginners at Pine Needles Club. A new world opened up. I got to know Peggy Kirk Bell, a famous female golfer, a strong advocate and supporter of the Women's Golf Tour, and a legend in golf instruction throughout the U.S. Her daughter, Bonnie, and her son-in-law, Pat McGowan, a competitive pro himself, were instructors among a legion of well-known golfers on Peggy's staff. Lots of students and lots of instructors gathered to hear the wisdom of Peggy and to learn her techniques.

One afternoon for my individual lesson, my new instructor came over to me and said, "Hello." Even that one word had a familiar ring, sounding straight out of Eastern Carolina.

"Where are you from?" I asked immediately.

"Tarboro," he said.

"I'm from Weldon. Tarboro is only 40 miles away and I had relatives there when I was a child."

"Yes. I know that town. I remember we used to play Weldon in baseball. Where do you live around here?" he asked.

"In Pinehurst down on the lake. How about you?"

"I live off McKenzie Road near the railroad tracks."

Suddenly an image of a yard with a golf hole flashed through my mind. "You are not that ol' fella who has a golf hole with a sand bunker in his back yard, are you?"

"Yup. That's me."

"You must be a pretty good golfer, then."

"Well, I like the sport and I've won a few tournaments in my life. I'm retired now and enjoy helping Peggy in the Golfaris. People come here from everywhere to learn a sport that's been important to me. I enjoy meeting and teaching them," he said.

"Well, it is nice to have you on board and I have enjoyed talking with you. Hope I have your help again," I said as we parted after my lesson. I'd forgotten to ask his name.

That evening at dinner, I asked my group, "Who is the man from Tarboro, the man with the golf hole in his Pinehurst back yard?"

"Where have you been, Alice?" exclaimed one of my new friends. "You don't know who he is? He's just the most famous amateur golfer in the country, maybe the world! Haven't you seen his pictures and trophies in the display case at the Pinehurst Country Club? His name is Harvey Ward."

On my way home, I dashed by the Club to look at the exhibits. Sure enough, there were several pictures of him at different times throughout his career and numerous trophies in the display case. He had been a celebrity for a long time.

The next day, I bumped into him, smiled sheepishly—and then we both laughed.

For the next several years, golf played a big part in my life, in hours if not in achievement. At the Club, I joined the Birdies, a novices group, and I took a few more lessons and joined a regular foursome for a game each week. People complimented me on my pretty swing. Great, I thought, except that I couldn't hit the ball much of the time. I tried hitting balls on the practice range to improve, but my smooth swing never progressed to the point of hitting the ball effectively.

The Birdies played all year: hot weather, cold weather, as well as in spring and fall. In winter, we got to the course as soon as the frost delays were over, which still meant "cold." Hats, ear muffs, shoes with foot warmers in them, gloves with liners that made hitting the ball awkward. I strove to break 100 on successive days, lamented my high handicap, and finally woke up to the fact I was supposed to be enjoying this game but somehow didn't get it. Wasn't retirement supposed to be relaxation and fun?

Learning to play golf is like learning to play the piano, which I had spent twelve years learning to do moderately well. "Oh, my gosh," I thought, "I may not have that many years left to give!" The sport requires daily practice of several hours, concentration on every stroke—no bird-watching—and ends in utter despair when things go badly, meaning almost every game. How could anyone enjoy a sport that turned anger inward? Why would anyone over sixty-five ever start? One morning I realized that, for weeks, I had been praying for rain every Tuesday when the Birdies approached the links.

"Enough!" I thought. I resigned from Birdies, gave up my handicap, reduced my membership in the Club to a social one, and slept as late as I chose. There are two kinds of golfers: experts and novices. I decided to remain a novice forever.

Then the game became fun. I joined friends once or twice a week to walk a nine-hole course or rent a cart for a longer game. Sara Hargrove kept me engaged by calling me often to join her in a pick-up round and by encouraging me to take lessons—again—from a teacher who was very good. My swing and productivity improved. Judy Thompson, one of my former Birdie companions, liked to walk nine holes once a week. She persuaded me to go on a couple of weekend golf outings to the mountains. And Farrell Bushing and his wife Pamela invited me to play nine holes with them every several weeks. That was just right: time to be with friends and not too much time on the golf course.

In time, as my hands showed signs of arthritis, my interest in playing waned, but I continued to enjoy volunteering at the national championships held in Pinehurst.

Life is more than golf, and more than swimming, boating, and watching the wildlife on the lake. But more what? Now that no alarm clock pushed me out of bed (except on Birdie days), no job required my full attention, no To Do list glared up at me, what would life be? It forced me to ponder not just what I was going to do but *who I was going to be.*

There was plenty to do. Everywhere a newcomer goes in Pinehurst, someone asks: "Can you help us? We need volunteers to...."

"Alice, can you serve on the Friends of the Library Board?" asked Betty Hurst. I like books, I thought.

"Sure, Betty, but I can't commit to more than one year." Two years later, I was still helping with the annual used-book sale.

Quickly I learned that retirement years can be busier than working years because, unlike the business world, there is no administrative assistant at your elbow. How I wished for Karen. Karen Buchanan was the person in Princeton I missed the most. Indispensable to me in my work, she could do anything with a computer and typewriter, and her brain was like a giant filing cabinet; she never lost anything. I now was so inefficient without her that I was forced to limit my time commitments. She and I still stay in touch, and though she is in New Jersey and I am in North Carolina, we find ways to see each other now and then. I cherish her friendship.

"How can I best find a niche that needs my skills and overlooks my shortcomings?" I wondered. Before I got depressed thinking about that, I got a call from a former colleague, Neal Kingston.

"Alice, I am now with a testing company in New Hampshire, Measured Progress, and we are planning to establish an outside board of directors and transition the company from the original owners to a not-for-profit organization. We would like you to serve on the board and help us with the transition," he explained. Neal had left ETS to become vice president of the young company.

The company developed custom-made tests for states to administer to students at multiple grade levels to monitor their achievement. Having spent much of my career in the field of educational testing, I knew the business. One of the owners and CEO, Stuart Kahl, wanted to position the company to offer its services nationally. He had a worthy vision and a sound plan. The appeal of Measured Progress's talent base, its outstanding reputation, and its commitment to high professional standards made me overlook my fatigue from years of working and travel. I jumped at the chance to stay involved. That initial serendipity led to a fifteen-year relationship with an exceptionally talented and dedicated group of educators and executives.

A second door opened, closer to home, from UNCG, my alma mater. Having been out of state for almost forty years and disconnected from the university and higher education more generally, I was thrilled to have a chance to be reintroduced to the university administration, faculty, and alumni.

At a dinner on campus, I met Walter Beale, Dean of Arts and Sciences.

"Walter, I notice that the residential college Warren Ashby dreamed about, proposed, and ultimately created is not named for him. Why?"

"It costs money—private money—to name any building or program or scholarship now, more money than the alumni of that college can afford. The college has not been around long and, while the alumni are dedicated, they are young and not yet established in their professions to have deep enough pockets for such an effort."

The Residential College is different from what one usually finds in a state university. A residential college within the university, it focuses not only on student learning but on self-governance and student participation in devising the curriculum. It embodies an approach to learning that establishes a close relationship among students and cross-disciplinary faculty.

"How could the years have passed without public recognition of Warren's contribution? That omission needs to be corrected," I told Walter.

Walter agreed and set about finding out what was involved by way of approval and fundraising. It appeared that more money and more red tape were involved than we thought because the university had just established new guidelines for naming opportunities. We needed $500,000! Even though that was about twice what we had envisioned, we set about working with the Advancement Office to raise money and secure pledges. It took several years and the tireless devotion of friends, alumni, and UNCG staff to realize our dream, but it did come to pass on September 6, 2007.

Today, the Warren Ashby Residential College prospers. Lively, intellectually curious students study with dedicated, stimulating faculty from academic departments across the university. The enrollment is limited to 125 students, all of whom are housed in one dormitory.

That initiative led to my serving on the Excellence Foundation Board, whose members are drawn from all over the state to support and advocate for the university. Under its aegis, capital campaigns and fundraising were undertaken to enrich academic offerings and initiate new programs the State did not fund. For nine years, I pointed my car northwest to Greensboro several times a month to attend a meeting, to enjoy a special event, to see college-mates at reunions, and to dedicate the Margaret and William Joyner parlor in Cotten Hall, named for my parents. James and Andrea made the Joyner parlor possible by offering to forego part of their inheritance to provide the funding.

In time, a group of UNCG staff and alumni came to see me. Again my home on the lake provided a congenial setting for an alumni gathering. On a lovely summer day around 2005, about seventy-five people gathered to enjoy refreshments, to roam around the grounds and along the water's edge, and to hear the vice chancellor and foundation board president announce a new capital campaign. My neighbor who had a large pontoon boat took a group for a short ride on the lake. Once more, *The Little Easy* garnered new admirers and simultaneously offered the university a chance to expand its reach. The capital campaign was off the ground in Moore County.

In a few more ways, I tried to be useful to organizations in my community. I became treasurer of The Village Chapel and served on its board and Foundation Committee for several years. The local branch of the English Speaking Union appealed to me because of its commitment to the education of students and teachers worldwide. I presided over the local branch as president for a couple of years, then took on the role of director of our region and served on the national board.

When I returned to my original question, I asked again: *Who did I decide to be?* The answer is obvious: What I had been before: someone dedicated to education in its many forms and types of organizations. What is the saying about an animal changing its spots? The only spots that changed on me were a few more age spots.

In time, I overcame my reluctance to travel and decided to see parts of the world I had missed. I figured I needed to move before arthritis kept me from getting on a plane or train. A UNCG alum gave me the nudge. I attended a meeting of the Class of '54 reunion committee and announced to the small group that I wanted to go to Spain.

"Who would like to go?" I threw out there, not expecting an answer.

Barbara Parramore spoke up, "I'll go with you."

We went on an Elderhostel tour to Southern Spain and Morocco to study the co-existence there of three religions, Judaism, Christianity, and Islam during the 14th and 15th centuries. A year later, we designed our own itinerary and traveled across Northern and Central Spain, from Barcelona to Bilbao to Madrid. A major goal was to see the Frank Gehry-designed art museum, the Guggenheim, in Bilbao.

While sitting in a restaurant one evening in Madrid, eating the most elaborate chocolate dessert ever, a sculptured twelve-inch tower of a sheet of pure chocolate, Barbara asked, out of the blue, "When were you born, Alice?"

"On the hottest day in August 1932, the 29th. I was born at home on the second floor of a house with no air-conditioning. And there was an eclipse of the sun! Mother must have wondered, 'What do the Heavens portend?'"

"So was I," responded Barbara, "I was born on the same day in the same year!" It turned out, too, that we were born within a few hours of each other, I in the Coastal Plain and she in the Piedmont. She was born on a farm; I was born in a small farm community. We were also about the same size and height, both with brown hair. If you believe in astrology—we were both Virgos with a compulsion for order—you might say that is why we made good traveling companions. And we discovered that, even though we had different majors, we had had some of the same professors at the Woman's College and at Duke in graduate school.

Thus began an annual trip for us and a strong bond of friendship. First to Alaska to see Denali National Park, the Yukon Territory, and Glacier Bay. I was determined to see the Chilkoot Pass, made famous in the Klondike Gold Rush.

Then, to the Southwest to see national parks: The Grand Canyon, Zion, Bryce, and Arches. Views from both sides of the road on Route 12 in Utah arrested our senses and ignited our attention: more rock formations than one can imagine, more variations in hue than on the color chart, and more sharp images against a clear blue sky than the eye can scan. To that, add heat that can melt anything in the open sunlight. We had to stay in the bus to eat our lunch; the park, even with trees overhanging picnic tables, was vacant. No one was venturing out, not even the animals.

After that, Andrea and I took off for Panama on a small ship that went all the way through the Canal. Some of the locks we traversed by day, others by night. Coming to understand the engineering and human labor that went into building the Canal around the turn of the twentieth century made watching the mechanical "horses" guiding the ships through the locks all the more extraordinary. I understood how and why President Teddy Roosevelt, TR, bragged about the Canal's success after the French had failed at the task.

Then to the Canadian Rockies with Andrea, canoeing on Lake Louise and riding horses in Jasper. Never have I seen such unusual lakes, bright aqua in color and entirely still under the bright sun.

A couple of years later, after I got my pacemaker, James escorted Andrea and me to the Greek island of Ikaria, where James's father's parents grew up. Then James was our tour guide to Athens, Crete, and Santorini. I still have my traveling shoes on today, ready to head out for the world at least once a year.

Exceeding all other times, the happiest time for me in my Pinehurst home, the time the walls burst with sounds of joy and cheer, was the wedding reception for Andrea and Cecil on January 23, 2010. Originally the wedding was scheduled for the following May in Charlottesville at the chapel on the University of Virginia (UVA) campus. Andrea had graduated from the university, and Cecil, an N.C. State professor in the Poole School of Business, liked UVA and Charlottesville. The Chapel on Grounds, as the campus is called, was reserved for the ceremony; the flowers had been chosen; the Alumni House had been scheduled for the reception; the band, the hotel, and restaurants for dinners had been reserved; and all deposits had been made.

Then, in late December, the clocks stopped ticking for us, quite along with our hearts. Andrea learned that she had breast cancer and might be going through chemotherapy in April and May. The surgeon recommended moving the date of the wedding to late January, before the surgery, or to later in the year, perhaps fall.

"How could we have plummeted so fast from the happy days of December when we were sending out save-the-date cards?" I moaned.

I was filled with guilt, convinced that I had caused her illness. My own breast-cancer surgery had been long ago in 1988, and, while I was now enjoying good health, I knew family on my father's side suffered from colon cancer caused by a defective gene. Further, I had been told that breast cancer could be associated with familial polyposis, the disease stemming from that gene.

As recently as the 1990s, two breast-cancer genes had been discovered, one of them at Duke University. Tests had been developed to identify the two genes.

"I must have transmitted BRAC-1 or BRAC-2 to Andrea," I feared.

"We can find out," responded her oncologist, Dr. Mark Graham, a specialist in genetic testing and counseling who had done his residency at Duke. "We can conduct a test on you for the gene and that will indicate whether Andrea has it."

The test revealed that I did not have the gene, meaning that Andrea's treatment would not have to be as aggressive as it would need to be otherwise. My sanity recovered; Andrea was reassured about her prospects; and we looked forward to the wedding.

Cecil was the Rock of Gibraltar during these anxious times. Having lost his first wife to cancer, he now faced a second marriage marred by it. Andrea felt it might be unfair to him to go through with the marriage and offered to call off the engagement. I remember being with him when we took Andrea for a consultation with her oncologist-surgeon.

As we waited in the outer room for Andrea to return from the doctor's examination, Cecil turned to me, put his hand on my knee, and said, "Mrs. Irby, I don't love Andrea because of her breasts. I love her because of who she is, and I want her as my wife."

Right there, on the spot, I let the tears roll down my face. I knew he and Andrea would be fine together in meeting this challenge.

For two weeks from the day Andrea and Cecil decided to marry—before, rather than after the surgery—I became the Perle Mesta of Pinehurst, "the Hostess with the Mostest," in arranging the wedding and the reception. They were to be married in The Village Chapel by a minister who was a friend of mine, Reverend Larry Ellis. The guest list of family and a few friends—a total of 35—ballooned into a total of 75, including children. *The Little Easy* would bulge at its walls.

My talented friends did it all: flower arrangements and house decorations prepared by Jean Webster; wedding cake donated by my niece, Karen; invitations addressed by my sister Margaret in her exquisite handwriting; bartending by Chuck and Sherri Grantham; hostess greeting guests at the door, Isabel Parish. My favorite caterer made time in her schedule to prepare the dinner, and the photographer rearranged his schedule to be on site. George and Gwen, my sister-in-law, helped with any and everything from the moment they arrived.

The house could seat 65, counting crowded corners and steps into the sunken living room. With the piano bench, the raised hearth of the fireplace, and the children on stools and small chairs in the bedroom, we had a place for everyone. It was cozy and warm, even in wintertime on the unheated glassed-in porch.

As her bridesmaids and I helped her dress for her departure, my mind returned to the day Andrea was born at 7:15 in the morning on February 28, 1961. Heralded by the powerful sounds of Franck's "Symphony in D Minor," I awoke that day to the face of a newborn girl, so tiny and fragile, lying in my arms, with small features, blue eyes, and a shock of light-brown hair. She was long compared to other babies in my family, 22 inches, and just the right size: 7½ pounds. Life has truly been better ever since Andrea arrived!

My doctors thought I needed rest—I had worked until the night she was born—and kept me in the hospital in Greensboro for five days. The rules then did not push new mothers out in a day. I relished all the attention offered by cheerful nurses and by a kind and gentle pediatrician, and, of course, the feeding of my baby girl while holding her slender hand. She had delicate, long fingers that wrapped around my first finger.

My LP records spun round and round on my phonograph, resting on the floor beside my bed. Over and over I played Franck's "Symphony in D Minor," because to me, it signified my wonder at the fullness of life. I will always think of the joy of Andrea's birth when I hear the expressive themes of that symphony. What was paradise like, if not this?

My protective cocoon lasted a couple of weeks longer with Mother's help when I got home, and Andrea herself made motherhood a dream. She slept when she was supposed to sleep and ate ravenously. Only once in her life did she have colic. Though it was not proper in those days to do so, I could have taken her with me anywhere: to restaurants, on planes, or to meetings. Later, the only risk in taking her to those places, as a toddler, I learned, was her propensity to visit with everyone around her. It was hard to keep her in her chair.

I remember one Easter Sunday, in Lambertville, N.J., when Mother and Dad were visiting. Andrea, about eight years old then, looked like a princess in her Easter clothes. Our reservations at The River's Edge restaurant, run by the famous star of the radio soap opera *"As the World Turns,"* Stella Dallas, provided us a river view. The spring run of shad stirred the waters, and sunlight brightened the dining room, now packed with guests. No wonder Andrea could not sit still: too many people to greet, too much going on at the river's edge, too good an opportunity to get away from a mother's leash. Besides, what do fashion models do if not show off their pretty clothes?

That was the beginning of Andrea's life as a people person and a lover of fashion. I don't know how she has done it—to have become such a caring, resourceful, life-giving friend and counselor to so many people.

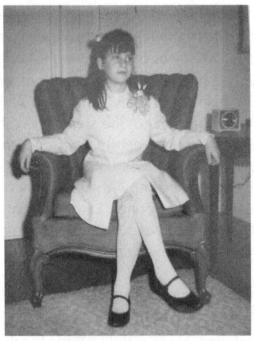

ANDREA IN HER EASTER OUTFIT, PRINCETON HOME, AGE 8

I am much more reserved, and, to my regret, much more judgmental. Much as Mother did, Andrea takes people as they are, loves them, helps them, supports them, grieves with them, and celebrates with them. I admire her for it. I am even a little jealous because I wish that I had just a little of her inner strength and generous nature.

THE VILLAGE CHAPEL, PINEHURST, JANUARY 2010

As Gwen, my sister-in-law, says of Andrea: "Her ready heart reaches out to anyone in need." Gwen has always had a special place in her own heart for Andrea, probably because of Andrea's big smile, friendly face, and open heart. She invites you in, minus all defenses.

That big, open heart has made her vulnerable from time to time in relationships and has led to suffering and feelings of betrayal. But, on her wedding day in my parlor, I thought to myself, "All that is past, and now she can look forward to a trusting life with Cecil. He is an honorable, impressive man who will love and protect her. I am at peace now, and

I can enjoy without judgment or fear the celebration of their new life together."

Even though the newlyweds had to postpone their honeymoon because of Andrea's upcoming surgery, that wedding night, no one was thinking of doctors and hospitals. As Andrea stood on the steps of my sunken living room when guests had congregated, she was surrounded by the three VIPs of her life: Cecil, her husband; James, her son, who gave her away; and Philip, Cecil's son and best man.

With her blue eyes sparkling and a radiant smile, she proclaimed, "Here is my family—my men—whom I love with all my heart. With them, I can face the future with confidence and hope." They, and everyone else, wrapped her in love and affection, and Reverend Ellis blessed them in a moving prayer. There were a few tears, especially mine, but mostly cheers, laughs, and praise.

Seeing Andrea in her going-away outfit prompted me to look into her future, seeing her life filled with excitement and great expectations. She looked like a New York model— but also much happier than a fashion model generally does. Soon we were weathering the cold outside in front of the house, lining the walkway to send Andrea and Cecil off with ribbon and confetti sprinkling down upon them.

My life in Pinehurst was full in all the ways anyone would wish, and my home on Lake Forest Drive, S.E., was a special place. Anyone fortunate enough to live there after me will be blessed with all that Nature offers and all that friendly neighbors provide. Were I to be forever young, I would choose to be in that spot for life. But life is a series of stages, and the next stage of my life required a different home and town. I grieved the loss of my Pinehurst home but have found joy in knowing that one day someone else inhabiting that place will find pleasure there and will love it as I did. I am mindful of a quote from Cicero about aging:

"I follow nature as the best guide and obey her like a god. Since she has carefully planned the other parts of the drama of life, it's unlikely that she would be a bad playwright and neglect the final act. And this last act must take place, as surely as the fruits of trees and the earth must someday wither and fall. But a wise person knows this and accepts it with grace. Fighting against nature is as pointless as the battles of the giants against the gods."

I live in Raleigh now in a spacious apartment, decorated by the original owners with rich Italian décor. Yet my Early American furniture fits well. Mark, my next-door neighbor, calls it The Ritz. The only thing the apartment lacks is a lake out back. Peering down into the backyards of townhouses from the third floor is quite a letdown from admiring my pool and the lake from my porch in Pinehurst. I keep trying to close in my balcony with vines and drooping flowers over the railing to block the view. Nothing seems to work.

Being close to my daughter and a few friends from college days makes up for the loss of landscape beauty in Pinehurst, however, and Raleigh has enlivened my life with book discussions, a few movies, lunches, dinners, the symphony, and ballet. Just down the road a mile is the North

Carolina Museum of Art, with an impressive permanent collection and a good restaurant. I go to the art museum much more than I go to my doctors, and that is a good thing.

Until 2016 I was busy with the testing company in New Hampshire, traveling north at least four times a year. And in North Carolina, like many retirees, I still could not say *No* to lending a hand in organizations that needed help. Being useful is not a false goal. I was doing my duty: "giving back," as they say.

Now I have days in which I have nothing scheduled—or at least nothing until noon—except entering my library to read and write. I enjoy the quiet of silence when rambling thoughts roll around in my head among cobwebs that want to block characters from my past and cloud my imagination. But, then a sentence in an article, a line in a poem, or a letter from a friend connects me to the honorable people in my past who revealed to me daily the power of goodness. They possessed the old verities of honesty, fairness, and truth—such a contrast to the reckless divisiveness of our society today. My people of memory, all of them, were people of distinction. They knew from reason and experience that courting division was wasteful, destructive, and downright unhealthy.

Eventually I am headed back to Weldon. I was born there, grew up there, was married in the Weldon United Methodist Church there, and lived or visited in the house in which I was born until my mother died when I was almost sixty years old. And there is a spot for me in Weldon cemetery next to my father in the Whitfield-Anderson plot shadowed by a blossoming magnolia tree that spreads its sweetness across the surrounding fields.

Several miles away, the town of Halifax is gradually being restored to assume its rightful place among important historic sites, having been the location of the first official resolution for independence among the colonies. Passed on April 12, 1776—almost three months before the Continental Congress's July Declaration of Independence—the Halifax Resolves put the Colony of North Carolina on record in declaring its independence, with all the associated risks of its citizens being accused of treason and hanged. The date is on the North Carolina state flag. Every April 12, Halifax Day, the Founding spirits join the living in celebrating the creation of a land of liberty, equality, and self-rule. They were *First in Freedom*! May it endure.

The corner of North Carolina I knew and called home is ageless. It will always look the same to me. The landscape continues to display its broad, flat fields of peanuts, cotton, still some tobacco, and now soybeans spreading across the horizon. And the Roanoke River, with its turbulent rapids, continues to spill its black silt on the banks to form rich arable bottomland. The people from home are as independent and true and steady as ever.

I came of age in a man's world—or so they told me after I had made my way. All the while, I thought it was My World! That's still the way I see it...enjoying every day and what it brings, looking forward to every new opportunity, and every day eating a few roasted peanuts out of the full bowl on my kitchen table. Life has been one great, big ever-full bowl of salty, savory peanuts...and a life of satisfying happiness, too.

Alice Joyner Irby

A quotation printed below my senior-year picture in our 1950 high-school yearbook reads:

> "Now my task is smoothly done,
> I can fly or I can run."

Almost seventy years later, I am inclined to add:

> "Now the race is almost done,
> I have flown and I have run."

To astonishing places around the globe that have generously fed my curiosity.

But after I roam? I always do turn South toward home.

December 2017

EPILOGUE

Twice in his young life of twenty-eight years, James' presence has brought hope and calm to my deep, penetrating sorrow. He has been the light of life returning to my room of darkness.

When just a year-old toddler, he was scampering around the lobby of the hospital in Rocky Mount, N.C., while my mother was dying of pneumonia on the third floor. I stopped to observe him and hug him, then moved toward the elevator. I was suddenly aware: death on the third floor contrasted with his new life on the first. I was struck by the contrast of death balanced by life anew—the continuity of life with its promise and hope.

James brought muted joy to my angry heart filled with grief for one of the two most important women in my life. The other, my daughter Andrea, was here beside me.

James was always an observant child, sensitive and perceptive. Like his mother, he enjoyed meeting and talking with people. He would have made a good baseball player because he had a strong arm with exacting aim, but in games he might abandon his position to wander off and talk with the second-base referee. He'd be out of position and miss a play!

He loved animals and all living things—including snakes! The complexities of nature intrigued him; its harmonies invited him to explore the natural world, too. In that regard, he also took after his mother, who has housed horses, dogs, rabbits, turtles, gerbils, mice, and birds for periods of time during her life. People who love animals love life, and they understand its promises and threats.

On two successive days, when James was about ten years old, he and I joined the safari at the Animal Kingdom in Disney World. He reveled in identifying and describing animals far away across the fields, deep in a pasture or wooded area. Even the professional naturalists on our game-viewing vehicle were impressed by his ability—unaided by binoculars or pictures—to see and identify the animals. They couldn't see the distant animals without binoculars.

JAMES TAKING A BREAK FROM GARDENING, 1993

I couldn't see them using *both* my eyeglasses and binoculars. James' eyesight is as good as mine is bad.

Ever mindful of that for a few years now, James routinely assists me by extending his arm as I try to navigate strange or uneven walkways.

At the age of two, he became my assistant gardener: "Come on, Nana, get the tools, let's work." He'd try any ploy to get outside, to be among the creatures hiding in the flower beds.

He also liked to plant any kinds of seeds and bulbs. Nothing in open spaces bored him, and now he is in Kenya working on a research project studying guinea hens—not our domesticated guinea hens, but large, royal-blue birds that migrate after they hatch in the wild.

JAMES IN KENYA WITH GUINEA HEN, NOVEMBER 2019

James spent hours "reading" stories—memorizing them as Andrea read to him each night before bedtime. He became fluent at an early age, a tribute to his mother's insistence on reading. James surprised his nursery-school teachers with the word "admonish," which he had learned from memorizing the story of Dumbo, the Flying Elephant. Having read about Dumbo many times, he might say to you in telling a story, "We must obey our mothers. Mrs. Jumbo admonishes her baby elephant, Dumbo, to stay close to her. She almost punishes him." Reading animal stories of high interest to him certainly contributed to James's early mastery of syntax in speech and writing.

Twenty-seven years after that day in the Rocky Mount hospital, James' presence softened the shock of Cecil's sudden death in May 2018—Cecil Bozarth, Andrea's husband of eight years. Andrea, my beloved daughter, had faced so many blows during her youth and adulthood that I was driven to ask the familiar question: "How could God visit such devastation on her?" Is it because she is strong? It's sometimes said that God does not visit on us what we cannot bear, but that is little comfort when vicissitudes accumulate as they had in Andrea's life.

James brought to us not just himself, which was enough, but the news of his intended engagement to Samantha, a young graduate student at the University of Michigan working toward an M.F.A. in writing. After they marry, she will join him in Germany when she finishes her degree. For me in May 2018, James gave shape to a vision of family continuity and of the celebration of a new coming-together of man and wife, of future generations.

He did not erase our sorrow or emptiness over the loss of Cecil, however. The anchor of our small family, Cecil was 55 years of age, at the peak of his professional career at N.C. State University, and a much-loved teacher, researcher, antique-car restorer and aficionado. But James's presence did keep my focus on the gifts of his humanity that Cecil had given us during the decade I had known him.

Colleagues and friends poured in from all over North Carolina as well as other states—students, faculty, antique-car enthusiasts, neighbors, and Andrea's horseback-riding friends—to support Andrea, James, Philip, and Cecil's family. Cecil was first and foremost a family man. He took seriously his obligations to mentor his son and support his wife.

His sharp wit and sense of humor softened many delicate situations. His business savvy combined with his academic expertise in management helped numerous companies improve their processes, thereby saving money and time. His love for—indeed, his fascination with—antique cars, especially those of the 1930s, resulted in his winning time and again in car shows, taking first in class with his 1937 Lincoln Zephyr coupe because of his unceasing attention to preparation and detail.

But these extra-curricular projects did not detract from his commitment to his teaching and to his publishing. Though many full professors rest on their laurels, Cecil worked hard each day, developing new pedagogical techniques and advancing the knowledge-base of his field, supply-chain management.

ANDREA AND CECIL, CHRISTMAS 2017

He was so highly regarded by his colleagues, students, and former students that they initiated an endowment for a scholarship in his memory. Already, two deserving undergraduate juniors have received grants.

There were other losses last year, too, cutting and wounding ones. My friends Mary Bowers and Jerry McDonald died. Her death was in January, Jerry's about the same time. Bobby George died several weeks after Cecil. Clarence Lindsay, a close friend in Pinehurst, died about the same time as did Bobby.

CECIL WITH PRIZE WINNING ZEPHYR

And James, the source of so much of my emotional strength and my hope for the future, suffered the deaths, not only of Cecil, his stepfather, but of both grandparents on his father's side of the family—all within a year. His strong fortitude and calm demeanor shielded us from what must have been for him life-altering changes.

While it seemed sometimes as if we were trembling at Dante's Gates of Hell, there were times we were on top of the mountain—literally, as in Machu Picchu, Peru. Those were good times. James got his master's degree from Konstanz University and the Max Planck Institute of Ornithology in Germany. To celebrate that milestone, Andrea, James, and I went to the Galapagos Islands and to Machu Picchu in April 2018. Even at age 85, with a heart condition, I was able to enjoy almost everything, except a few hikes at the top of the world in the Inca ruins. On the islands of the Galapagos chain, populated only by animal life—no humans allowed—and in Peru, with the Andes Mountains dripping with moisture from the rain forest and birds flying everywhere, we felt as if we were in Paradise.

And there, in Machu Picchu about 8,000 feet above sea level, I experienced one of the happiest afternoons of my life.

Limited by the altitude and a sudden spike in my blood pressure, I was unable to take the four-hour walking tour among the ruins. James insisted he would stay with me while the others hiked the trails.

"But, James, this place is what this trip is all about! This is what we came to see, the Inca ruins—to experience being in the region of an ancient civilization with its artifacts and edifices such as the Temple, imagining how the Incas thrived. You must go with the others," I insisted.

"No, Nana, I will stay with you here at the gardener's hut while Mom hikes with the others." I had been guided to a bench under a thatched roof of a gardener's hut on the edge of the ruins.

"James, the animals, the Temple, the species of birds you have never seen—you must see them."

"No, Nana, my priorities are clear. You first, birds second, Machu Picchu ruins third. That's the way it is."

Little did we know the bench under the thatched roof of the gardener's hut would provide a perfect view of the Temple ruins—a picture like the one on so many post cards and travel brochures. Neither did we imagine that many species of birds, some unknown to James, would put on a dazzling show in front of us as they soared among the lush green mountain peaks towering against the bright sky.

JAMES ON LEDGE AT GARDENER'S HUT, MACHU PICCHU

James's camera, with its long-distance lens, captured birds' markings in close focus: some familiar to James, already catalogued in his mind's library; some entirely new to him. Some were tiny, others giant size—almost hawk-like—all colorful and each unique. How exciting to observe their soaring silhouettes framed by the giant mountains and the blue sky's scattered thunderheads.

"Look, Nana, a new one, one I don't recognize," James explained as he consulted his ornithology guide. A click of his camera captured and stored the image for future study.

Every minute brought a new discovery as we tracked birds, noted their behavior and then, suddenly witnessed a small herd of llamas emerge from a cave in the ruins onto a plateau among the terraces of the site. Playfully, they teased the attending shepherd, defying him in his efforts to disperse them. Finally, after about 30 minutes, he was able to steer the llamas away from the tourists.

People of every nationality, size, shape, and dress filed along the path below us toward the exit. We looked and looked for Andrea, but after three hours, we decided to abandon our perch and seek a bus to take us back to our hotel, about 45 minutes away. We were in need of a restroom and, by design, there are no restrooms in the historic site. Once outside, there was no re-entry because tourists are limited to four-hour tours.

In an unexpected way, the best for me was yet to come. On the bus, James and I talked about issues of the day, his future in his profession of ornithology, and his maturing relationship with Samantha. As we talked about his future and our family life, he held my hand, signaling in my mind the transfer of responsibility from me to his generation. We spoke of his becoming the head of our small family, along with Cecil, and the importance of protecting and caring for his mom as the years unfolded. I felt assured that he would be an attentive son to his mother, a compassionate husband and father, and that one day he would fulfill his dream of heading his own research laboratory in animal behavior. An afternoon of pure joy, of experiencing love without having to say a word, and of mutual respect—that's the only way to describe it. James had become an engaging, knowledgeable, and impressive young man.

And, the next day, James got to walk among the ruins. He arose early and went on a self-directed hike into the historic site, climbing the hills and mountains and observing and recording sightings of birds along his way.

The last morning in Peru, standing in our hotel room in Cusco, I stood before Andrea and James with outreached hands and tears in my eyes.

"I am so happy. This trip is like a reunion, harkening back to our trips when you, James, were a small child," I declared.

"Now, I can die at peace with the knowledge that each of you will be okay: you, Andrea, have a full life with a generous, capable, and reliable husband in Cecil. You can look forward to a long life together.

"And you, James, are set on a fascinating course for a productive professional life and a happy future with Samantha.

"All is well in my world. I can rest on the knowledge, too, that all is well for you."

That was two weeks in May 2018 just before Cecil died suddenly in his sleep. Andrea's discovery of him in the early morning hours rocked our world. All too soon, James did become the acknowledged head of our family.

Almost as if to tie up the loose ends of my journey, a year after Cecil died, in May 2019, seven of us who grew up together—"our gang" we called ourselves—gathered in Weldon.

"Alice, I want to test an idea on you," Sonny Hines' voice rang out when I answered the phone one February day. "What do you think about trying to get the surviving members of our gang together one more time in Weldon?"

"I think it is a great idea. Who's left? When?" I asked.

"One weekend in May. Henry Johnson is all for it. He and Jenna can come. Harriett will come with me. And, there's Bill Pierce who still lives on his farm outside Weldon with Sally, his wife. Susan Shepherd Smith is in Pensacola, Florida, but says she is not well enough to make the trip. Blanche Selden Bullock is still in Chadbourn but I have been unable to reach her. Can you try to get in touch with her?" Sonny started naming those still around.

"I know Peggy Draper is still in Roanoke Rapids, and I believe Jimmy Coker, her husband, is still around. But I have no idea how to contact her," I said.

Sonny added, "I haven't seen Peggy since we graduated from high school. And what about Katherine Waynick Bastian? Where is she?"

"She's in Weldon, a widow now, living in the Vaughn house. Martha, her sister, lives in the old Allen home on Washington Avenue. I may be able to locate her through my cousin who knows Martha."

Sonny, chief organizer and delegator, enlisted Henry to lay out a weekend schedule, Bill to honcho local arrangements, and me to get the scoop on our lives since graduation.

Mother's Day weekend found us, along with spouses and two daughters—Blanche's daughter Susan, and my daughter, Andrea—gathered at Ralph's Barbecue, a local institution going back to our childhood. For our taste, it offers the best barbecue in North Carolina, without a doubt!

We had lost a couple of friends to illness or disease along the way, but the rest of us retraced our footsteps in the sands of time along the banks of the Roanoke River, and its aqueduct and canal paralleling the river.

A "must-see" on the itinerary were the restored buildings in historic Halifax, the site of the 1776 April Resolves declaring the independence of the North Carolina colony from the Crown. Patterson Wilson, a young daughter of Glenn Dickens, a high-school friend of ours, had come back home from her worldwide business travels to open a popular restaurant on the main street of Halifax. On Saturday night, she gracefully accommodated us, knowing, I'm sure, that our chatter might forestall other guests from dining there.

Our gang was augmented by a dozen or so additional childhood friends and their spouses, some local, others coming from out of town—the oldest being Charlie Daniel—we called him "Charlie Boy"—age 89, a nationally-honored cartoonist living now in Knoxville, Tennessee. He was accompanied by his lifelong love and wife, Patsy Stephenson from Garysburg, a small town a stone's throw across the river in Northampton County.

These friends are all people of distinction, individuals who have found ways during their long lives to be useful in and contributing to their communities. But this night, our group of age-eighty-plus men and women acted as if we were teenagers, talking about who dated whom, who played practical jokes on our elders, and who got punished for breaking into the high school on Halloween. For a moment, our vision clouded through our thick-lens glasses to help us imagine we were as good-looking as we remembered.

High school friends know each other better than friends made later because they live and grow up together, unadorned and with no pretense or guile in a place of simplicity, candor, and civility—long before they face the many demands of the external world, college, or the workplace. We played and studied together in protected surroundings before we suffered failures, big and small, and before we confronted barriers that blocked our way. A bond like no other binds us together still, a bond created by common standards of behavior, similar instructive punishments from our parents, and the same expectations of success in school and work. Being together again offered a temporary reprieve from thoughts of the ever-hovering Grim Reaper— a time of belonging, a time of pure, innocent pleasure.

The climax of the weekend came for me the next day, Mother's Day, when Andrea and I donned our red and white roses, attended the Rosemary Methodist Church in Roanoke Rapids, and afterward made our way to the park in Weldon on the bank of the Roanoke River. I had planned every detail, including the wide-ribbon bow and exquisite wrapping paper encasing the gift I had for Andrea. She had experienced such grief and unexpected difficulty since Cecil's death that I wanted her to be cheered by tangible expressions of my love and respect for her. I wanted the day to be unusual and memorable, and it was, despite the light rain that fell as we approached the riverbank.

We sat on a covered picnic bench as she unwrapped the gift. It was my booklet, *A Caring Heart*, that contains two stories from this book.

ANDREA OPENING THE BOOKLET, MOTHER'S DAY 2019

They describe her youth and scenes from her adult life. It was my gift of love to her, an expression of a mother's admiration for a remarkable daughter, and a hope that the deep, unconditional love I feel will shine through any memories of difficulties I have caused for her through the years. Is there any better place for a celebration like that than back at home in Weldon where it all began?

Having reflected in these collected stories on my quests and wanderings of four-score and seven years, I see what set me on my unlikely journey: my father's fearless confidence in himself, his willingness to take risks to achieve worthy goals, and his will to serve others. Mother bequeathed me courage and resilience, but it was my father's DNA—and his modeled behavior through his business, his respect for others, his devotion to his brother—that sent me venturing out, excited about testing the unknown. Grounded in faith and love of family, Dad and Mother opened my heart and quickened my mind to seek the full meaning of life's boundless journey.

Turning to the present and closing this glimpse of the past, I have one last scene tying it all together in my best way: filled with song.

As George Deaton, the tenor whose voice touched my heart in Jerusalem, sang "O, Divine Redeemer" in a concert on November 3, 2019, at Highland United Methodist Church in Raleigh, the people in my stories walked back into my life. Their images joined me when I stumbled around cragged hills, and at other times as I walked in the smooth sands of warm, calm beaches; they are as real to me now in the tenor line of song as they were to me in the days long ago.

Today, I feel gratitude for the love of my brother and sister, hoping the three of us can make one more trip looking for ancestors—or just get together for another weekend. I am also encouraged by the young people in my family—studying hard, learning the importance of work by doing chores for the family or starting careers, participating in church or community programs, or advancing the study of nature. At school or on campus, these young people are too busy to pay attention to extremists' protests and won't be taken in by the claims of those who see virtue in victimhood. They are confident, filled with ideas of hope, not anger. Well-grounded, they know who they are; they are optimistic about what they can achieve, setting ambitious though realistic goals and helping others along the way.

KARA, PHILIP, JAMES AND GIGI, CHRISTMAS 2019

Thanksgiving this year will be a different family time but a happy one. I was touched by an unanticipated and undeserved expression of Southern kindness by the proprietor of Mrs. Lacy's Magnolia House Tea Room in Sanford, N.C. When I presented myself at Mrs. Lacy's to pick up a sweet-potato pie I had ordered for Thanksgiving, Ms.

Schulz recognized me and remembered our conversation during my first visit in late October.

"Ladies," she addressed us then as she approached our table. "We are known for our desserts." Then, when recommending her pies, she assured me that her sweet potato pie was as good as any I had ever tasted.

"I am sure it is delicious, but I still remember my mother's as the best I ever had," I responded.

"Just try mine. I bet you will like it because I use the very best sweet potatoes from Eastern North Carolina."

"The very best are from Tabor City," I said, to which she responded. "Of course, that's where I get them when I can." I put her to the test by ordering a piece of her pie. It was superb, almost identical to Mom's, I discovered, when she told me the ingredients she uses.

At the counter to pick up the pie, I waited for her to bring it from the pantry. "I want you to have this pie," she said as she handed it to me.

"That's $20 plus tax, right?"

"No, this is for you. I want you to have this pie as a gift, and I wish you and your family a very good Thanksgiving."

She saw, before I even thanked her, that her kindness and appreciation of my family's tradition had brought a tear to my eye. Thanks to this gracious lady—I think her name is Faye—Mother's spirit will be with us this Thanksgiving.

I look forward to being at Andrea's home with her, with Kara, her law-school student live-in, and with Philip, her stepson. Kara, a mature young woman, has been an indispensable companion to Andrea since Cecil's death, residing in her home much of the time. Kara became especially fond of Andrea and Cecil when they provided housing for her during an interlude between jobs. Just two years older than James, Kara has become another loyal young member of Andrea's family.

JAMES AND SAMANTHA'S ENGAGEMENT

Cecil would be proud of Philip, now living in his own apartment, working full-time in a job that utilizes his mathematical skills, and on the side, tutoring mathematics to high-school students. Like his father, he is a hard worker, though he does take time off to spend evenings with Andrea, play card games with his work colleagues, and go to the gym to exercise.

We look forward to Kara's graduation from law school in December and to James' and Samantha's wedding in February.

I continue to marvel at Andrea's resilience—given the trials of her life during the past few years—and her enduring ability to be optimistic about the future, ever confident that good things will happen. And I know way down deep that her new family—her children James, Samantha, Kara, and Philip—will care for her, share their lives with her, and fill her life with purpose and happiness.

I am at peace, then, in the visible knowledge I have that people related by caring *do* find ways to meld and weave their lives together for even more shared ventures and adventures down the roads they travel together. They will tell their stories about what they've seen and done, too, and they will, like me, feel this great peace of knowing that all is well.

November 27, 2019

ACKNOWLEDGMENTS

I want to thank...

The fountainhead of this project, Ron Rhody, executive and author, who had the idea, who insisted I tell my stories to an audience beyond my family, and who persisted as I dawdled over months, even years. He introduced me to my editor and to my publisher. He would not let me give up. He has been more than a mentor. He has been my advisor and my friend.

Linda Whitney Hobson, Ph.D., my editor, who also persisted in giving me encouragement as well as sound advice. She not only edited the contents of this book but taught me how to transform barebones essays that family might recognize into stories someone else might enjoy reading. She, too, stood by me when there were blocks of time I could not write or work. She never failed to have pen and protractor in hand when I showed up.

Jane Hobson Snyder, who with a practiced eye and pinpoint accuracy insured the integrity of the manuscript and its presentation. The professional expertise she brought to bear on the project enabled me to rest easy.

Anthony Policastro, whose patience with a first-time author was endless and who calmly guided me through the logistics of moving words to print. He is imaginative in his work, but also constant in his focus on tasks I needed to learn to get it right.

Brent Miller, the man behind the scenes, who made sure I could deal with every technical challenge I faced—and there were a few. He is my go-to technical consultant and never fails to respond to my need and solve my problems, always with a happy smile.

Friends who read the manuscripts of several stories to ensure accuracy and to provide clarification: Paul Ashby, Louis Horne, Steve Koffler, Ellen Mappen, Richard Nurse, and Richard Swartz. I am indebted to them.

The people I have profiled in these stories: The words on these pages cannot describe fully the rich and varied lives of the people who shaped my life. Remembering them, writing about them, admiring their qualities, and appreciating their complexities brought me to a fuller awareness of myself. I acknowledge and appreciate them for enlivening, enriching, and gracing my eighty-plus years. I am deeply grateful. They gave me their faith, hope, and love.

January 2020

ABOUT THE AUTHOR

ALICE, LEFT, WITH HER DAUGHTER, ANDREA, DURING A TRIP TO CANADA

Before moving to Raleigh in January 2016 to be closer to her daughter and family, Alice lived in Pinehurst, NC, where she focused her interests on her profession, her alma mater, and her community.

She chaired the board of a testing company in New Hampshire. At UNCG, she was a member of the Excellence Foundation. Locally, she served on the board of Friends of Given Library, was president of the local branch of The English Speaking Union and served as Treasurer of The Village Chapel.

Her determination to "retire from retirement" when she moved to Raleigh has been partially successful in that Alice has made time to write stories for her family and friends—now the chapters of *South Toward Home*.

Alice, a native North Carolinian, was born in the small town of Weldon in historic Halifax County. She grew up in what was then the Methodist Episcopal Church, a church in Weldon co-founded by her ancestors.

In 1950, she moved to Greensboro, graduated with honors from the Woman's College of the University of North Carolina (now UNCG), and moved to Durham for graduate work in Economics at Duke University.

After several years of working with Merrill Lynch and teaching at UNCG, she moved into academic administration as Director of Admissions, UNCG. In 1962, she moved with her young daughter, Andrea, to Princeton, New Jersey, to join Educational Testing Service (ETS). For the next 36 years, she lived and worked in New Jersey and in Washington, D.C.

In 1964-65, she was on leave from ETS to assist in the establishment of the Job Corps during the Johnson Administration.

During the 1970s she joined Rutgers University as the first female vice president of a major university, returning to ETS in 1978 to lead its field offices and oversee its legislative relations.

Alice's family consists of her daughter, Andrea, and grandson, James, in the Raleigh area; her sister, Margaret, in Southern Pines; and her brother, George, in Morehead City.

APPENDIX

Names of Family and Friends

Andrea: Andrea Leigh Irby (author's daughter)
Dr. Ashby: Warren Ashby (Professor of Philosophy, UNCG)
Mrs. Ashby: Helen Ashby (lifelong friend, weaver and musician)
Bobby: Bobby George (lifelong friend from childhood)
Cecil: Cecil Chester Bozarth III (Andrea's husband)
Claud: Claudius A. Irby (author's former husband)
Daddy: William Bridgeman Joyner (author's father)
George: George David Joyner (author's younger brother)
Granny: Alice Anderson Hudson, née Alice Belle Anderson (author's grandmother)
James: James Klarevas-Irby (author's grandson)
Kara: Kara Claire Foster (close friend of Andrea and author)
Louise: Louise Farber (piano teacher and friend)
Monk: Margaret Joyner Kinker, née Margaret Ray Joyner (author's younger sister)
Mother: Margaret Hudson Joyner, née Margaret Green Hudson (author's mother)
Philip: Philip Neilson Bozarth (Cecil's son and Andrea's stepson)
Samantha: Samantha Bares (James' wife)

ABOUT THE COVER

Like the stories in this book, the photograph on the cover is part of my life. Years ago, at the River Mall in Weldon, I purchased a greeting card featuring this photo. I saved it because it is stunning, breathtaking, and real. It sparks memories of my growing up on the Roanoke River, capturing faithfully the essence of life there: beauty, turbulence, danger, bounty, and pleasure.

My publisher and I knew the image would make a perfect book cover, but I had no idea who took the photograph—no name, date, trademark, or seller was listed. And Outer Banks Publishing Group was not about to use it without attribution. How to find the owner? Where to look? We began sleuthing.

I called Glenn Dickens, a friend in Halifax who offered to go to the Mall to inquire about it. I sent a note to Karen Vaughn, president of Friends of Historic Halifax and a well-known artist in Roanoke Rapids. I put in a call to the mayor of Weldon. My daughter Andrea posted it on the Weldon Facebook page. On the website of the Halifax Arts Council, I saw the name of a photographer, Les Atkins. Could it be his? I left a message on the Arts Council's website. It was not.

Was the photographer someone from Weldon? Halifax? Roanoke Rapids? Littleton? Merely a fisherman visiting for the day? Someone long gone?

Incredible! Within twenty-four hours, Facebook solved the mystery. The photographer's wife, a Weldon native, saw the post and responded to Andrea. Simultaneously, Nancy Topham Mueller, an artist who received my inquiry via Les Atkins, sent me an email: she thought she might know.

His name is Lee Copeland, a well-known photographer in Weldon, married to Dee Riddle, the daughter of John and

Janie Riddle, a couple I knew growing up. (I can picture their precise house on Maple Street, Dee's family home.) I reached Dee by phone, listening eagerly to every bit of news about her parents and other folks in Weldon. And Lee graciously gave permission to use the photograph.

It turns out, too, that Nancy Mueller is the great-granddaughter of Mrs. Nannie Spiers, who was a devoted member of Weldon Methodist Church and lived in a spacious, wood-frame home right behind the church. Mrs. Spiers is featured in the first story in my book. To seal the connection, Nancy sent me an engaging photo of her mother with Mrs. Spiers when they were both young.

Just through one photograph, I discovered new acquaintances who link closely to my past life in Weldon. I hope to see those new faces soon—in Weldon or thereabout.

That's what the Roanoke River does for those who live on or around it: brings people together in time, across generations. But the river itself is timeless, with its jagged rocks, swirling rapids, and powerful currents—seemingly the same, day in and day out over decades and centuries.

Rushing water shapes its banks and the lives around it, but it records no account of what has gone before. Its ceaseless, cascading, uninterrupted flow erases forever the family celebrations, personal tragedies, capsized boats, fugitives' escapes, and battles of war that have gathered upon its banks over time. It has no memory, but those of us who grew up there do.

Lee Copeland has captured the timelessness of the River: in beauty, power, and energy. I cannot imagine a more fitting cover for my stories. I am ever grateful to him.

Alice Joyner Irby
March 2020

Made in the USA
Monee, IL
20 July 2020